D1431352

MARK
THANKS FOR YOUR
HELP WITH THIS CLASS!
KENT

Applied
Portfolio
Management

Applied Portfolio Management

How University of Kansas Students Generate Alpha to Beat the Street

CATHERINE SHENOY

KENT C. McCARTHY

John Wiley & Sons, Inc.

Published by John Wiley & Sons, Inc., Hoboken, New Jersey

Published simultaneously in Canada

For general information on our other products and services or for technical support, please contact our Customer Care Department within the United States at (800) 762-2974, outside the United States at (317) 572-3993 or fax (317) 572-4002.

Wiley also publishes its books in a variety of electronic formats. Some content that appears in print may not be available in electronic formats. For more information about Wiley products, visit our Web site at www.wiley.com.

Library of Congress Cataloging-in-Publication Data

Shenoy, Catherine, 1952–
    Applied portfolio management : how University of Kansas students generate alpha to beat the Street / Catherine Shenoy, Kent C. McCarthy.
        p. cm. – (Wiley finance series)
    Includes index.
    ISBN 978-0-470-04172-7 (cloth)
1. Portfolio management.   2. Investment analysis.   3. Stock price forecasting.   4. Investments.   I. McCarthy, Kent C., 1958–   II. University of Kansas. III. Title.
    HG4529.5.S535 2008
    332.6–dc22

                                                            2007039473

Printed in the United States of America

10 9 8 7 6 5 4 3 2 1

KCM:

In memory of Clark Hestmark. In 25 years of managing money, one client stands out. Clark had a great sense of humor, a great outlook and philosophy on life, and most of all was loyal—especially when the chips were down. I was a young broker at Goldman Sachs when Clark became a client and wanted some safe, income-producing investments. I bought him some Bethlehem Steel Preferred Stock yielding 9 percent. Two weeks later this "safe" investment was cut in half. Later I tested Clark's loyalty by being short the Japanese market two years too early. If that wasn't enough, in the late 1990s, I was short the Internet stocks. This mania caused a lot of long-term clients to lose confidence in me—but not Clark. I will never forget a dinner with Clark in those "dark" days of 1999 when he encouraged me to stay the course and hold to our convictions. It's easy to be a loyal friend when things are good, but I will always remember Clark's loyalty during the hardest times.

Clark became a special friend and mentor to me. He was beloved by his family. I can only hope that I can become half the husband and father that Clark was to his family. One final thing: Clark knew that the Applied Portfolio Management class meant a lot to me. Even though he was a graduate of Utah and lived in Lake Tahoe, he made several financial contributions to the class. And in typical Clark fashion, he did so anonymously. I did not find out about his gifts until many years later.

CS:

For my parents, Jerome Allen and Mary Helen Smith.

Contents

Preface

I n 1988 Kent McCarthy returned to Lawrence, Kansas, after several years in San Francisco. The last four had been spent in the Private Client Services division at Goldman Sachs. During his six-month sabbatical he taught at his alma mater, the University of Kansas, and planted the seeds for the Applied Portfolio Management program. Kent went back to Goldman for another six years but kept thinking about his teaching experience and ways to make bright, ambitious but sometimes naive Kansas students more knowledgeable investors.

Kansas students are typically smart and hardworking but aren't always as sophisticated as their brethren on either coast. They tend to believe the best of everyone and aren't always as skeptical of investment ideas as they need to be. They share many of the same traits as ordinary investors. Initially they are too quick to believe the "conventional wisdom" and end up as followers in the mainstream of the investment community. Kent's very successful career at Goldman wasn't sparked by following the crowd, and he wanted to share with students the basics of investment success that he has enjoyed. The story of the APM class is the story of educating individuals to be successful investors with hard work, patience, and persistence.

Cathy Shenoy has a Ph.D. in finance from the University of Kansas. In 1999 she visited with Kent to discuss a research idea that involved how successful portfolio managers made decisions. Kent convinced Cathy to begin teaching the APM class instead. The class had been on a hiatus for about a year and a half. Kent and Cathy taught the class together for the first time in the fall of 2001. It was a time of turmoil in the world and in the market. September 11 rocked the world and students. The fall of Enron introduced the importance of corporate governance to the masses. In class we had our first online chat and conference call with a new Chinese Internet company.

Lots of investing books have a winning formula. The biggest problem in investing is that the winning formula changes. How do you pick the right winning formula for today? One of Kent's favorite phrases in class— "Investing is dynamic"— captures the idea that you need to adjust your investment strategy as investment conditions change. In this book we provide some case studies of how to recognize when to change course. Changing your course does not mean timing the market but recognizing when fundamental changes in a company's business means a shift in investment strategy.

APM investing is not a story of market timing or benchmarking through market capitalization or sectors. The benchmark is hard work to dig deep to figure out a company's real story through detailed business analysis. The time to invest may be when the tide of opinion is swinging in the opposite direction. That's the time to have the courage to follow your own convictions and believe in your analysis. In the end the market always rewards good businesses. In the short term the market can get carried away with minor details or the fad of the moment.

A large part of the APM story is in teaching how to dig behind the facade of public numbers, press releases, and spin to figure out what's really going on. How does a company make money? What numbers from the financial statements and other public information demonstrates how well a company is accomplishing its mission? What are the people like who are running the company? Each week students in the APM class dig into these three questions. Each week they learn a little more about the best way to view a new situation. Another favorite APM phrase is "peeling the layers of the onion." Each quarterly report, each news release provides a little additional information to confirm or refute the original investment hypothesis. In investing, experience is important. In the APM class the students begin building experience by learning what type of information is important and how to answer the fundamental three questions.

At the beginning of every semester students typically fall into three main groups:

1. Students who don't know a lot about investing and have enrolled in the class to learn make up the majority.
2. Students who have been investing, have had some success, and think they can show the class how it's done make up the next group.
3. Students who have been investing and haven't been as successful as they had hoped make up the third group. They want to learn more and avoid the mistakes they've made.

All of these students have had investments theory courses. Most of them still don't know how to answer all of the big three questions: How does a company make money? What numbers from the financial statements and other public information demonstrates how well a company is accomplishing its mission? What are the people like that are running the company? We are writing this book because many people who are interested in investing fall into the same categories as our students. Those readers can learn to answer the questions just as the APM students have learned. Almost everyone can become a better investor with hard work and persistence.

At the end of the semester, students typically fall into two groups. The majority now realize that investing takes time, persistence, and hard work. Quite a few have been inspired or strengthened in their inspirations to pursue careers in the financial industry. This group realizes that the market isn't a get-rich-quick game. They come away from their experience ready to dig in some more. Many of these students stay in touch and stay connected to APM by offering the class new ideas, keeping up with the newsletter, and even coming back to present a case in class. There are always a few students who decide Cathy and Kent really don't know what they are talking about. Many times these are the students who want a "popular" strategy. The popular financial press stands ready to help all of those people who feel the need to join the crowd.

Another important part of the story is building a network of contacts. Each semester the APM program has a network of guest speakers that rivals any investment group's contacts anywhere. Speakers fall into two categories. The first group is investment professionals. This group includes mutual and hedge fund managers, traders, investment bankers, security analysts, and other asset managers. All are generous and provide the class with their best ideas. Even more important, they provide the class a glimpse of their decision-making process. Decision making isn't a one-time idea; these experts explain to students how to come up with ideas, what to read, and how to interpret what they read. The other group of speakers in class comes from the corporate side. This group includes chief executive and chief financial officers and other decision-making and operating professionals from firms. These people provide insiders' perspectives on what it takes to run a firm: what the industry is like, what the economic environment of the firm is, what variables can be controlled and what ones cannot be controlled.

Building a network of contacts is a significant advantage for any investor. No one can know everything about the many different industries, countries, and markets. Better information breeds better investment decisions. APM speakers are just the beginning of the network of contacts. Students form lifelong relationships in college. As they graduate and go on to work for different companies, they can provide the basis for a most productive network.

No one really knows how many universities have student portfolios. One estimate is there that there are over 200 student funds. Thirteen years ago, when APM began, there were probably fewer than 25 funds. APM was unique then in its emphasis on building a network of contacts, on discovering the fundamental drivers of business success, and on buying at the right price. Today as the number of student portfolios expands, the

most common management technique is sector benchmarking, which most
mutual funds and other large asset management companies follow.

There are two problems with this type of asset management.

1. It's very difficult to earn above-market returns using sector benchmarking.
2. This technique doesn't take advantage of a small fund's (or individual's)
   flexibility. Any megafund or individual can invest in Microsoft. However, a megafund will not invest in Chinese company trading on the
   Hong Kong Growth Enterprise Market (GEM) exchange with a market
   capitalization of less than $US 500 million.

APM takes advantage of its smaller size to invest in some areas that others do not. The APM advantage makes our approach ideal for an individual
investors willing to go against the grain of conventional thinking.

In this book we relate case studies and ideas from speakers that illustrate
the key ideas from class. Our hope is that readers will be able to experience
some of the same learning that goes on in the APM class. We'll peel some
onion layers away to show where the value lies and how to find it.

Acknowledgments

The authors would like to jointly acknowledge the students and speakers who since 1994 have made the Applied Portfolio Management class such a vibrant experience.

Class speakers we'd especially like to thank are Victor Almeida, Bob Ceremsak, Grant Donovan, Steve Farley, Steve Glennon, Jack Golsen, Clark Hestmark, Scott Jones, Andy Mathieson, Simon Michael, Edmund Miller, Mark and Betty Morris, Todd Preheim, Penny Pritzer, Josh Selzer, Brad Shoup, Tony Shelby, John Svoboda, Pat Terrell, and David Walthall. Many other speakers have also made a tremendous contribution. Lots of them traveled many miles at their own expense to share their wisdom with the class. We'd like to thank them all.

Faculty members at the University of Kansas who also helped make this possible are Jack Gaumnitz, Paul Koch, and Allen Ford. Without their initial and ongoing support, this class wouldn't have happened. Two deans of the Business School also deserve special mention. Joe Baumann was the dean who made the class possible initially. Bill Fuerst, the current dean, and Keith Chauvin, associate dean, are tremendous supporters and deserve a big thank you.

We would also like to thank the wonderful people at A.G. Edwards, especially Al Simmons and Gene Diederich, who have been supporters of the class since inception. They go the extra mile to find information to facilitate our trades. The traders who work our orders; Darrell Collins, who plans visits to A.G. Edwards headquarters; Scott Wren; and all the analysts who answer our questions have been a tremendous resource.

Thanks to Alberto Bassetto, Joe Onofrio, Michael Raupp, and John Thompson. Discussions and e-mails with Mark Fleischhauer and Kara Tan Bhala were especially helpful because of the clarity of their thinking.

We would also like to thank Bill Falloon, our editor, for convincing us that this book really was a good idea. The entire team at Wiley has been helpful and encouraging. Emilie Hermann has been a wonderful editorial assistant, as has Laura Walsh.

Thanks to Scott Jones, John Naramore, and Sushila Shenoy for reading and offering advice, comments, and suggestions. Sushila provided great assistance and editing on any questions or problems with the graphics. Also thanks to Todd Preheim for his energy, enthusiasm, and encouragement. George Bittlingmayer helped put things in perspective. Jim Guthrie, word-smith, also offered lots of useful suggestions, and Keith Chauvin helped with the bigger issues.

Cathy Shenoy would also like to thank the Garage Gang for their encour-agement and suggestions. They are Ann, Dave, Eileen, George R., George P., John, Joyce, Steve, Surendra, Vicky, and especially Loren. Finally, big thanks go to my family: Prakash, Chandra, Sushila, Nick, Dusty, Piper, Landrie, Libby, and my mom and dad, Jerome and Helen Smith.

One

Introduction to the Applied Portfolio Management Class

Lots of universities have investment management classes that manage money. Some are older than our program, some have more assets under management, but we feel that the Applied Portfolio Management (APM) class at the University of Kansas is unique in the quality of the information that the students receive. "Quality of information" isn't exactly the catchiest slogan, but for investors the quality of the information is the key difference between average returns and extraordinary ones. Information drives the investment process. Getting great information and evaluating and interpreting it correctly is a major theme in the APM class.

In the first part of this book, we outline how we've gotten to where we are today and how what we do is different. In Chapter 1 we review how the class started and how it's changed. What worked that we kept and what changes we've made to make it better. "Investing is dynamic" is a phrase that APM students hear frequently. Teaching young investors is dynamic also. In Chapter 2 we discuss how the class guidelines work now. They will almost certainly evolve as we think of new and better ways to combine investing and teaching investing. In Chapter 3 we review finance theory and how breakdowns in the theory create investment opportunities. In Chapter 4 we illustrate "surface analysis" and how in the APM class, we try to make sure that we rely on the best-quality information in our investment decisions.

CHAPTER 1

APM History

When the Applied Portfolio Management (APM) class started, there were not a lot of student-managed portfolios. There were no "best practices" to follow. We think it's instructive to go through the history of the APM class because in designing the class, we've helped educate many future successful investors. As a class, we've also succeeded in generating great returns. We've also had a firsthand look at the thinking of beginning investors. Through the APM class, we've learned a lot about the mistakes typical investors make, and we think our experience in helping students overcome these mistakes is useful to all investors.

In managing their own portfolio, individual investors make many of the same mistakes that students make at the beginning of the semester. Fortunately, it didn't take too long to hit upon a workable strategy for the APM class that encourages what we consider the right kind of decision making—one that makes money over the long term. We've managed to earn a great return over the last 13 years. APM began with $230,000. As of this writing in mid-2007, the portfolio is valued at close to $1.5 million. That's an annual rate of return of more than 20 percent, 10 percent per year higher than the return on the NASDAQ index or the Standard & Poor's 500 Index (S&P 500). Figure 1.1 shows how APM's return has compared to NASDAQ's over the life of the portfolio.

The class strategy has changed over time. During the 1990s the portfolio strategy was more event driven. Now we have a more value-oriented buy-and-hold philosophy. The philosophy has changed because market conditions have changed. In class we focus on understanding what's going on in the market, what's happening in a company, and how those events can interact to create investment opportunities.

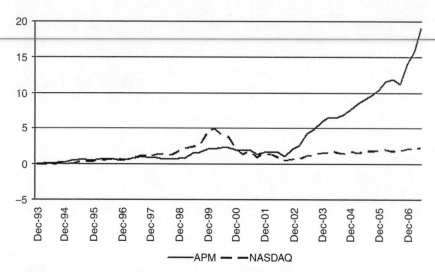

FIGURE 1.1   Cumulative APM Return vs. NASDAQ Return 1994–June 2007

IN THE BEGINNING

Kent McCarthy retired from private client services at Goldman Sachs in 1993 at the ripe old age of 35. At the time he retired, he was the largest producer ever for Goldman Sachs Private Client Services. He generated those fees because he decided to base his business on generating performance for his clients. He found good investment returns for his clients in many overlooked areas. Kent felt that the Japanese market was overvalued and Hong Kong stocks were undervalued. Consequently, he managed more trades with the Hong Kong Exchange than anyone else at Goldman. That time marked the beginning of his love affair with China.

He was ready for a change and decided to come back to his under-graduate alma mater, the University of Kansas, to teach classes about investing. He donated $230,000 to start the APM class. Professors Allen Ford, Jack Gaumnitz, and Paul Koch were instrumental in persuading the faculty and administration to accept Kent's seed money for the portfolio. The KU Endowment Association didn't rush to embrace the idea of a class portfolio. Jack met with Jeff Davis, the endowment's chief investment officer, and pitched the idea. Jeff was open but cautious. After reviewing investment management programs at other universities, such as Wisconsin's ASAP and Texas's MBA Investment Fund, KU Endowment was on board.

That first fall semester in 1994 Kent, along with Jack and Paul, taught two sections of Applied Portfolio Management to a select group of 30 students. One class was held at the main Lawrence, Kansas, campus, and the other at the Kansas City Regent's Center. The semester started with the $230,000 from Kent's gift in the fund. The students were divided into groups of four, and each group was allocated $10,000 to invest. At the end of the first semester, the APM portfolio stood at almost $275,000.

STUDENT COMMENTS FROM KENT'S EARLY CLASSES

Todd Preheim

APM Fall 1994

The APM class was very intense. I remember being very worried that Kent would call on me. When we talked about the cases, he would randomly call on people and pepper them with questions until the student could not answer one. I was always on edge and remember getting performance anxiety after Kent called on me to answer questions—even if the questions were elementary. I spent significantly more time preparing for the class versus others but still felt I never prepared enough.

My favorite case was International Speedway (ISCA). Guest speaker Steve Farley asked students how ISCA could increase sales in the coming years. A classmate answered they should not allow fans to bring their own coolers into the raceway. When determining what the additional revenue would be from this plan, another classmate suggested we model each fan will drink 10 beers.

Kent's teachings of aggressive event-driven strategies were way ahead of his time and are very prevalent today with many hedge funds. He challenged most claims of the buy-and-hold strategy and emphasized the importance of strong management. The case format along with Kent and his speakers' experiences allowed students to better understand how Wall Street works.

Paul Koch taught the class from inception with Kent until 2000. He was instrumental in laying the groundwork in the expectations of hard work and rigorous analysis in the class. Cathy Shenoy started teaching with Kent in 2001. By this time student groups were no longer allocated $10,000 to invest, but the idea of stock mentors guiding student decisions was starting to form. The switch away from active student management happened for several reasons. The first reason was poor decision making by students, especially early in the semester. The second reason was to encourage a longer-term mentality.

HOW DO BEGINNING INVESTORS THINK?

Let's examine what happens at the beginning of the semester. We'll focus on the poor decision making first and then get to what we hope is a cure for poor decision making. Several times Cathy starts the class by putting the two simple charts shown in Figure 1.2 on the board and asking students which stock they would prefer as an investment.

Almost universally, students pick Stock A with no hesitation. Cathy started putting up the charts after she noticed students coming to class saying "Why does the portfolio hold Stock X? It's a big loser." A lot of times the previous semester's class had picked Stock X. Students had selected the stock because they felt several things might happen in the future that would

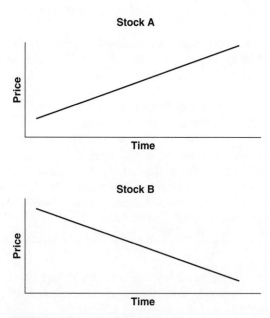

FIGURE 1.2   Where Would You Invest?

change its prospects. Selling now when it was down was exactly the wrong thing to do.

Psychologists have identified this type of behavior by investors, and call it the "recency effect." Kent calls it "ruler analysis." Generally, when people forecast stock prices, or anything else, it's easiest for them to assume that the past will be like the future. However, in stock markets, individual stocks, economies, and lots of other areas, cycles and changes in directions are very common. Because so many people like to jump on the bandwagon and invest in stocks with rapidly increasing value, those stocks with recent price increases are more likely to be overvalued.

A big example of ruler analysis is the recognized trading strategy of momentum investing. Momentum investors are those who look at recent trends and ride those trends up or down, selling stocks with recent poor returns and buying ones with recent good returns. During the bubble of the late 1990s, momentum investors made a lot of money because there was an extended trend (bubble?) upward. During the shake out in 2001–2002, momentum investors lost a lot of money.

We find that new students in the APM class are especially prone to ruler analysis because they are afraid to trust their own judgment. A student once said, "Everyone else thinks that things are great. What do I know about anything?" The story of the Emperor's New Clothes comes to mind. In a Danish fairytale, two con men sell an Emperor a new suit of clothes. They convince him that the suit is the latest and greatest, but emphasize that the most special property of the suit is that it is invisible to people who aren't fit for their position. Of course, there is no suit, but no one wants to say they can't see it. Finally, a child speaks up and asks why the Emperor isn't wearing any clothes. Sometimes it just takes a few clear-thinking people to see through the hype of the Street's new favorite stock.

"Buy high and sell low" happens when investors get stuck in a ruler analysis mode. People want to wait until others provide confirmation an investment is sound. By that time prices have gone up. They end up buying high—toward the end of Stock A's price increase. John Bogle, the longtime chairman of the Vanguard Group, testified before Congress in 2004 about the phenomenon. He calls it a "timing and selection penalty."[1]

[S]hareholders have paid a heavy timing penalty, investing too little of their savings in equity funds when stocks represented good values during the 1980s and early 1990s. Then, enticed by the great bull

---

[1] Statement of John C. Bogle before the United States Senate Committee on Banking, Housing, and Urban Affairs, February 26, 2004.

market and the wiles of mutual fund marketers as the bull market neared its peak, they invested too much of their savings. Second, because they have paid a selection penalty, pouring money into "new economy" stocks and withdrawing it from "old economy" stocks during the bubble, at what proved to be precisely the wrong moment.

The result of these two penalties: While the stock market provided an annual return of 13% during the past 20 years, and the average equity fund earned an annual return of 10.3%, I estimate that the average fund investor earned just 3% per year. It may not surprise you to know that, compounded over two decades, the nearly 3% penalty of costs is huge. But the penalty of character is even larger—another 8 percentage points. $1 compounded at 13% grows to $11.50; at 10%, to $7.10; and at 3%, to just $1.80. A profit of just eighty cents!

It's not just mutual funds where people chase returns. It happens in all types of investing. Few people want to invest in a company that hasn't had good performance, especially if analysts or the media are not saying good things about it. So how does the APM portfolio avoid falling into this trap? The short answer is education. We educate students to think for themselves and do their own analysis. We also educate them in the "ways of Wall Street." By "Wall Street," we mean all of the participants in the investment industry. Some of the participants that influence investments and stock prices are mutual funds, investment banks, hedge funds, and private equity funds. Since these participants make up a large part of all the transactions in the market, understanding why and how each of these market participants makes money and their institutional incentives helps students unravel the mystery of stock prices. Another big influence on investment decisions is the financial media. The media, especially since the advent of CNBC, want to create a sense of crisis to keep viewers or readers tuned in to each tiny gyration in the market. How do they pick stories and stocks to follow? By understanding each participant's incentives, students can see when there may be some influence on prices outside of a stock's intrinsic value. In class we try to focus on making our own decisions about stock valuation and not being too influenced by temporary price aberrations caused by one of the market participants or the media.

We believe that a company's fundamentals eventually will be reflected in its price. Sometimes it takes longer than expected, but eventually a company's intrinsic value will align with its stock price. For this reason, education in two areas is important. First is education in the valuation techniques that many research analysts and portfolio managers use. The main valuation methods that we use in class are discounted cash flow valuation and relative valuation. Both of these have lots of variations, but the core ideas in the two methods remain constant. The second area is education in what drives the decisions of the market participants. If students understand all of the different Wall Street participants and their incentives, then they will understand more objectively why some stocks linger in the dumps while others soar to mysterious new highs.

We discuss these ideas more in upcoming chapters, but here is a brief example of where and how mutual funds invest and how individual investors or a small portfolio like APM can find value where mutual funds cannot. A 2007 study by the Investment Company Institute estimated that investment companies managed about $11 trillion in assets.[2] That's around 14 percent of the world's securities. In the United States there are at least 105 mutual funds with more than $10 billion in assets and 35 with more than $20 billion. That's at least $1.5 trillion in assets right there! In funds that are so large, it is hard to move in and out of a stock quickly without affecting the price. It's not worthwhile for funds to own just a few thousand shares; usually they need to own a significant percentage of shares in a company. Funds have quarterly reporting dates. An unscrupulous fund may not want to report a loss on a position even when it doesn't like the long-run prospects. Right before the end of the quarter it might enter the market and buy a lot of shares to drive up the price of a stock. After the reporting date the fund will slowly unwind that position, and the price will come back down, as well. For those who have studied the company fundamentals, the situation represents an investment opportunity.

STUDENT GROUPS: SHORT-TERM INVESTING AND PORTFOLIO CONTESTS

For the first few years of the APM class, each student group received $10,000 to invest at the beginning of the semester. The rest of the portfolio was managed by the class and called the core fund. The core fund held approximately 70 percent of the total assets. From 1994 to 1996 there were 25 student groups managing $10,000 each. Table 1.1 shows that of the 25 groups, only 6 had a positive return, and only 1 group each year beat the core portfolio performance.

Table 1.2 shows the groups actual returns versus the core portfolio. A couple of groups did better than the core, but not enough to make up the difference in the poorly performing groups.

---

[2] 2007 *Investment Company Fact Book*, May 2007, http://www.icifactbook.org/

TABLE 1.1 Number of Groups with Positive and Negative Performance

Date	Negative Returns	Positive Returns	Total Groups	Groups beating Core
1994	8	1	9	1
1995	7	2	9	1
1996	4	3	7	1
Total	19	6	25	3

Why were the student group returns so dismal? We think there are a couple of reasons. First, many of the students were beginning investors, and they made many of the mistakes that novices make. The biggest mistake is the one that we mentioned earlier in this chapter: chasing returns instead of looking for good values. The other mistake that we made was in setting up a de facto competition among the groups. There is a logical strategy to follow in a competition: Bet a lot on a risky investment and hope it comes through. If it pays off you look like a genius, but the odds are low and many times the bets didn't pay off.

Every year there are a lot of sponsored investment competitions. Usually the rules are simple. Everyone starts with the same amount of money. The person with the most money at the end wins. The contest typically lasts three months, about the same as an academic semester. Winners in portfolio contests usually need to double their money in a few months to win. How do you double your money? You take a big bet in a few companies. To have the highest odds of success, pick just a few companies with the best chances of a big change. You want to look for a company that is waiting for drug approval, a big technology breakthrough, or some other impending event that will either make or break it. You have to be right on two counts: on

TABLE 1.2 Early Portfolio Returns: Groups and Core

Date	Average Negative Returns	Average Positive Returns	Group Average	Group with Highest Return	Core Fund Return
1994	−9%	15%	−10%	15%	18%
1995	−15%	9%	−10%	18%	16%
1996	−10%	12%	−7%	18%	14%
Total	−12%	12%	−9%		

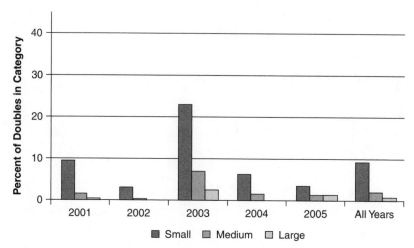

FIGURE 1.3 Percent of Stocks that Doubled or Better in Each Market Capitalization Category, 2001–2005

the timing of the event and that the outcome of the event was in the right direction. If you are wrong on either count, your returns will be flat in the best case. More likely, if you are wrong you lose a lot of money.

What's the chance of picking big winners? On average about 7 percent of all stocks double in value in one year, so just picking at random you have a chance to find a big winner. Figure 1.3 shows the percentage of stocks that doubled or better in each year over 2001 to 2005. If you pick from small companies with a market capitalization (market cap) of less than $1 billion, your odds increase to just over 9 percent. Two percent of companies with a beginning market cap from $1 to $10 billion doubled and 10 (less than 1 percent) large-cap firms with market caps over $10 billion doubled.

If you aren't going for a double, you still can do pretty well with returns of 50 percent or better. Figure 1.4 shows the percentage of companies earning an annual return of 50 percent or better for each market cap group. Overall, 17.6 percent of firms from 2001 to 2005 had at least one year with an annual increase of 50 percent or better. They may have decreased later, but a fairly large proportion of firms make significant moves every year, and every year there are more small-cap firms making the big move.

If you have some skill or knowledge, you may improve your chances even more. The 60th percentile is the level of return where 60 percent of stocks did worse and 40 percent did better. In Table 1.3 you can see that if you can perform in the 60th percentile over time, you will have a return that's well above average. There is still plenty of variability over the years, but by

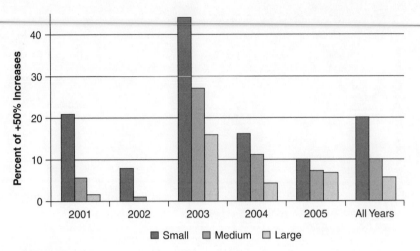

FIGURE 1.4 Percent of Stocks with an Increase of 50 Percent or More in Each Market Capitalization Category, 2001–2005

eliminating the bottom 60 percent, your return is significantly improved. In most years, it is still the small stocks that are the best performers. In all years, the small- and medium-cap firms do better than the large-cap ones.

Some of the student groups turned out to be right in the long run but missed the timing that the semester constraints put on them. For example, Jeff Brueggemann and Greg Baugh from Group 1 in 1994 invested in Duracell at $45.75. By the end of the semester, when they sold, the price was $45. A year later the price was $53. If we had held to the next year, including the generous dividends that were paid, we would have earned a 40 percent return.

TABLE 1.3 60th Percentile Returns by Market Capitalization, 2001–2005

	2001	2002	2003	2004	2005	All Years
Large cap (>$10B)	−7.8	−14.5	29.9	13.9	7.9	7.6
Medium cap ($1–10B)	2.1	−5.4	38.7	19.8	9.6	13.9
Small cap (<$1B)	15.5	−0.8	56.3	16.0	3.3	16.7
All firms	11.4	−2.2	50.7	17.0	5.1	15.4
Median return	−4.6	−13.7	30.9	13.9	4.1	6.4
Total firms	7,112	6,704	6,388	6,228	6,228	32,660

As we said earlier, an investor has to be right on two counts: on the timing of the event and the outcome has to be in the right direction. But probably the biggest obstacle to better returns was and is the difficulty of tuning out conventional wisdom and getting close to the information.

GETTING CLOSE TO THE INFORMATION

Jack Gaumnitz feels that Kent's biggest contribution to the students is his ability to dig into a company and get close to the information. What Jack means by "get close" is understanding what drives a company's business. Wall Street is fixated on earnings per share (EPS) numbers. Research analysts' forecasts of EPS are trumpeted everywhere. Just watch CNBC for a few minutes during earnings season. The buzz is all about whether the company made its earnings numbers, that is, did EPS match analyst forecasts of EPS? If the company comes in at forecasted EPS, then the stock price usually stays the same. A miss, when actual EPS is below forecast, usually means a stock price drop; and when actual EPS comes in higher than expected, the stock price usually is higher.

Getting close to the information is looking at the all the pieces that go into the EPS number and understanding what the most important component is. In later chapters we have some extended examples, but here are a couple of simple illustrations of this idea. In the late 1990s wireless companies were starting to take off. Companies were signing up loads of new subscribers. Many of them weren't profitable yet, but revenue growth was spectacular and stock prices were soaring. A closer look at the numbers revealed that ARPUs—average revenues per user—were declining significantly. At the same time, costs to sign up users were also increasing. Some companies actually were losing money for every customer they signed up. For some of these companies, EPS was increasing because they were selling other assets or had one-time income unrelated to their wireless businesses. Of course, those gains were not sustainable. When the wireless businesses had to stand on their own, it became clear that the competition to sign up customers had driven the ARPUs down. Since then we have seen a lot of consolidation in the industry with just a few economically viable companies emerging.

Before the wealth of information was available on the Internet, Kent would bring piles of documents to class: analyst reports, annual reports, and industry information. He would also make arrangements for the students to listen to companies earnings conference calls. He would bring in speakers who were key players in the industry. All of these information sources were hard for an individual investor to access in the mid-1990s. Access to analyst reports was limited to portfolio managers; individuals with sizable accounts could get some reports from their broker. Many times those reports were limited to the broker's own firm. Access to earnings conference calls was even more limited. Top analysts and a few others in privileged positions were invited to participate. It was rare indeed for students in a class to be listening to a CEO explain corporate strategy and expectations for the next year. Nevertheless, students had to examine the statements and decide on the CEO's credibility.

One of the biggest changes in investing is access to information. Today all corporate filings are available electronically at the Web site of the Securities and Exchange Commission (SEC). Every company is required to have a Web site with the same information available. In October 2000 Regulation Fair Disclosure, called Reg FD, became effective. Reg FD prohibits companies from making disclosures to selected individuals. If a company wants to report some information, it must make it available to everyone. Earnings calls have to be announced in advance with access provided to anyone who wants to listen. The SEC's idea was to provide a level playing field for all investors.

Regulation FD and the explosion of information available on the Internet provide students and individual investors mountains of information not generally available in the 1990s. Are we all better investors because of the wealth of information? Maybe not. Now that we have a lot more information, the task is to organize, synthesize, and recognize what is going to drive the stock price; what is fundamental to a company's success, and how is the street interpreting the same information. It is the same task that successful investors always had, but now there is more chaff to sift out to get to the grain. (Sorry about the Kansas analogy.)

A big part of the APM class now is learning to sift through the mountain of information available to get to the pertinent information quickly. When students first enter the class, many rely heavily on finance.yahoo.com or moneycentral.msn.com. Both of these Web sites, and many others, provide lots of information about stocks. The sites provide stock quotes, a multitude of financial ratios, financial statements, historical prices, estimated earnings, business summaries, ownership information, analyst ratings, news, charts, competitors, message boards, and even more. We look at the APM portfolio everyday on finance.yahoo.com. We can scan the news releases and find quotes on foreign stocks that other sites don't have.

It seems to be a one-stop shop for all you would ever need to know about a company. What else would anyone need? How much closer to the information can you get? These financial summary sites are great at providing a fairly in-depth summary of lots of information quickly. You can keep up to date on all the news about a company and find out when earnings calls will be and how to participate. The sites provide a financial and market snapshot of where things stand right now. What you cannot find is how a company arrived at its current state and what its prospects for change are. How many lines of business does a company have, and how are they doing? The profile lists all lines of business or products but gives no qualitative or quantitative information on the relative or strategic importance of any product or business line. Figuring out an investment catalyst is one of the most important jobs for students or any investor. Here the financial summary sites are of little value. They do not interpret the information for investors.

LSB Industries is a longtime holding in the APM portfolio. Currently it manufactures chemicals in one division and HVAC (heating, ventilation, and air conditioning products) in another division. In Chapter 6 we outline how each of these segments has provided different strategic opportunities and challenges to the company. It is not possible to understand LSB as a long-term investment without understanding its business segments separately and how they interact. Figure 1.5 shows LSB Industries' income statement from finance.yahoo.com. This summary provides no clues about whether each of the businesses is performing well, nor does it give the kind of financial information that would indicate good or bad performance. To find that level of detail you need to go directly to the source of the information, the financial filings with the SEC.

10-Ks are the annual financial statements that must be filed with the SEC by every U.S. company listed on a stock exchange in the United States. 10-Qs are quarterly statements. The notes that accompany the financial statements are required parts of 10-Ks and 10-Qs. The notes explain how a company reports items in the financial statements or provide more details about certain items. Companies must provide financial information for their significant business segments in the notes section. The footnotes to the financial statements generally report three types of information: what accounting method a company uses when there is a choice, detailed information about some items, and other required disclosures. If the ability to pay interest on bonds is of particular interest, the footnotes contain details about scheduled bond payments.

The management discussion section provides a narrative of more qualitative information about segments. Every 10-Q and 10-K must report four parts:

1. Financial statements including notes
2. Management's discussion and analysis of financial condition and results of operations (called MD&A)
3. Quantitative and qualitative disclosures about market risk
4. Controls and procedures

LSB Industries Inc. (LXU)	On Jul 21: **8.42 0.00 (0.00%)**

Make investing easier with MarketWatch.com.
- **Visit now to find out why!**
- **MarketWatch.com**

Income Statement   Get Income Statement for: [   ] [GO]

View: **Annual Data** | Quarterly Data   All numbers in thousands

PERIOD ENDING	31-Dec-05	31-Dec-04	31-Dec-03
Total Revenue	396,722	363,608	317,263
Cost of Revenue	330,651	310,497	267,831
Gross Profit	66,071	53,111	49,432
Operating Expenses			
Research Development	-	-	-
Selling General and Administrative	53,456	50,541	41,745
Non Recurring	(2,350)	-	-
Others	-	-	-
Total Operating Expenses	-	-	-
Operating Income or Loss	14,965	2,570	7,687
Income from Continuing Operations			
Total Other Income/Expenses Net	1,561	6,061	983
Earnings Before Interest And Taxes	16,526	8,631	8,670
Interest Expense	11,407	7,393	5,559
Income Before Tax	5,119	1,238	3,111
Income Tax Expense	118	-	-
Minority Interest	-	-	-
Net Income From Continuing Ops	5,746	1,906	3,111
Non-recurring Events			
Discontinued Operations	(644)	-	-
Extraordinary Items	-	-	-
Effect Of Accounting Changes	-	(536)	-
Other Items	-	-	-
Net Income	5,102	1,370	3,111
Preferred Stock And Other Adjustments	(2,283)	(2,322)	(2,327)
Net Income Applicable to Common Shares	$2,819	($952)	$784

FIGURE 1.5   LSB Financial Statements from Finance.Yahoo.com

10-Ks have additional discussion requirements, but each of the four is always in both 10-Ks and 10-Qs. Unless students dig into the filings, they would miss a basic understanding of how LSB operates. Note that Figure 1.5 contains a link to the SEC filings.[3]

---

[3] Foreign companies listed on U.S. exchanges may elect to file an annual 20-F instead of a 10-K. Companies that file 20-Fs usually do not file 10-Qs, although they may still report quarterly information on their own Web site or in some other unofficial format.

ONIONS, POKER, AND ANTS

When students get close to the information and understand what the invest-ment thesis is and what drives a company's operating results, the next step is to step back and see how things unfold. Kent uses two different analogies to describe that process: peeling onions and playing poker. When you carefully peel the skin off an onion, another layer is revealed beneath the skin. You can take off more and more layers to reveal what's beneath. New press re-leases and earnings statements are like peeling the layers off an onion. With each new piece of information, a new layer of the onion is revealed.

The poker analogy is similar. When you play five-card stud, some cards are revealed to the whole table. As the dealer reveals more and more cards, you have a better idea of where all the cards lie. Again, once you understand the investment thesis, each month will bring new evidence to support or refute that hypothesis. If you understand the company's business and critical issues, the new information is more valuable and more informative.

In 2001 we invested in Sohu, one of the first publicly traded Chinese Internet companies. The investment thesis was that the Chinese economy was developing rapidly and that increased spending by the Chinese consumer would not be far behind. As the middle class developed in China, Internet usage exploded. At the time most of the news stories about Sohu and other Chinese companies focused on the risk of investing in China or the poor financial reporting practices in China. Never mind that Sohu traded on the NASDAQ and had to follow U.S. reporting requirements and was audited by U.S. firm accounting firm PricewaterhouseCoopers. Once we had made a decision to invest in China, the Chinese Internet sector, and Sohu, that type of news story was irrelevant. What was relevant were operating results. When quarterly statements and conference calls were available, we wanted to see rapidly increasing numbers of users and increasing gross margins. We did see those things, but the market did not react to them for quite a while. Table 1.4 shows Sohu's year-end stock price, cash per share, and annual stock return. It also shows the revenue growth rates for the two main segments of Sohu's business, advertising and wireless.

Sohu started trading on the NASDAQ on July 12, 2000, at $13. By year-end it was down to $2.38, an 82 percent drop in price. Sohu did have negative earnings but positive cash flow. Advertising revenues and users were growing rapidly. The table shows that reported revenues were up over 200 percent. The fundamentals looked as if they were going according to plan with the APM investment thesis. However, those numbers were not good enough for the market in 2000. Sohu introduced advanced wireless services in 2000, and both advertising and wireless revenue segments were up 58 percent and 3,345 percent, respectively. Still, the stock price was down

TABLE 1.4 Sohu Stock Return and Sohu's Growth in Business Segments

Date	Year-End Stock Price	Cash Per Share	Annual Return on Stock %	Advertising Revenue Growth %	Wireless Revenue Growth %
1998	–	–	–	505	–
1999	–	–	–	243	–
2000	2.38	2.12	–	261	–
2001	1.20	0.82	−50	58	3,345
2002	6.40	0.62	433	50	1,153
2003	29.91	3.56	367	113	364
2004	17.71	3.47	−41	89	−23
2005	18.34	3.49	4	27	−28

50 percent from the previous year-end price. The stock closed at an all-time low of $0.60 on April 9, 2001. The APM portfolio was buying all during this time. Little news—good, bad, or indifferent—was reported about Sohu. Even when the company reported great numbers, nothing happened with the stock. No one was paying attention.

In 2001 there were some generally negative stories about investing in China. Conventional wisdom about investing there was negative. Big economic changes had been taking place for the past 10 years, but lots of stories in the United States said that investing in China was too risky. The comments ran like this: It was a communist country; they could change the rules; and you would lose your money at any time. Kent challenged that type of negative thinking. Through his guidance, the APM fund has had a significant portion of the portfolio invested in China since 2000.

By 2002 and 2003 the rest of the world started to pay attention, as you can see from Sohu's stock price increase. In the third quarter of 2002 Sohu achieved positive earnings. Still, it took until mid-April 2003 until the price was over its $13 initial public offering level, almost two years. Little about the fundamentals had changed, the investment thesis held, but it took the rest of the market a few years to catch up to the fundamentals. Every quarter an onion layer was peeled away, a new poker card was shown.

WHAT ABOUT THE ANTS?

Another side of getting close to the information is sorting through ants on elephants. The financial press reports just about everything that happens to public companies, but it is especially interested in bad news. All company news releases are filed with the SEC as 8-K filings. There is so much corporate news that it's hard to filter out what will affect fundamental value from news that is just a part of doing business. The doing-business news is something that happens in the due course of running a business. You should expect some negative things to happen to a company, and you should expect that good management knows how to deal with the situation. That's their job. Plants get shut down because of accidents or natural disasters. In our litigious society, lawsuits are filed all the time.

Beginning students pay a lot of attention to current news reports and not enough attention to how the news affects the investment thesis. It's not uncommon for a student to say that we need to get out of a company because a lawsuit has been filed. It's bad news, and the stock price has dropped. Most lawsuits are part of doing business. Usually they do not affect the overall fundamental value of the company. Sometimes the more sensational the story, the less it will affect the value of the company. Fingers in food or hot coffee aren't going to bankrupt a large restaurant chain, but they certainly grab the headlines. Focusing on the small stuff is the ant on the elephant. The elephant does not even know the ant is there. Getting close to the information is learning to recognize the ants and the elephants.

Another example is that one line of business is not working out and the company has decided to drop it. Many times that line of business is a very small percentage of the overall company, and it has been losing money. It's actually good news that the drag on earnings is going to be relieved, but the news isn't pitched that way, and students may pick this up as bad news.

THINGS TO COME

We discussed a lot of ideas in this chapter. In the rest of the book we expand on these ideas and provide some detailed examples to illustrate these ideas more carefully. We seemed to dwell on mistakes that beginning APM students typically make, but it is important to recognize mistakes so we can become more astute investors. Fortunately, by the end of the class, most students recognize their mistakes and have a handle on the analytical tools to help them succeed.

The returns on the APM portfolio since inception have been exceptional, especially compared to the market. Since inception through mid-2006 our cumulative return is 1,568 percent compared to 235 percent for NASDAQ. That's a compound annual return of 23 percent for APM versus 9.3 percent for NASDAQ. The alpha or "excess" risk-adjusted return is almost

16 percent (refer to Figure 1.1). In Chapter 5 we'll delve deeply into the numbers.

The goal of the APM class is to provide a hands-on investment education and make money at the same time. We think that we have hit on the right balance of oversight and education that makes a long-run successful portfolio and investor.

CHAPTER 2

APM Guidelines

Before 2004, the APM class did not have any explicitly stated guidelines for the portfolio. Toward the end of the fall 2003 semester, we asked the class to discuss what they had learned and what they considered the APM investment philosophy to be. Here are the four major points that they highlighted:

1. Purchase stocks with an educational value. Do our own analysis. Do not rely on outside experts for advice.
2. Develop and maintain good relationships with alumni, friends, donors, and corporate guests.
3. Maintain a small number of stocks and monitor them closely.
4. Maintain a global focus.

The students succinctly stated the lessons that we hoped they would learn from the class. These four statements plus one more form the basis of our current guidelines.

1. The investment is a learning experience.
2. The stock mentor keeps the class updated on the stock.
3. Limit the "names" in the portfolio.
4. Earn an adequate return on the investment.
5. Maintain international diversification.

These guidelines are very different from most professional money manager guidelines. They are also very different from most class-managed portfolio guidelines at other universities. Other school portfolios are set up to teach students how professional money managers manage a portfolio. We don't want to mimic professional money managers. We want to do better. A small fund has some significant advantages. We want to exploit those advantages.

PROFESSIONAL MONEY MANAGERS

There are two broad categories of portfolio management: active and passive. Passive management is a fund that follows an index and takes human judgment out of the picture. APM follows an active management strategy. We'll discuss the different active strategies to see where APM fits and why it has adopted that niche.

Mutual funds and many other professional portfolios typically have a theme or a specialization beyond the active/passive label. For example, there are large-cap value funds where the theme is investing in stocks of companies with market capitalization above a specified level and that have price/earnings (P/E) values below a specified level. Unless you read the prospectus carefully, you may not find out that a fund actually has only a fairly small percentage of assets invested in that class. There are some checks on keeping funds in the advertised category that we discuss later.

Table 2.1 shows an example allocation for a small-cap equity focus. Note that as little as 15 percent of the total assets at any time actually may be invested in small caps. The policy range for the portfolio manager is 30 to 60 percent. The manager doesn't have to rebalance until the portfolio gets under the minimum threshold of 20 percent. If it gets below 20 percent, then the manager immediately has to reallocate to add more small caps.

This type of allocation seems pretty reasonable. A manager has a theme, but there is some diversification from having other asset classes in the portfolio. The APM guidelines don't include anything like this. Think about why you would be at the minimum 20 percent threshold in the portfolio. One reason might be that your small caps have increased in price and grown out of the category, and now they are in the Other Equities category. You many think they are still good investments and it might not be time to sell. Other times market conditions may dictate that holding cash or bonds is a better strategy than small caps, so you load up there. Any predefined allocation

TABLE 2.1　　Example Asset Class Allocation

Asset Class	Policy Range	Policy Target	Minimum Threshold	Maximum Threshold	Current Allocation
Small-cap equities[a]	30–60%	50%	20%	100%	30%
Other equities	10–40%	25%	0%	50%	20%
Fixed income	0–30%	15%	0%	50%	41%
Cash	0–15%	10%	0%	20%	9%

[a]Small cap is defined as less than $1 billion in market capitalization.

is arbitrary. Instead of trying to find the best investment, the investment manager is spending a lot of time trying to fit in a category.

This type of asset class allocation is a way to try to have your cake and eat it, too. Professional managers want to advertise a portfolio with a theme. They also want to be diversified. Modern portfolio theory and folk wisdom values diversification. Modern portfolio theory says it's risky not to have a well-diversified portfolio. Folk wisdom from Sancho Panza says, "It is the part of a wise man to keep himself today for tomorrow and not risk all his eggs in one basket." Diversification is good advice for an individual. Most of the time individuals are well diversified. They own lots of different assets—a house, savings accounts, mutual funds, art, stocks, and bonds. They are able to diversify by themselves just fine. They don't need a money manager to diversify for them.

An asset allocation discipline is also a way to hedge the portfolio manager's bets when the primary investment focus is out of favor. Most traditional managers don't manage to earn absolute return; they manage to beat a benchmark. The benchmark is an index related to the style of the portfolio. For example, a small-cap manager wants to beat the Standard & Poor's (S&P) 600 Index, the Russell 2000, or the *Morgan Stanley Capital International* (MSCI) 1750 Index. These are three indices that track small-cap stocks.

Several companies follow and rank how well mutual funds and other money managers, such as hedge funds, perform in each category. Lipper and Morningstar are two examples. They provide an independent check on a fund's self-stated category. Funds have to report quarterly holdings. The reporting services track the holdings of each fund from their required quarterly reports. If a fund is too far away from its stated target in terms of holdings, the reporting company sends the fund managers a letter stating that the fund needs to track target style more closely or the reporting service will reclassify the fund. Funds, especially those doing well, want to be listed with others in their target group for marketing purposes.

Lipper and Morningstar provide data to the major personal finance Web sites: Yahoo!Finance, MSN Money, and many others. They also provide the information that is used in the *Wall Street Journal, Forbes*, and many other financial publications for their stories and quarterly rankings of funds. Figure 2.1 shows a Morningstar-style box for the Birmiwal Oasis Fund (BIRMX). A Morningstar-style box identifies where a fund is classified in terms of market capitalization and valuation.

Lipper rates funds on five criteria within their style category. Birmiwal Oasis Fund is rated in the top 20 percent in Total Return and Consistent Return relative to their peers: other small-cap core funds. The checkmark and Lipper Leader indicate top 20 percent in the category. The numbers

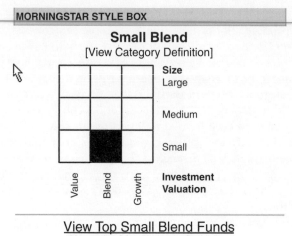

FIGURE 2.1   Morningstar Style Box from
Finance.Yahoo.com

2 to 5 indicate the next 20 percent categories. A 5 represents the bottom
20 percent. The Birmiwal Oasis Fund has 5s for the rest of the categories:
Preservation, Tax-Efficiency, and Expense (See Figure 2.2.)

Why are we discussing actively managed mutual funds, when they are
only one piece in the investment management business? They may be only
one piece, but they are a large piece. Other large investment managers manage money in a similar way. Many active institutional money managers have
similar backgrounds and philosophies. Some of the other large institutional
money managers with similar management styles include those at privately
managed accounts for not-for-profit institutions or partnerships, and trust
accounts. All of these taken together represent a good chunk of money

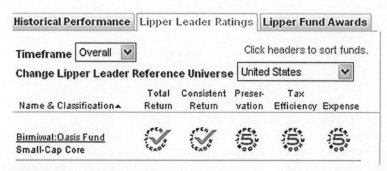

FIGURE 2.2   Lipper Ratings

managers. While they don't all do the same thing, and it's usually not a good idea to generalize, we will do it anyway while recognizing that there are exceptions.

TACTICAL ASSET ALLOCATION AND SECTOR BENCHMARKING

Once active portfolio managers have identified a category and some allocation targets, they use three common strategies of fundamental analysis to choose which stocks go in the portfolio: tactical asset allocation, sector benchmarking, and stock picking. In APM we believe in fundamental analysis and stock picking. Another active strategy that doesn't rely on fundamental analysis is technical analysis, which we'll save for other authors. First we'll discuss tactical asset allocation and sector benchmarking, and then we'll get back to stock picking.

Tactical asset allocation and sector benchmarking are top-down approaches to stock selection. The portfolio managers start with macroeconomic analysis. In tactical asset allocation, managers adjust weights in assets classes in response to changes in the relative values of the asset classes. Managers can focus on many different classes or just a few.

On October 9, 2002, Andrew Hornig, director of research, F&C Investments, London, called in to class and gave us an example of strategic asset allocation. Table 2.2 shows how much of the world's assets were invested in equities, fixed income, real estate, and cash in October 2002. Each of these categories was divided into finer groups in different areas of the world: the United States, Western Europe, Japan, and Emerging Markets. The students' job was to decide whether to be over/underweight in each class. The table shows each group's allocation strategy until the end of class. We told them that we'd evaluate their results on November 28. As you can see from the

TABLE 2.2 Asset Benchmark Weights on October 9, 2002 (weights in %)

Asset Class	October 9 Benchmark Weight	Group 1 Weighting	Group 2 Weighting	Group 3 Weighting	Group 4 Weighting
Equities	50	40	40	45	40
Fixed income	37	43	40	40	50
Real estate	11	12	10	5	5
Cash	2	5	10	10	5
TOTAL	100	100	100	100	100

FIGURE 2.3   NASDAQ Index from 1999 to October 9, 2002

table, all of the groups were extremely pessimistic about equity over the next two months. They decided they should significantly decrease equity weighting and increase debt and cash.

Why were the students so pessimistic about equity? Figure 2.3 shows the NASDAQ up to October 9, 2002. Equity markets in the United States had been in free fall since the March 2000 peak—down 48 percent. The third quarter of 2002 was the worst quarter since 1974. Over that quarter, bonds were up 4 percent and stocks were down 18 percent following a second-quarter decline of 9 percent. Investors were worried about a possible second war in Iraq. Stocks were at 1996 levels. P/E ratios were back to 1990 levels.

The NASDAQ chart shows the free fall in the market since the peak in March 2000. The world benchmark equity weight was 50 percent in early October 2002. All of the groups thought any portfolio should be less than the benchmark weight of 50 percent. That means that all groups would be selling down from the benchmark. It turns out that the markets bottomed on October 9, the date the allocations were due. The NASDAQ closed at 1,114.11.

All of the groups underperformed the benchmark index return because they had decreased their positions in equity—a classic case of ruler analysis. Things were bad in equity, so they decided to move out of equity at exactly the wrong time. All of the groups also increased holdings in fixed income.

The double whammy of chasing fixed income returns and moving out of equity at exactly the wrong time showed up in poor performance of all the groups relative to the benchmark portfolio, as shown in Table 2.3.

Of course there are successful portfolio managers who use tactical asset allocation successfully. Just because the class wasn't particularly successful with this exercise doesn't mean that someone can't do it well. However, there is a tendency to be more backward looking (ruler analysis, again). It's hard for investors to forecast turning points. When an investor does think the economy is in for a change, she has to overcome what most other investors are doing. If the stock market is going down, most investors are selling.

A contrarian has to have some courage and patience to get out in front of the crowd. Every day, the market gives you a report card. It can be a long wait sometimes for the turning point. If you are too early, then you receive a long string of poor grades, even if it's long-run performance that matters. Perhaps it is easier for a seasoned professional than for most students or individual investors to have that kind of courage and patience.

The asset allocation exercise did not have any relation to what we actually did in the portfolio. On October 9, 2002, the APM portfolio was fully invested in equities with no short positions and only 0.4 percent in cash (see Table 2.4). On that day the portfolio was valued at $167,374.29, just about at the lowest level since its inception. However, the main reason we were down was not the investments. During that year we had $80,000 in withdrawals from the fund. Some were for scholarships and some were for administrative expenses. The year 2002 had started with the APM portfolio around $300,000. Year to date in the third quarter, after adjusting for the withdrawals from the portfolio, performance was down 20 percent, while the NASDAQ was down 36 percent for the year.

The class's experiment in tactical asset allocation did not show big performance gains. It was an effective way to learn. Several factors made the timing of this exercise unique. Hornig pointed out several areas as he wrapped up the exercise:

- October 9 was a very significant low point in equity markets globally.
- The rise in stock markets in the following month was one of the largest four-week rallies ever.
- Asset class behavior turned around 180 degrees.
- Since all of the groups were underweight equities, it was almost impossible to beat the benchmark.
- The benchmarks and guidelines forced investors heavily into the weakest bond market in the United States over this specific period, detracting from overall absolute performance.

TABLE 2.3 Benchmark Weights and Returns, October 9 to November 28, 2002

Asset Class	November 28 Benchmark Weights	Asset Class Return	Benchmark Index Return	Group 1	Group 2	Group 3	Group 4
Equities	55	18.60	10.24	7.28	7.14	8.48	7.43
Fixed income	33	−4.00	−1.32	−1.77	−1.43	−1.83	−2.02
Real estate	10	1.00	0.10	0.12	0.10	0.05	0.05
Cash	2	0.25	0.01	0.01	0.03	0.03	0.01
TOTAL	100		9.03	5.64	5.84	6.93	5.47

TABLE 2.4 2002 APM Portfolio Values and Returns

Date	Beginning Value	Ending Value	Net Contributions or Withdrawals	APM Quarterly Return	APM YTD Return	NASDAQ YTD Return
Q1 2002	312,101	303,613	−15,410	2%	2%	−5%
Q2 2002	303,613	237,685	−67,500	1%	3%	−26%
Q3 2002	237,685	179,862	0	−24%	−22%	−38%
Q4 2002	179,862	271,034	0	51%	18%	−32%

Hornig concluded the exercise by saying:

Global balanced portfolios are not the way to play the very short term in global markets, but they will end the full year 2002 with a relatively good performance compared with equity funds because of their bond weightings and because the U.S. dollar gave back some strength, which boosts returns from non-U.S. markets.

Sector benchmarking is similar to asset allocation in that the first step in allocating money in the portfolio is observing what the industry sector benchmarks are for different sectors of the economy. There are several different industrial classifications, but the most popular one right now is published by S&P in collaboration with MSCI. It is called the Global Industry Classification Standard (GICS®).

GISC has four levels of detail: sector, industry group, industry, and subindustry. S&P assigns a company first to a subindustry based on its principal business. A company can belong to only one subindustry regardless of its different lines of business. Usually the company is classified based on its revenue source. Some companies with multiple lines of business can be classified as Industrial Conglomerates or financial Holding Companies. Companies are reviewed annually and can be reclassified at that time, if the business model has changed.

In 2002 S&P reported 10 sectors, 23 industry groups, 59 industries, and 122 subindustries. The sectors are assigned a two-digit code; industry groups, a four-digit code; industries, a six-digit code; and subindustries, an eight-digit code. Here is an example of the GICS code, the North American Industry Classification System (NAICS) code, and the Standard Industrial Classification (SIC) for Anheuser-Busch (New York Stock Exchange [NYSE]: BUD).

GICS Sector	30	Consumer Staples
GICS Group	3020	Food Beverage & Tobacco
GICS Industry	302010	Beverages
GICS Sub-industry	30201010	Brewers
NAICS Code	312120	Breweries
SIC Code	2082	Malt Beverages

Sector benchmarking is also called sector rotation since different sectors are supposed to perform better or worse in different market and business cycle environments. During the early part of an economic expansion, the traditional wisdom is to buy Consumer Discretionary and Financials, especially retail, consumer durables, transportation, and housing. The idea is that consumer spending will pick up after a downturn, and you want to be

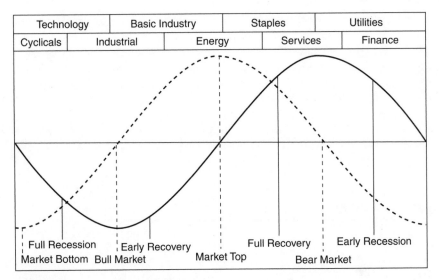

Technology	Basic Industry	Staples	Utilities
Cyclicals	Industrial	Energy	Services	Finance

Full Recession   Early Recovery   Full Recovery   Early Recession

Market Bottom   Bull Market   Market Top   Bear Market

FIGURE 2.4   Sector Rotation Model
Source: Chart courtesy of Stockcharts.com.

ahead of the game. There are similar strategies for each stage of the economic cycle. Figure 2.4 shows how the market cycle and economic cycle interact.

Almost all investment theories sound great and can work, but there are always difficulties in implementation. Big problem number one: It is difficult to tell exactly where in the cycle we are. Just as the students discovered in the strategic asset allocation exercise, the impetus of the moment is hard to overcome. When things look bad, it's hard to envision how they are going to change. Ruler analysis strikes again.

The next big problem is that each cycle looks slightly different from previous cycles. Changes in technology and in the global economy overwhelmed some of the traditional cyclical patterns. Advances in fiscal and monetary policy have changed some economic responses so that growth and inflation are no longer synonymous. Technology influences costs and margins, so what was once a stodgy industrial is now a high-technology growth company. An example is the steel industry. Restructuring of the steel industry allowed for much greater efficiency, much better turnaround time, and higher margins. During bull markets, people are very optimistic and say: "This time it's different. We've put bad times to rest because of technology."

Both strategic asset allocation and sector rotation depend on identifying which market and economic stage we're in. Then you place your bets. Those bets are hedged because you aren't usually out of an asset class or sector, but underweight. Portfolio managers who use asset allocation and sector rotation can end up looking a lot like the market and returning close-to-market returns. Because of the human tendency toward ruler analysis, it's hard to go against all the news reports and recent history. We all know a change is coming, but it's easier to predict the change will be later. We like some confirmation that things are turning up or down. By then it's too late. The worm has turned.

There are, of course, investors and strategists who can make this approach work really well. Sam Stovall at S&P always has some great ideas in his column. Peter Lynch was a master at sector rotation.

APM APPROACH

There are many ways to provide practical investing insights to students. We could run the portfolio using asset allocation or sector rotation, but we've chosen to manage the portfolio using a stock-picking approach. The goal of stock picking is straightforward. We want to seek out and invest in companies that are fairly priced that will provide a good investment return. It doesn't matter what is happening in the stock market or the economy, there will always be some firms that provide a good investment return. Market and economic cycles matter because they may make it harder or easier to find those investments. Stock picking means that it's important to understand how a company is supposed to make money, evaluate how it is doing that job, and then evaluate whether the stock price reflects our belief in how well or poorly the company is performing.

In the rest of this chapter we briefly discuss how our stock-picking approach fits in with our five guidelines. In subsequent chapters we focus on some extended examples of how we find and evaluate companies for the portfolio.

Guideline 1. The Investment Is a Learning Experience

APM's first priority is to provide educational value to the students. We are more likely to purchase stocks that we can understand and analyze. For example, General Electric (GE) is a fine company and may be a very good investment. However, with its multiple divisions and multiple acquisitions every year, it is almost impossible for students to begin to understand the pieces and properly analyze the company's prospects. The only way that we might begin to understand how GE creates value and to recognize when

TABLE 2.5   APM Market Capitalization, August, 2007

Category	Capitalization	No. of Stocks	% of Portfolio
Micro	Less than 250 $M	7	23%
Small	250–1,000 $M	12	36%
Medium	1–5 $B	9	28%
Large	5–25 $B	1	5%
Giant	Greater than 25 $B	4	8%
Cash			1%
Total		33	100%

that value is misunderstood is to have a senior GE executive explain the key components. A GE analyst at a research firm or investment bank also might be able to help us. Since we don't have alumni or friends of the school doing either of those things, it's not cost-effective in terms of time and energy for us to study a company like GE.

Instead we might focus on a company like H&R Block. Its main business is to provide tax services, in addition to two other smaller divisions. It is possible for students to come up with a demand for tax services and have a good idea about the competitive environment. A smaller company like H&R Block may be more willing to come and speak with our students in class. This requirement does result in a portfolio that probably would be identified as a "small-cap" portfolio. Table 2.5 shows the APM portfolio's market capitalization breakdown as of August 2006. It's been similar for quite a few years.

MARKET CAP DEFINITION

Brokerage companies and mutual funds differ on how they define market capitalization categories. Some define small cap at a distinct level, such as less than $2.5 billion (Value Line) or $3 billion (Tocqueville Small Cap Value Fund). Others use the market capitalization of the S&P 600, Russell 2000, or MSCI 1750 indices to define small cap. Currently, the largest market capitalization in the S&P 600 is Frontier Oil at $4 billion.

Guideline 2. The Stock Mentor Keeps the Class Updated on the Stock

In the APM class, stock mentors fill several different roles. One way to be a successful stock picker is to build an information network of different people who know about a particular industry or company really well. By drawing on that network, the class can get close to the information. The mentor can help the students understand the nuances of an industry, or why a company's convertible debt offering might not have been a good idea at the time.

Many times stock mentors are alumni of the class who have been working in an industry for several years. Since the class began in 1994, some of our alums are reaching a point in their careers where they have significant responsibility and insights they are willing to share. Some mentors are speakers in the class who aren't APM alums, but perhaps they are University of Kansas alums or other interested parties who are willing and able to help out. Sometimes we've had a mentor from a company who wasn't an alum, had no connection to KU; but we've called the company or analyst, and they been so happy to spread their story that they've turned into a valuable mentor.

We don't rely just on the mentor's opinion. The students are expected to trust but verify. They are encouraged to form their own opinion while taking into account what the mentors have to say.

The mentors also provide an example of how students can build their own network after they graduate. Many of the mentors still keep in touch with friends they made while in school. Kent is a great example of keeping in touch with classmates and friends. He has built a great network beginning with his undergraduate classmates. Many times in class he'll give a student a name and number to call to get more information about a company. An example of how he uses his network is with Brooke Corporation (BXXX). Brooke's business is retail insurance franchises. To find out more about the details of retail insurance, Kent asked several friends in the retail insurance business about margins, which companies provided the most generous premium sharing with retail brokers, and other specifics of the business before deciding whether to invest in the company.

Finally, the mentors play a role in helping student make contacts that will provide jobs. Mentors who don't have jobs to offer have helped prepare students with mock phone interviews, resume reviews, job leads, and in many other ways. Having a successful alum visit class and share her story about how she found her job after graduation is inspiring to many students.

Guideline 3. Limit the "Names" in the Portfolio

This rule is in place to make sure that the students can get to know each company in the portfolio. The target is 25 to 30 names. A name can be two different securities for one company. For example, the APM portfolio has held both the common and the preferred stock of LSB Industries for several years. A covered call position (holding the common stock and writing a call on the stock) would also be counted as a "name." One aspect of the class is understanding the economics of the company, then understanding how to invest when there is a choice of several securities.

It's very unusual to have fewer than 25 companies in the portfolio. Students and mentors are much more likely to recommend buys over sells. Having the target is one way to enforce some sell discipline and deeper evaluation of current holdings. This guideline and the previous one tend to work in opposing directions. If a buy recommendation comes in and the portfolio is at the target level of names, the students have to go through several different types of analysis. They have to evaluate the current names in terms of investment opportunities. Those at the bottom of the list need to be compared to the new recommendation with respect to all five criteria.

Guideline 4. Earn an Adequate Return on the Investment

Determining an adequate return on investment entails examining the risk and return of the stock. Much of the rest of the book involves the specifics of how we determine what an adequate return should be.

Guideline 5. Maintain International Diversification

There are lots of investment opportunities throughout the world. With our U.S.-centric media, it is more difficult to find the good investments in other markets. Currently about 46 percent of the APM portfolio is invested in international stocks.

There are many varieties of international investing. The easiest way for U.S. investors is to buy a foreign company that is listed on a U.S. exchange. Many foreign companies are listed on U.S. exchanges. Current foreign holdings in the APM portfolio that are listed only on U.S. exchanges include Garmin (GRMN), Linktone (LTON), and Sohu (SOHU). Each of these companies is headquartered in a different country. Linktone and Sohu do business exclusively in China. Garmin produces GPS systems for many retail outlets in the United States and is nominally a Cayman Island corporation with headquarters in Kansas. Garmin has a large manufacturing facility in Taiwan and one in Kansas. Since the company sells most of its products in the United States and has a headquarters in this country, is it a foreign company? Technically, yes, so Garmin is included in the 46 percent. In class we use Garmin to illustrate the difficulty of defining a foreign company because most people might think of it as a U.S. company.

There is less ambiguity with Linktone and Sohu. Many Chinese companies have chosen to bypass their domestic capital markets and raise money in the U.S. equity markets. The first to do so was called chinadotcom in 1997. The APM portfolio invested in 2001 when the stock was less than $2. It had nosedived after reaching $78.00 on March 6, 2000.

Another way to invest in a foreign company is through sponsored American Depository Receipts (ADRs). ADRs are shares of a company that trades on a foreign exchanges bundled through an investment bank or other sponsor to trade in dollars on an American exchange. It is usually seamless for an investor to trade ADRs. Sometimes there are some liquidity issues. The ADR may not trade with the same liquidity as the home exchange shares. The APM portfolio held ADRs in Internacional de Ceramica, a Mexican tile company. Its ADR ticker symbol was ICM. The primary shares traded on the Mexican Bolsa de Valores, and one ADR was worth five B shares and five D shares. On December 23, 2004, Internacional de Ceramica delisted its ADRs. The primary reason was that the company did not want to incur the expenses related to Sarbanes-Oxley (SOX) reporting requirements. Since it is a small company the several millions in SOX expenses would be significant. The portfolio still owns the shares. We received the five B shares and five D shares for each ADR. Our shares now trade in Mexico.

Other ways to trade foreign companies are on the local exchanges or in the gray market. Recently the "gray" market has expanded significantly, yet very little information about it is available. The gray market trades unsponsored ADRs on the Pink Sheets, a centralized quotation service. The Pink Sheets are not technically an exchange, and the rules governing the quotation service are not always clear. A broker can make a market in any type of shares he wishes on the Pink Sheets. For example, suppose a broker buys some shares on the Hong Kong exchange. He can offer some of those shares for sale in the gray market at a specified price. He does not have to post a bid, nor does anyone else. For an investor, the upshot is that you might be able to buy shares one day but then not be able to sell them on the gray market. We'll discuss this market in greater detail in Chapter 11.

WRAPPING UP

Our guidelines work pretty well, but that doesn't mean they are set in stone. The class has changed over time because we've thought of better ways to do things and because investing is dynamic. Things change in the market, but we are always trying to think of better ways to educate students and run the portfolio at the same time. What won't change is the hard work and clear thinking that's required from students in the class.

CHAPTER 3

Conventional Wisdom

Finance theory came of age shortly after World War II. Some of the pioneers of that age—Harry Markowitz, Merton Miller, William Sharpe, John Lintner, and others—started building financial theories using mathematical tools honed during the war. They applied statistics and statistical analysis to the stock market to come up with a body of knowledge called Modern Portfolio Theory. The foundation of Modern Portfolio Theory includes work on diversification, specification of types of risk, the efficient frontier, and the Capital Asset Pricing Model (CAPM).

Before Modern Portfolio Theory, investment professionals looked at the risk and reward of individual securities without considering whether things change when you combine individual securities into a portfolio. Markowitz started the modern age of portfolio management in 1952 by applying the statistical notion of correlation to stocks. His insight showed that investors can reduce risk by combining stocks into portfolios because stocks don't all move in the same direction at the same time. Diversification wasn't a new idea, but Markowitz's formal proof using statistical concepts was.

Statistical measures, including correlation, and other analytical techniques were developed into useful tools in the late nineteenth century, but their application was limited until the introduction of computers during World War II to perform the needed computations. After the war smart people armed with computing power were set loose to think about things other than bombing algorithms. Quite a few of them ended up pondering the stock market.

Markowitz's insight and formalization of risk and diversification in statistical terms was groundbreaking, turning finance into a science. Other researchers picked up the thread, and the race was on. Universities started and expanded business schools in the 1960s. Finance theory entered the classroom. New PhDs based their research on Markowitz's theories and developed new ones. In the 1960s efficient diversification led to the Capital

Asset Pricing Model (CAPM) and the Efficient Market Hypothesis. By the 1970s empirical work testing the models was going full bore. In the classroom, students were taught the theories and were the first generation to implement them in the markets. Financial education and practice were revolutionized in less than 15 years.

There was no question in the finance community that the theories were generally correct. There was a little quibbling at the edges over a specification or two, but as soon as the quibble surfaced other researchers would show an elegant way to get around it. In 1985 a conference held at the bastion and birthplace of Modern Portfolio Theory, the University of Chicago, afforded the quibbles some legitimacy. In October a conference called "The Behavioral Foundations of Economic Theory" was held. Its aim was to examine some systematic evidence that called into question the foundation of Modern Portfolio Theory. A growing number of studies documented departures from rational economic behavior. The upshot of the conference was that even if some individuals weren't rational economic actors, markets overcame any problems with individual rationality. The conference did spark additional inquiry and systematic research into behavioral issues in economics and finance. In the 1980s and 1990s individuals who called into question market efficiency were dismissed either as misinformed practitioners or as misguided and perhaps dangerous academics who might corrupt students' educations.

In this chapter we review the implications of Modern Portfolio Theory for individual investors. Modern Portfolio Theory is the current conventional wisdom. Following any conventional wisdom leads to subpar results, especially the stronger and more widely received the conventional wisdom is. Why? The reason is simple: If everyone is acting (investing) the same way, everyone is going to receive average returns. After subtracting the costs of investing, returns will be below average.

DIVERSIFICATION AND RISK

Harry Markowitz is the father of Modern Portfolio Theory. Using the statistical concept of return variability to define risk led Markowitz and others down the path of mathematical certainty with proofs, theorems, and more proofs. Markowitz shows us why and how to diversify. Finance professors love teaching the theory. It's neat, clean, and wraps things up very nicely, thank you. Students may not love it as much as professors, but they do like the certainty it affords. Ambiguity in a classroom isn't popular. Students like it when their professors have the answers. They can learn what the professors are teaching and have the answers too.

Let's review the two principles of diversification and risk:

1. Risk is defined as standard deviation of return—a statistical measure of return variability.
2. There is an optimal way to combine stocks to form portfolios with the lowest level of risk for a given return. In a portfolio stocks have two types of risk: market risk and idiosyncratic risk. Market risk is measured by beta, and that's all that matters.

These two principles were expounded and expanded by Markowitz and his successors. A few more types of risk were added, but the idea that we can measure risk and combine stocks into an optimal portfolio is still key. We'll discuss these two foundations of investing, how they are still at work in the world. In the past 10 years, others have criticized the "theory," but the investment industry still relies heavily on these notions, so it's worth understanding exactly where they fail.

Risk Defined as Standard Deviation

As mentioned, risk is defined as standard deviation of return—a statistical measure of return variability. It's great to be able to calculate the risk of a stock. When people are asked to assess risk subjectively, studies show that all kinds of personal biases can creep in. One of those is a familiarity bias. If you spend a lot of time studying a stock, you become familiar with its warts. You may tend to become more comfortable with its warts and give it a lower risk rating than less familiar stocks. So when Markowitz discovered a way to calculate risk using standard deviation, many rejoiced. At last, an objective measure of what's really going on with risk! Jack Treynor and William Sharpe, almost simultaneously, developed the risk measure further, and with others' input the whole idea came to be known as the Capital Asset Pricing Model. The CAPM breaks risk as measured by standard deviation of return into two parts: market risk and idiosyncratic risk. The theory says that market risk is what investors really need to worry about because idiosyncratic risk can be diversified away by forming a portfolio.

Standard deviation measures how spread out returns are. Figure 3.1 illustrates this concept. Both have zero as expected return, but one is more spread out than the other. There is a greater chance that you'll receive a return of 5 percent or higher in the return distribution with the bigger spread or standard deviation. At the same time, in this case, there's a bigger chance that you'll lose 5 percent or more in the distribution with a larger spread. The tall, skinny return distribution has a standard deviation of 1, and the shorter, fat distribution has a standard deviation of 2.

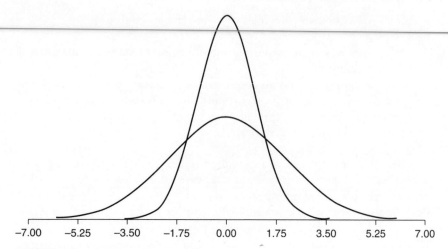

| -7.00 | -5.25 | -3.50 | -1.75 | 0.00 | 1.75 | 3.50 | 5.25 | 7.00 |

FIGURE 3.1 Two Return Distributions

Investors really care only about the losing-money part. Risk really isn't the chance that you'll make money but the chance that you'll lose money. Standard deviation is okay, if the upside and downside are symmetric. The theory predicts that higher risk is and should be associated with higher returns. Some of the best investors in the world disagree. Warren Buffett is a pretty well-regarded investor and is known for following a very-low-risk strategy in his investments. He looks for limited downside with very good upside potential. He accomplishes this partly by not overpaying for his investments. His mentor, Benjamin Graham, schooled him in the art of finding good deals. Using standard deviation as a measure of risk for Buffet's portfolio would be misleading because the source of variation comes primarily from the upside.

In March 2001, the APM class invested in a small Chinese company called chinadotcom, which ran a Chinese Internet business. The company had bypassed the Chinese equity market and became the first Chinese company to list directly on the NASDAQ in the United States in July 1999. After the Internet bubble burst, the share price had fallen from $73 in March 2000 to $1.86 in July 2002. It seemed like just another Internet bubble stock biting the dust, except chinadotcom had $3.42 of cash per share on its balance sheet and no debt. The APM portfolio initially purchased chinadotcom in September 2002 at $1.99 per share. At the time the company had a net loss of 12 cents per share, but it was breaking even on a cash basis so it didn't need to rely on the cash on the balance sheet to keep going. The downside was limited, but there was lots of upside. We discuss chinadotcom in more detail later, but this investment illustrates one way of limiting downside.

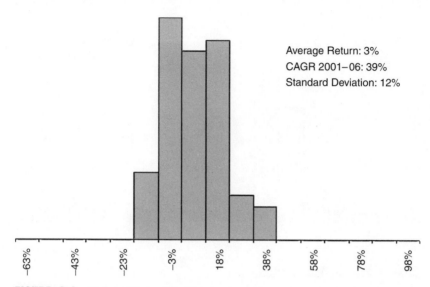

FIGURE 3.2 Valero Return Distribution

Generally, though, standard deviation doesn't look like too bad a risk measure for stocks. Figures 3.2 and 3.3 show the distribution of monthly returns from 2001 to 2006. Valero's average monthly return was 3 percent, and the company returned a compound annual return (CAGR) of 39 percent with a standard deviation of 12 percent. Sohu's standard deviation is just about twice as big as Valero's, but so is the average return. The CAGR is bigger also. Higher risk, higher reward is how the theory is supposed to work.

Forming Optimal Portfolios

There is an optimal way to combine stocks to form portfolios with the lowest level of risk for a given return. In a portfolio stocks have two types of risk: market risk and idiosyncratic risk. Market risk is measured by beta, and that's all that matters.

Sharpe and Treynor took things further than standard deviation. Because almost all stock returns are correlated with market returns, they are correlated with each other. Idiosyncratic or stock-specific risk can be minimized by combining stocks into a portfolio. Market risk is measured by beta (β), which is pretty easy to calculate and very popular. It's on all the financial Web sites. Beta is also easy to interpret. The market's beta is 1, so a stock with a beta close to 1 would have average risk. Stocks with betas

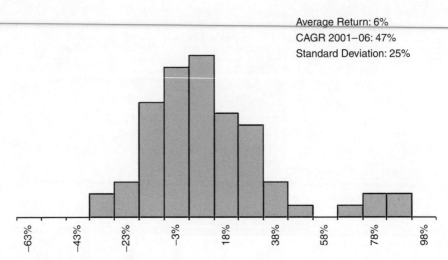

Average Return: 6%
CAGR 2001–06: 47%
Standard Deviation: 25%

FIGURE 3.3 Sohu Return Distribution

higher than 1 are riskier than average, and stocks with betas less than 1 are less risky than average.

Students learn to use betas to calculate the cost of equity capital for firms. The cost of equity for a company is important because it is the same as the return that an equity investor should receive on an investment in the firm. The CAPM equation to find the cost of equity is:

$$Cost\ of\ equity = Risk\text{-}free\ rate + \beta \times (Expected\ return\ on\ the\ market$$
$$- Risk\text{-}free\ rate)$$

where   Risk-free rate = U.S. Treasury bill or bond rate
β = Beta
Expected return on the market
= Subjective estimate of what someone
thinks the long-term return in equities is going to be

Over the past 50 years, the annual average market return has been around 10 percent, so lots of people use 10 percent for the expected return on the market. The Treasury rates are posted daily. The only piece of the equation left is the firm's beta. Students learn the equation to calculate the cost of equity, but they don't always learn how to evaluate beta. (A note to our colleagues: We know you teach this. It's the learning part that doesn't always come through.)

The first semester that we (Cathy and Kent) taught the class together was fall 2001. The students had a case due on LSB Industries. Yahoo!Finance reported that LSB had a beta of −0.24. Negative betas are very rare, and it's not entirely clear how to use them in the CAPM. A negative beta means that a stock is moving in the direction opposite of the market. However, it's not clear that this means that the cost of equity capital should be low. Most of the time companies with negative betas are just statistical flukes driven by a few odd days. Using a risk-free rate of 5 percent for 10-year Treasury bonds and 10 percent expected return on the market, the students calculated the cost of equity for LSB to be 3.8 percent.

According to the theory, LSB should be an extremely low risk company for a portfolio. Because it has a negative beta, it should offset risk from other portfolio investments. A couple of pieces to the puzzle didn't quite fit. Students wrote in their reports that LSB was a very risky company because of its high debt load. LSB had approximately $150 million in debt with an equity value of only $36 million. The company issued debt at 10.75 percent around this time; that's the cost of debt. In bankruptcy, debt holders are paid before equity holders. Typically the cost of debt is lower to reflect that priority in the capital structure. Comparing a 10.75 percent cost of debt to a 3.8 percent cost of equity doesn't compute. The cost of equity should be higher than the cost of debt. Kent told the class he thought there was about a 30 percent chance of bankruptcy for this firm. Not a great comfort to equity holders! Certainly equity holders should be expecting a return of more than 3.8 percent. You could get almost that in dividend yield on any number of very safe, stable stocks.

So what's going on with beta? Why isn't it giving us a reasonable number? Beta is estimated by comparing a company's returns to market returns over one to two years. Beta isn't a precise estimate, but almost everyone reports a point estimate. That point estimate gives the impression of "truth" when in fact the estimate may not be very good at all. Statisticians look most often at an interval estimate, or the likely range of values, instead of a single point estimate. Interval estimates have a couple of advantages. They drive home the point that have an estimate, and the width of the interval gives an idea about how precise we the estimate is. If we have a range of our interval estimate from 0.76 to 0.78 for a beta, that's a very precise estimate. We have a good idea that this company is about two-thirds as risky as the market. If we have an interval of 0.5 to 1.5, however, we can't even say whether the stock is more or less risky than the market.

The interval should contain the "true" beta with a certain degree of confidence, and any point in the interval is equally likely to be the "true" estimate of beta. Most of the time people use a 95 percent confidence interval. That means that 95 percent of the time, the interval will contain the "true"

TABLE 3.1 LSB Betas Using Different Market Indices

	NASDAQ Index	S&P 500 Index
Point estimate	0.70	1.10
Lower limit of 95% confidence interval	0.15	0.31
Upper limit of 95% confidence interval	1.26	1.90
Adjusted r^2	5%	6%

value. There's still a 5 percent chance you could be wrong. You can construct a 99 percent confidence interval, but the tradeoff is that it will be wider (less precise). The 95 percent confidence interval for LSB's beta in 2001 was −2 to 1.6! That's a huge range. The midpoint of the interval was −0.24. The financial reporting sites on the Web just report the midpoint (the point estimate). Since any point in the interval could be the true beta, we could use −2, 0, or 1.6 for a beta to calculate the cost of capital. Such a wide interval means that any estimate of beta is meaningless for LSB and shouldn't be used. Still, because it's published, students and most others don't question whether it's a good estimate or not.

It gets worse. When you estimate beta, you have to decide how many years, months, or days to use. You also have to decide whether to use daily, weekly, or monthly returns. Finally, you have to decide which market index to use: NASDAQ, Standard & Poor's (S&P) 500 or something else. Depending on your choice, you can get very different point and interval estimates. Table 3.1 shows an example of two different ways to estimate beta for LSB in November 2006. Each way uses weekly returns for two years. One is to estimate using NASDAQ as the market index, and the other uses the S&P 500. Just looking at the point estimates, you would draw different conclusions about the company's current riskiness. The point estimate of 0.70 indicates that LSB is less risky than the market, while the estimate of 1.10 indicates that it is slightly *more* risky than the market. The last line of the table, adjusted r^2, measures what percent of the variability in LSB returns is explained by the market index. As you can see, NASDAQ explains only 5 percent of the LSB's return; the S&P 500 is slightly better, at 6 percent. Approximately 95 percent of LSB's return is explained by something other than the market. Figuring out that other 95 percent might be more important than worrying about beta.

The rest of the world is pretty confused about beta also. In Table 3.2 we show betas for three APM stocks, LSB Industries (LXU), CDC Corp. (CHINA), and Valero Energy Corp. (VLO), from different Internet sites and

TABLE 3.2   Betas for Three Stocks from Different Financial News Sources

	LXU	CHINA	VLO
moneycentral.msn.com	NA	1.84	0.92
Yahoo!Finance	0.06	2.35	0.32
NASDAQ.com	0.32	1.82	0.79
Bloomberg Raw	0.46	1.26	2.05
Bloomberg Adjusted	0.64	1.17	1.70

from Bloomberg, a professional financial information service. These betas were all collected on the same day in 2006. The point estimates vary widely. None of these sources provides any way to tell anything about the precision of the estimates. You can see that the sites probably are making very different choices in how the betas are estimated.

So what's the bottom line with beta and the CAPM? They sound good in theory, but they're very tough to implement in practice. A lot of finance professors have spent quite a bit of time trying to come up with variations on the CAPM that explains risk better. Conditional CAPM with time-varying betas and Consumption CAPM are two variations. Other extensions add other variables besides the market return. Some of the variations work better in some time periods or on some set of stocks, but nothing works well all the time. In Chapter 10 we present a few simple rules that work to benchmark a company's risk.

EFFICIENT MARKETS

Markets are efficient and investors are rational economic actors. Investors, because they are rational and don't like to lose money, don't make a lot of mistakes in pricing securities. Stock prices are the best estimates of the underlying value of the company. So goes the Efficient Market Hypothesis (EMH) as formulated by Eugene Fama of the University of Chicago. By implication, investors shouldn't worry about things like stock prices because the market has set them and they are right. Chicago (along with many other universities) has long been the bastion of efficient markets. One joke was that a finance professor from Chicago was walking down the street with his graduate student. They saw a twenty-dollar bill lying on the sidewalk. The student leaned down to pick it up. The professor said, "Forget it. If it really were a twenty-dollar bill, someone would already have picked it up."

The EMH is a paradox. Markets are efficient because lots of really smart people are out looking for the twenty-dollar bills or analyzing stocks. As soon as a twenty is spotted, it's gone; in other words, as soon as a good trade on a stock is spotted, it's snapped up. If smart traders aren't out there trying to beat each other to the punch, then the market can't be efficient. The EMHers feel that for most of the world, it's not worth trying to figure stocks out unless you have some sort of special advantage that you can exploit that isn't illegal. They argue that for most of us, it's not worth the bother. We wouldn't be compensated well enough for our time. We should leave it to the professionals. They are faster, smarter, and have lower cost than the rest of the world. We can put our money in a well-diversified, low-cost mutual fund and leave it there until we're ready to retire on our average gains from the market. Our main decision after that is how to withdraw it over our retirement.

The main message of the EMH is "trust prices." Smart people competing in the market make sure that the prices are accurate. "Accurate" means that they reflect the best consensus expectations of a company's long-term prospects. All relevant information is compounded into the stock price by the analysts, portfolio managers, and other investment professionals beating each other to the punch. There's no extra return that can be earned by individual, nonprofessional investors.

We don't believe in all efficient markets all the time. We try to show the class what drives institutional behavior. By understanding how institutions fit into the investment landscape and what drives their investments, the class, individuals, and students can earn returns that don't fit in the EMH beta/CAPM framework. The institutions that drive investment behavior are investment banks, mutual funds, hedge funds, and corporations. To understand what drives each, you have to look at the decision makers' incentives. We can categorize these into buy-side and sell-side incentives. Corporations don't belong in either of these categories but are influenced by both.

Institutions and the Efficient Market

Investment banks are called the sell side. They don't actually do much investing, and they aren't bankers. They make money on transactions. Traditionally, investment banks had two big transactions: helping companies raise capital and advising companies on mergers and acquisitions (M&A). Because these can be very large transactions, they can have a big effect on stock prices. We'll look at the investment banking business in some detail and how it affects prices.

Investment banking is a very competitive but profitable business. The top firms are called bulge-bracket investment banks, and they are measured by deal volume and reputation. Deal volume is tabulated in "league tables."

TABLE 3.3   M&A League Tables: Completed Global Deals

Adviser	Rank	Market Share (%)	USD Volume ($B)	Deals
Goldman Sachs & Co	1	29	617	292
Citigroup	2	25	527	277
JP Morgan	3	24	496	304
Morgan Stanley	4	23	490	294
Merrill Lynch & Co	5	18	384	233
Deutsche Bank AG	6	15	322	187
UBS	7	14	292	234

Source: From Bloomberg, calculated April 2006.

Table 3.3 shows a league table for global M&A deals. There are also league tables for equity offerings, debt offerings, and total underwritings. The investment banks use league tables as marketing tools. They pitch the idea that bigger is better in terms of doing an M&A deal or a public offering. Table 3.3 shows that Goldman is number one for M&A deals as of April 2006. There are many other league tables. For private equity M&A, Citigroup is number one, and Morgan Stanley is number one in equity underwriting. When you look at the leagues tables, make sure you know the calculation basis. The investment bank is always going to use a league table that conveys the right message.

Large M&A transactions and equity IPOs are very profitable. For the banks, it doesn't really matter if the deals make economic sense or not. They'll get their cut no matter what. On a large deal, such as Freeport-McMoRan acquiring Phelps Dodge Corporation, the initial price tag was $25.9 billion. J.P. Morgan and Merrill Lynch were the coadvisers, so they split fees of 1 to 1.5 percent (plus expenses) of the $25.9 billion. That's more than $250 million in fees split between the two firms. But initial fees are only the beginning. Typically then the investment banks start to make some real money on trading, lending, and advice on divestitures that typically come with acquisitions.

What does all of this have to do with Efficient Market Theory? Well, one part of the theory says that when a firm is mismanaged or wasting money, its stock price will reflect that mismanagement. A new team of managers will recognize that they can create value and will come in to take over the assets and optimize firm value. That should be a great situation for shareholders. A group of good managers is coming in to rescue the company. That's one scenario.

Another good reason for two good firms to merge is because of synergies—the firms together are worth more than they are separately. That's another good outcome for shareholders. Share prices of both firms should rise because they are worth more together than separately. The theory suggests that investment banks are the good guys, making the market more efficient by helping get rid of bad managers and getting the guys with synergies together.

What's happened in the real world? A 2005 study in the *Journal of Finance* found that in aggregate, acquiring firms lost $216 billion in shareholder value in the 1990s.[1] The 1980s were considered pretty bad for acquiring shareholders, but they only lost $4 billion in that decade. The 1990s were 50 times worse. Maybe the losses were only bad for the acquirers. The theory says that acquired firms' shareholders might benefit. But that's not the case. The study finds that after netting out gains from the acquirers, total shareholder loss was only $134 billion in the 1990s! Over both decades the total value paid by acquiring firms was $959 billion (in 2001 dollars). The study found that the dollar return on that investment was a loss of $430 billion (in 2001 dollars), a −45 percent return. All of these numbers are before fees. Investment banking fees were around 3 percent in the 1980s; today they have decreased to around 1 percent. That's about $19 billion in 2001 dollars for the investment banks just on the M&A part of the deal. Add to those numbers lawyer fees, accounting fees, and more, and it is clear that M&A activity has destroyed a massive amount of shareholder value!

It's not just the greedy investment banks going around destroying value for shareholders. The acquiring companies have to agree to do the acquisitions. That's the chief executive officer (CEO) and the board of directors who go into the deals knowing the bleak prospects for acquiring firms. What are they thinking? They are thinking of their own paychecks, of course. The biggest predictor of CEO pay is the size of the company. The bigger the company, the bigger the paycheck is for the senior managers. Board members usually see the same effect. But wait, there's more. Many times there is a provision in the CEO's pay package that she or he can cash out all options and deferred pay when there is a change in the ownership structure. So one CEO gets to manage a bigger company with bigger pay and the other gets paid off. Boards use the cover of efficient markets to proclaim that they are doing the shareholders a favor with the acquisition activity.[2]

---

[1] Sara B. Moeller, Frederik P. Schlingemann, and René M. Stulz, "Wealth Destruction on a Massive Scale? A Study of Acquiring-Firm Returns in the Recent Merger Wave," *Journal of Finance* 60, no. 2 (2005): 757
[2] CEOs and the board probably really want the acquisitions to work. Perhaps they figure, "This time will be different." It's hard to take off the rose-colored glasses when so much is at stake.

Who profits from acquisition activity? Usually the acquired firm's shareholders do because the acquirer tends to overpay, but shareholders of the target firm need to sell soon after the announcement of the deal. The investment banks certainly benefit from the fees—the larger the transaction, the higher the profits. The banks are mostly publicly traded, so their shareholders benefit also. Finally, management of both acquired and acquiring firms usually benefits through increased pay or golden parachutes. That's not to say that management is intentionally destroying value, but it makes it so much easier to be seduced by an investment bank's sales pitch when managers and directors have a theory that provides them a rationale for the deal. It doesn't hurt that they'll get rich(er), too!

WRAPPING UP

It's important to understand the beliefs and motives of different market participants. A company's stock price is an indicator of those beliefs, but in the long run, value usually is determined by a company's operating performance. We point out to the APM class the times and situations when investment banks or other large institutions have incentives that might lead to share prices deviating dramatically from their "true" value. A firm being acquired at too high a price is one situation. It's not a new idea. Lots of hedge funds have figured this one out. It's called merger arbitrage (merger arb for short). Traditionally targets are bid up and acquirers are shorted. So in one sense the market does help even things out, but it doesn't close the gap completely. The gains from merger arb aren't quite what they used to be.

Another example where it pays to understand participants' motives is regarding the other lines of business of investment banks. Sometimes a bank has an inventory from an IPO; sometimes it helps arrange a Rule 144 private placement for institutional buyers. Usually there are some trading restrictions, called lockup periods, on the shares that the bank holds. Many times the bank will unload its shares at the end of a lockup period. When that happens, the stock typically drops because a relatively large sale has occurred. Investors think that the bank has better information than they do. If the bank sells, its managers must know something. Perhaps, but maybe they are just cleaning out some inventory.

When students realize that some of the institutional details matter, they start becoming smarter investors.

CHAPTER 4

How Students Find an Investment Edge

A big edge that the APM portfolio shares with individual investors is that it's not that big! Super-investor Warren Buffett spoke to University of Kansas students in 2005 and told them he wished he was starting over again because it would be easy to double or triple his money. Small investors can invest where big funds don't want to bother.

In this chapter we discuss how to find an investing edge by building an information network and further questioning of conventional wisdom. We also discuss how surface analysis hinders students and investors. Getting close to the information is the remedy for surface analysis, but understanding who and why others may only skim the surface is important in understanding when getting close to the information will pay off.

BUILD YOUR OWN INFORMATION NETWORK

A big part of the APM class is devoted to building relationships. We try to foster ties between current students and alumni and between current students and investment professionals who speak in class. A good information network is a good way to find an investment edge. Individually we can read only so many publicly filed documents and listen to a limited number of earnings calls. A network of friends looking for good investments is one way to expand your information horizon. Those friends may work in different industries, live in different parts of the world, or just have a fresh perspective on a new investment idea.

The APM Web site and quarterly newsletter are two of the ways that alumni can keep up with the current thinking of the class and its speakers. Each week a student group is responsible for writing up the class notes and getting them up on the Web site. Whenever there is a delay in getting the notes, likely we'll get an e-mail from an alumnus asking about the holdup. The Web site also has an up-to-date listing of portfolio holdings, transactions, and performance and contains two or three of the best student reports each week. The quarterly newsletter reports in a little more depth about what the class speakers had to say. It also contains an update on portfolio performance and any news that alumni care to share.

You don't need an information network if you're going to invest in the companies that are featured on CNBC and other popular press outlets. Those companies usually have lots of research available from the big investment banks. You do need a network to separate the hidden investment gems from the lumps of coal. One way to do that is to look at so-called neglected firms. In Chapter 15 we go into the specifics about how APM alums keep us informed about the latest thinking.

NEGLECTED FIRMS

Neglected firms are those that aren't followed by research analysts or are underinvested in by institutions. Research analysts don't follow just good investments; they follow investments that institutions are likely to invest in. So there's a high correlation between the following of a firm's analyst and institutional investment. Neglected firms were first identified as providing superior returns in the 1980s.[1] The Efficient Market Hypothesizers (EMHers) explain the superior returns as lower liquidity or higher risk. Again, let's look at the motives of the players to see how APM and small investors can benefit.

Institutional investors have to worry about being second-guessed. The second-guessing mostly comes when an investment doesn't work. Clients are like armchair coaches who don't look at the overall strategy but look at the blown plays or underperforming players. The best managers and coaches block out the inevitable criticism and stick to their plans. Unfortunately, the incentive for many money managers is to play it safe and avoid criticism. Playing it safe means that many funds end up performing about as well as the market less whatever fees the managers charge.

What motivates this behavior? Let's examine the upside and downside of making an investment that is out of the mainstream. In 1999 Berkshire

---

[1] Avner Arbel and Paul Strebel, "The Neglected and Small Firm Effects," *Financial Review* 17, no. 4 (1982): 201–218.

Hathaway's stock significantly underperformed the NASDAQ and most other indices. CEO Warren Buffett said in his annual letter to shareholders:

> *The numbers ... show just how poor our 1999 record was. We had the worst absolute performance of my tenure and, compared to the S&P, the worst relative performance as well.*[2]

Investment gurus interviewed in the media were saying that Buffett had lost his touch in the world of modern technology. He just didn't "get it." A lot more people were investing in Amazon instead of Berkshire Hathaway in 1999 and 2000. A manager who invested in Berkshire Hathaway from mid-1998 until 2000 had to be able to explain to shareholders why he was forgoing the impressive returns from technology companies in order to invest in a has-been operation. After all, Warren Buffett was old and losing his touch.

If the manager invested in Berkshire Hathaway and was wrong, then he or she would look like an idiot. Everybody knew that the company was headed nowhere. The manager most likely would be underperforming the benchmark by going against the crowd. Figure 4.1 shows that Berkshire's stock was going up nicely with the market until mid-1998. Especially in 1999 and 2000, its cumulative returns lagged the NASDAQ cumulative returns. The manager would have to keep explaining his or her reasoning for going against the crowd. For most managers, it isn't worth the extra effort to invest in something unpopular, even if they think it's a good investment.

If the manager invested in Berkshire Hathaway and was right, he or she would need to wait until the bubble burst and a little while longer to see the fruits of being right. A year is a long time to wait in the investment world. It's a long time to have to explain an unpopular holding. It wouldn't be until mid-2001 that the cumulative return on Berkshire would look better. The problem is that investors don't have much of a long-term focus. With quarterly reporting, it's a question of how have you performed this quarter. Figure 4.2 shows that Berkshire lagged the NASDAQ index for seven straight quarters from Q3 1998 to Q1 2000.

Berkshire Hathaway isn't exactly unknown in the investment world. But at the time, we classified it as neglected since institutions were staying away in big numbers. Most people would think of neglected firms as small and not very well known. Early finance researchers identified neglected firms as those with few or no research analyst coverage. That was in the 1980s, when there were a lot of research analysts working for investment banking firms, large and small. Today there are fewer analysts, but information is more widely

---

[2] Quote from Berkshire Hathaway Inc., 1999 Annual Report, 3.

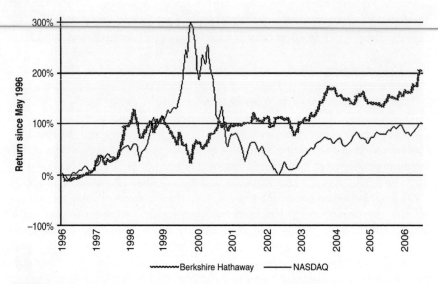

FIGURE 4.1   Berkshire Hathaway Returns versus NASDAQ Returns, May 1996–December 2006

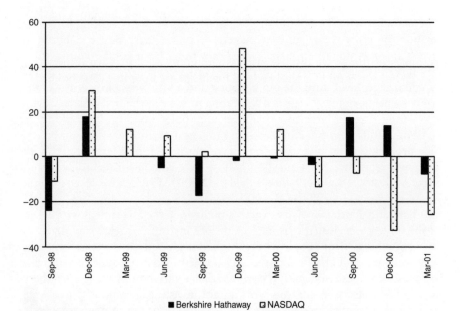

FIGURE 4.2   Quarterly Berkshire Hathaway Returns versus NASDAQ Returns, Q3 1998 to Q1 2000

disseminated. The Internet puts information in the hands of the masses. The Securities and Exchange Commission (SEC) has every single corporate filing available to any and all. The information explosion has made it easier for students and investors—and harder at the same time.

Now it's possible to get all kinds of information about any publicly traded firm. It's hard to imagine that some would really be "neglected." What's missing from an investment perspective is context. It's easy to do a surface analysis of a company, but you need to dig deeper to investigate products, prospects, management and the investment potential. That's what the APM students start to learn in class.

SURFACE ANALYSIS

Surface analysis is great for parties, where a sound bite makes you seem like a real investor. Surface analysis is what many investors, individual and professional, do. They know a stock "story," but they don't always know the numbers or what really will make the business move and the stock take off. They don't always know the real risks either. Early in the semester, it's common for students to come to class very enthused about a great stock. They'll know the story, but they won't know the company's market capitalization, valuation metrics, or other important details.

Here we discuss three examples of surface analysis. These are typical examples of things we discuss in class and companies that we've invested in. LSB Industries and Capitol Federal Financial are longtime class holdings. The LSB case is examined in much greater detail in Chapter 6, but in this chapter we provide an overview of how and why it has been a misunderstood investment opportunity. Here, we also discuss why Capitol Federal is usually misunderstood by investors. The last example we touch on is investing in China. We highlight only a few points about Chinese investing here, but again examine this topic in greater detail in Chapter 11.

LSB Industries

LSB Industries is headquartered in Oklahoma City. It has two divisions, the chemical division and a heating and air-conditioning manufacturing (HVAC) division. The chemical division manufactures ammonium nitrate fertilizer and a few specialty chemicals. The inputs for ammonium nitrate fertilizer are natural gas to fuel the reaction, ammonia, and nitric acid. LSB pays for natural gas, but in many places around the world it is a by-product of refining that is being burned off at refineries around the world. Some places do use natural gas to manufacture their own fertilizer at a much lower cost than ammonium nitrate producers in the United States. LSB's chemical business, as well as other U.S. fertilizer manufacturers, is in a long-term secular decline. Over the last 10 years, at least eight U.S. ammonium nitrate producers have declared bankruptcy, been taken over by another company, or shut their doors. Why has LSB survived and become one of only a few remaining manufacturers in the country? The company has survived because of great management and because it's got a nifty little HVAC division that keeps chugging along and keeping the firm's head above water.

Because LSB has survived and others have failed and because of better regional agriculture conditions in LSB's market region, it is making some money with its chemical division. The real money probably will come from the HVAC division. If the two divisions weren't part of the same company, HVAC would probably be a sexy little high-growth company that small-cap managers would be really, really interested in. That hasn't happened because investors have not really figured out LSB's business. In December 2006, after an 84 percent year-to-date increase in LSB stock price, Jon Markman mentioned it at the end of an article for TheStreet.com.

> *There are many interesting micro-caps in the chemical business for extreme risk-takers to consider. One is LSB Industries (LXU), an industrial conglomerate that has a large division selling ammonium nitrate and nitric acid to the fertilizer industry, and another large division that's a major manufacturer of commercial explosives.*
>
> *Shares are up quite a bit this year, but the stock is still cheap at a price-to-sales multiple under 0.3 and insiders buying heavily in the past month. But with so many inexpensive large-caps to buy, it may not pay for most investors to throw the dice on the bit players.*
>
> *DuPont used the slogan "Better living through chemistry" for three decades in the middle of the last century before it was turned on its head by LSD-popping hippies. Maybe it's time to trot it out again, at least for stock-popping investors.*
>
> . . .
>
> *Please note that due to factors including low market capitalization and/or insufficient public float, we consider LSB Industries to be a small-cap stock. You should be aware that such stocks are subject to more risk than stocks of larger companies, including greater volatility, lower liquidity and less publicly available information, and that postings such as this one can have an effect on their stock prices.*[3]

---

[3] Jon D. Markman, "In a Word: Plastics," Special to TheStreet.com, December 1, 2006, www.thestreet.com/newsanalysis/investing/10325324.html.

This short article is illuminating for a couple of reasons. First of all, it's a very good illustration of surface analysis. None of the facts in the short article is wrong. LSB does have a chemical division that produces explosive chemicals and ammonium nitrate, but that's not where its profits are coming from. The bulk of the profit comes from its HVAC division, which is not even mentioned.

Why do stories like this get written? When a company has had a big run-up in price, some stock screens start to pick it up. LSB's primary industry code is its chemical division's industry code. So it gets identified as a chemical company. The price/earnings (P/E) ratio is easy to calculate and is one of the first things that people look at. They don't go any further. Low P/E, high realized returns, chemical company: That's the story. Of course, there has to be a disclaimer since no one else has talked about LSB. So a generic small-cap warning is tacked on to the end of the story. There is only one part of the story that's incorrect. The author says that there is "less publicly available information" on small-cap stocks. That might have been true at one time, but now all companies provide the same information to the SEC. Small companies don't have the press coverage, but the same information is available to all.

LSB is a risky company because it has high operating leverage in its chemical division and high financial leverage, but it's not risky because it's a small-cap company. We'll do a full analysis of LSB in Chapter 6 to show how the students go beyond the surface analysis of this company to see what the real value drivers are.

Capitol Federal Financial

According to MSN.com, at the end of 2006 the APM portfolio holding with the highest P/E ratio was Capitol Federal Financial (CFFN). It topped the list with a P/E of 58. That's up there with the dot-coms and high-flying growth stocks. Capitol Federal, or Cap Fed as it's known in Kansas, is a Topeka, Kansas–based savings and loan company. It is a solid, consistent performer with a good dividend, but it didn't blow anyone away in 2006. No plans have been announced to expand beyond its base in Kansas. The flat yield curve makes it tough for many financial institutions whose primary business is mortgage lending.

As Table 4.1 shows, Cap Fed is profitable, but 2006 wasn't as good as 2005. The year 2007 wasn't forecast to be that great either; earnings per share (EPS) were forecast to be only 55 cents. That translates into a reported forward P/E ratio of 70. So what's up with the stratospheric valuations?

Capitol Federal has a special corporate structure called a mutual savings bank. About two-thirds of its common shares are held by a mutual holding

TABLE 4.1 Capitol Federal Financial's Important Numbers

	2005	2006
Interest and dividend income ($M)	156	127
Net income ($M)	65	48
Dividend per public share	2.30	2.09
Shares outstanding (millions)	74.30	74.0
Public shares (millions)	20.50	20.4
EPS—reported	0.90	0.66
EPS—adjusted	3.17	2.35
P/E—reported	36.6	58.7
P/E—adjusted	10.4	16.5
Dividend yield (%)	5.9	6.2
Stock price—year-end	32.94	38.42

company. Those shares don't receive dividends. Common shares are divided into two categories: public shares and the holding company shares. To compare Cap Fed to other types of companies, either the EPS numbers should be compared only to other mutual holding companies, or the shares should be adjusted to reflect only the public shares. None of the data services is set up to adjust the numbers to account for this type of corporate structure. When data services provide EPS and all the other financial numbers to the financial Web sites, they don't make any adjustments for the structure. Data providers don't actually read and think about how to calculate things. They download the data and publish them. Some providers do make some common adjustments, but not all. The lesson is that some important numbers can't be calculated en masse.

What should Capitol Federal's P/E ratio be? That depends on the expected number of shares outside the holding company. Mutual holdings companies can do a second conversion to raise additional capital with the shares held in the mutual holding company. Capitol Federal's chief financial officer, John Dicus, has spoken in the APM class several times. Each time he's said that Cap Fed has no plans to carry out a secondary offering or expand beyond its core competencies. If you agree with Mr. Dicus and think it's unlikely to have more shares outstanding, then the P/E ratio is around 16. If you think it's very likely that Cap Fed will convert all the holding company shares, then the P/E ratio that you'd use would be 58.

What if you're not sure about the conversion? Suppose you think there's about a 20 percent chance of a full conversion, a 60 percent chance of no conversion, and a 20 percent chance of a partial conversion with 20 million of the shares in the mutual holding company. You would calculate your P/E ratio in this way:

$$Cap\ Fed\ P/E\ ratio = 0.2 \times 58 + 0.6 \times 16 + 0.2 \times 32 = 24$$

Many students start APM thinking there is a fixed and immutable way to calculate a P/E for a company, and it's easy just to look it up on Yahoo!Finance or their favorite financial Web site. P/E ratios are clues to getting close to your own measure of company's valuation. Since it's your own valuation, you need to come up with your own calculation.

Still, you need to know what others are thinking. One way to distinguish value and growth portfolios is by the P/E ratio. Value managers tend to invest in companies with low P/E ratios, while growth managers tend to invest in companies with high P/E ratios. Cap Fed isn't going to make it into any value fund, nor is it going to get picked up in a growth fund just because it has a seemingly high P/E ratio. It would need to have high earnings growth to make in a growth fund. Because Cap Fed doesn't fit neatly in a box, the growth pattern of its stock is likely to be fairly lumpy.

When earnings are flat, the stock won't do much even if it is paying a high dividend. When there is a good year with a special dividend, such as 2002, there is a big jump in the price. In Figure 4.3 you see Cap Fed's stock price since April 1999, when it initially went public. In 2002 it paid a large special dividend for the first time. The stock started increasing in early 2002 in anticipation of the announced dividend.

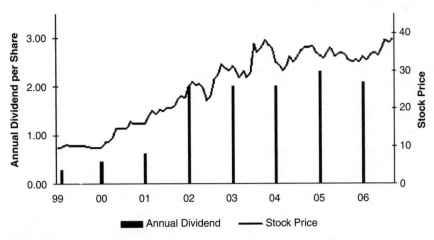

FIGURE 4.3 Capitol Federal Stock Price since Initial Public Offering

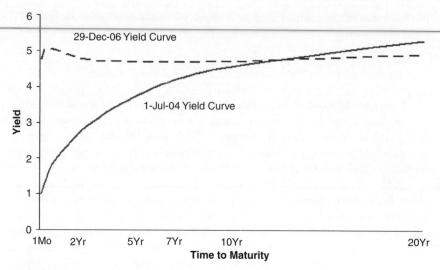

FIGURE 4.4   Treasury Yield Curves, 2006 and 2004

In 2005 and 2006 earnings of financial institutions and especially mortgage lenders were under pressure because of a flat yield curve. The yield curve is a chart that plots the interest rate (or yield) on the y-axis and time to maturity on the x-axis. Figure 4.4 is an example of the yield curve in mid-2004 versus the yield curve at the end of 2006. The interest that institutions pay on checking accounts and other short-term deposits is typically slightly above the one-month maturity on the yield curve. In 2004 mortgage lenders were paying 1 percent to their depositors. That increased to just below 5 percent throughout 2006. Mortgage rates are related to longer-term maturity yields on the curve. Mortgage lenders received a little more than 5 percent on mortgage loans in both 2004 and 2006. The spread in 2004 was 4 percent, but the spread in 2006 was very small because the cost of deposits was getting close to the amount received in interest on mortgage loans.

Since financial institutions can't control interest rates, it's important that they manage the areas that they can control, the largest of which is operating expenses. Cap Fed has always had a very low expense ratio compared to other savings and loans. When times are good, it will earn more than competitors. Another way that financial institutions increase earnings is by lending to riskier borrowers. They can charge high-risk borrowers a premium over conventional mortgage rates. Earnings will look good while the economy is good and there aren't a lot of the riskier borrowers defaulting. When times get tough, there may be more defaults and lower profits. Cap

Fed hasn't changed its credit standards much over the years, so in times of flat yield curves, as in 2006, earnings aren't great, but they do look good when the yield curve is in their favor.

We emphasize in class that nothing lasts forever. A flat or inverted yield curve will revert back to a more normal, steeper yield curve. Investors forget to look ahead, especially in cyclical industries like mortgage lending. Cap Fed has a great dividend yield. In the next cycle, earnings will increase. Then investors will sit up, take notice, and drive the stock price up. That's not the time to buy. The time to buy is during the tough market, when stock price is beat. Remember, it's buy low, sell high!

Misconceptions about China

The APM class has invested in China and Chinese companies since the beginning of the portfolio. Kent has been investing in China since 1993, the first year the Chinese market was opened to outside investors. He'd been in the Hong Kong market since 1984. He made several trip to China in the 1980s and early 1990s. In 1997 he attended an investor conference in China. He came away from the conference more convinced than ever that China was generally misunderstood by the investment community. Surface analysis and the stereotype of a communist country make it easy for investors to misunderstand what makes a good investment in China. The same issues make it hard for investors to understand the real risks involved.

Surface analysis is present in the disclaimers always found in any discussion of Chinese investments. A typical article starts off discussing how wonderful the company, how great the value is, then ends up with a half dozen disclaimers. Three common ones are: China is a communist country with little shareholder protection, corporate corruption is rampant, and financial statements aren't reliable. We examine investing in China and the Chinese financial system in more detail later, but here we discuss a few of the main reasons why would anyone want to invest in a country with problems of corporate corruption and fraudulent financial statements.

China has a communist government but a thriving market economy. The United States is the largest foreign direct investor in China. There are problems with corruption in China, but there are problems with corruption in the United States, Western Europe, Latin America, Japan, and India. Name a country, and there are problems, large and small. Perhaps because they are more familiar with the U.S. legal system, U.S. investors think they are safer investing in the United States, but not many equity investors have recovered any money lost from corporate corruption and misreporting. Just ask Enron and Tyco investors how much money they recovered.

And just who was minding the books at Enron and Tyco? Arthur Andersen was Enron's auditors. Tyco's auditing firm was Pricewaterhouse-Coopers. Listed Chinese companies and most major firms around the world are mostly audited by the same large auditing firms worldwide. How can we trust the books in the United States but not elsewhere when they are audited by the same firms? People everywhere have a home bias. We understand our own culture better; we excuse problems at home because we know that most people aren't crooks. We magnify problems outside of our own culture because we don't understand the rules or the context.

WRAPPING UP

In APM, we try to think for ourselves and evaluate information critically. It helps to understand the really poor investment choices that come from relying only on sound bites in the popular press. In the first four chapters, we've explained some of the background and touched on what we see as problems in current investment management that has created opportunities for APM. Next we'll expound more on exactly what we do in class and how we've developed our own investment philosophy.

CHAPTER 5

Alpha, Sigma, Beta

APM's Risk and Reward

Returns over time should be the primary measure of success of a portfolio manager. In this chapter we'll examine how the APM portfolio stacks up against the many different risk and return measures that risk managers use. Since we're primarily stock pickers, we don't really manage our portfolio using these techniques. Still, it's a useful exercise. It's very common for people to look at our portfolio and comment on how risky it is. They don't have any idea about the risk numbers, but they assume that it must be risky because we have some concentrated positions and we have a lot of names that they've never heard of.

This is the only chapter where we'll mention alpha. We've realized great alpha and great returns over the life of the portfolio, but we don't get the returns by focusing on the statistical techniques and obsessing about measurement. We realize our returns by staying focused on selecting good investments that are either temporarily out of favor, ignored, or for whatever reason priced right (in our judgment).

What do we measure? We look at the weight of each position in the portfolio. Positions with higher weights get more daily scrutiny in terms of fundamentals, news, and industry factors. Quarterly we look at our portfolio returns relative to the NASDAQ and the Standard & Poor's (S&P) 500 and S&P 600. For all positions, we track announcements and listen to quarterly earnings calls to see if our investment theses for our individual stocks are still on track. We stay focused on the fundamentals of each company. If all is well, then the stock price will fall in line. If things aren't panning out as expected, then it's time to sell.

Focusing on individual stock performance doesn't mean that we ignore what's going on in the market. If we think that the market may be in for a correction, we'd sell and realize gains on some holdings. We'd have a larger percentage of cash than when we think there are a lot good stock buys. When there's a correction in the markets, we see lots of good investments because prices have fallen. That's when cash is tight, because we have so many buying opportunities. We have to evaluate our positions relative to each other much more carefully. In bull markets we have a harder time finding stocks that are priced right. Then we'll have a boatload of cash to invest.

Lots of institutional portfolio managers have a big risk management team in place. They examine market risk, interest rate risk, exchange rate risk, equity price risk, inflation risk, commodity price risk, credit risk, sector risk, liquidity risk, business risk, model risk, regulatory risk, legal risk, political risk, accounting risk, and tax risk, and probably others. Some of these risks are market risks, and some are individual security risks. In APM we don't analyze market risk explicitly very often. We do examine the individual security risks as part of the case analysis when we evaluate companies. All companies have one or two significant nonmarket risks that we should pay attention to over time. We don't have a measure that is applicable for that type of risk. It's a qualitative assessment. Things that you can't measure aren't especially popular on Wall Street.

Lots of portfolios have guidelines for sector benchmarking or for asset allocation ranges. While it is important to pay attention to risk exposure, the class does not play the "closet-indexing" game of being sector neutral to any benchmark, nor are decisions made based on sector or capitalization weightings. In APM, the "benchmark" is hard work and detailed business analysis for investment decision.

In this chapter we measure the risk and return components for the APM portfolio and discuss each one. We summarize the formulas in the main text and put more detailed results and calculations in the chapter's appendix. While it's nice to know the numbers, it's more important to know how to generate the performance. The rest of the book focuses on the more important task of figuring out where the numbers come from.

RISK-RETURN TRADE-OFF

Efficient market proponents argue that long-term "excess" returns happen by luck. They do admit the possibility that some excess return can be earned by extra skill or knowledge, but that excess return should not persist because others will come in to copy the strategy. Higher returns are supposed to be associated with higher risk. APM has earned pretty good returns over the life of the portfolio. From inception in December 1993 through mid-2007,

TABLE 5.1 APM Portfolio Returns Compared to NASDAQ Returns 1994 to June 2007 (in percent)

	APM	NASDAQ	Excess Return
YTD 2007	33.2	7.8	25
2006	32.6	9.5	23
2005	17.2	1.4	16
2004	24.0	8.6	15
2003	123.8	50.0	74
2002	17.7	−31.5	49
2001	−10.9	−21.1	10
2000	−5.3	−39.3	34
1999	74.6	85.6	−11
1998	−8.2	39.7	−48
1997	30.6	21.6	9
1996	2.4	22.7	−20
1995	17.6	39.9	−22
1994	23.1	−3.2	26
Cumulative Return	1567.9	235.1	312.1
Annual compound return	23.1	9.3	11.0
Alpha	15.9		
Beta	0.64		
Standard deviation	36.8	34.8	32.1

the annual compound rate of return has been 23.1 percent. Table 5.1 shows the annual returns for APM compared to NASDAQ returns since inception.[1]

As you can see, APM has outperformed NASDAQ 10 out of 14 years. In two of the four underperforming years, APM returns were still 18 and 75 percent. APM lost money in three years. Only one of those years was a double-digit loss of 11 percent. NASDAQ lost money only in 4 of the last 14 years, but in 2 of those years, the losses were 32 and 39 percent. In 2000 and during the spring of 2001, for a variety of reasons, the class did not meet. APM teaching assistants under the supervision of a faculty member

---

[1] We calculate time-weighted returns before fees. On an after-fee basis the compound annual return is 22 percent, alpha is 15 percent, and beta is 0.61. The returns are adjusted for contributions and withdrawals. For example, a $10,000 contribution to the portfolio is not counted as a performance gain, nor is the withdrawal to pay for a $10,000 scholarship counted against performance. We are missing a few monthly statements in 1995 to 1997. For those years we were able to reconstruct most of the transactions based on the ending balances of the next month's statement.

functioned as portfolio caretakers, but no classes focused their attention on the portfolio.

The overall return of the APM portfolio since inception is 1,568 percent. That's a compound annual rate of 23 percent per year compared to the NASDAQ return of 9 percent. According to accepted financial wisdom, APM must be riskier than NASDAQ to have earned higher returns. APM's returns shouldn't be "excess" returns. Excess returns are those returns that a portfolio earns after considering the portfolio risk. Higher-risk portfolios are "supposed" to earn higher returns to compensate for that risk. Alpha and beta provide an idea of the risk and return. Alpha is the measure of excess return earned after market risk has been accounted for. Over an extended period alpha should be zero, unless you get lucky. APM's alpha is 16 percent, significantly higher than we should expect, according to efficient market theorists.

So is the APM portfolio riskier? Let's look at the two direct measures of risk in Table 5.1, beta and standard deviation. Standard deviation is total risk, and beta is a measure of risk compared to the market. Beta measures risk when assets are combined into a portfolio. When beta is equal to 1, that means a portfolio or an asset has the same risk as the market. APM's beta over this 14-year period is 0.64, about half as risky as the market. The second risk measure is APM's standard deviation, which is just slightly higher than the NASDAQ's and is about average risk: 37 percent compared with NASDAQ's 35 percent.

Table 5.1 reports risk over the life of the portfolio. Over the last five to six years, APM's beta has been quite a bit lower than NASDAQ's. Table 5.2 calculates the alpha and beta for the portfolio over three-year rolling averages from March 2002 to June 2007. You can see that beginning in 2003, APM's beta dropped from 1.44 to 1.10 and has been dropping over the period. APM's beta was at its highest level when its return was highest.

The Sharpe and Treynor ratios are two other risk-adjusted measures of portfolio performance. Neither of these has a benchmark number (like beta's 1), but you can compare performance from period to period or across funds. Higher is better. We computed the Sharpe and Treynor ratios for the NASDAQ index to provide some perspective. APM is always higher than NASDAQ, often by a very large margin.

Maybe it's not fair to compare APM to the market. Maybe we should compare to a successful mutual fund. When we screened mutual funds by five-year performance using Yahoo!Finance's mutual fund screener, we found that APM clearly has outperformed these funds based on alpha. We looked at 10-year mutual fund screeners from *USA Today* and MSN and didn't find any mutual funds with an alpha larger than APM's. That's not to say there isn't one. We couldn't find a screener that screened by alpha, so

TABLE 5.2 Quarterly Rolling Three-Year Performance Measures for APM and NASDAQ, 2002 to 2007

Period	Alpha	Beta	Annual APM Return	Annual NASDAQ Return	Excess Return	APM Sharpe Ratio	NASDAQ Sharpe Ratio	APM Treynor Ratio	NASDAQ Treynor Ratio
Q1 2002–05	8.7	1.20	46.1	2.7	43.4	2.08	−0.12	35.0	−1.6
Q2 2002–05	7.0	1.19	48.6	12.0	36.6	2.22	0.60	37.3	7.7
Q3 2002–05	8.9	1.44	66.1	22.5	43.6	3.12	1.63	42.8	18.2
Q4 2002–05	8.1	1.39	48.2	18.2	30.0	2.63	1.61	31.5	13.9
Q1 2003–06	10.3	1.10	45.8	20.4	25.4	3.35	1.96	37.8	16.2
Q2 2003–06	9.8	1.10	28.9	10.2	18.7	1.97	0.68	22.6	6.0
Q3 2003–06	7.8	0.53	22.6	8.1	14.5	2.79	0.54	35.0	3.9
Q4 2003–06	7.8	0.64	24.4	6.4	18.0	2.43	0.30	31.6	2.1
Q1 2004–07	6.1	0.50	25.2	6.7	18.5	2.70	0.35	41.8	2.3
Q2 2004–07	5.6	0.62	33.5	8.1	25.2	3.48	0.58	47.1	3.8
Average All 3-year Periods	3.1	0.54	21.9	10.7	8.6	1.2	0.8	27.3	5.3

we screened by long-term returns, which should be related to alpha. You've got to have return before you can have alpha. Table 5.3 shows a selection of some of the highest 10-year mean annual return mutual funds. All of the statistics are calculated over 10 years. As you can see, APM has the highest Sharpe ratio and the highest Treynor ratio by a wide margin.

OTHER RISK MEASURES

APM isn't a hedge fund. It's a student-run, primarily equity portfolio. When we have participated in student competitions, people have commented, "Oh, you're more like a hedge fund." We're not sure how we fit into the hedge fund category because we're not hedging anything. We don't benchmark, and we're not doing asset allocation. We do have some concentrated positions, so perhaps that's more hedge-fund like. Still, we're not like most hedge funds. Maybe it's not fair to use risk-adjusted measures for return. We look at some of the other measures that have been developed to manage risk in hedge funds.

Next we look at one absolute measure of risk that was developed about 15 years ago at J.P. Morgan called Value-at-Risk. Michael Brunnquell, a spring 2007 APM student, developed a VaR model for the portfolio. Then we look at the maximum drawdown and return over the maximum drawdown. Finally we look at the Sortino ratio. The bottom line for all of these measures is that APM doesn't look really risky.

Value-at-Risk

Value-at-Risk (VaR) has a somewhat cumbersome definition. It is the loss that the portfolio could be expected to exceed at a given probability over a specific time frame. The definition is confusing and is better illustrated with an example. We need to pick a probability for a loss over a future time frame. Usually probabilities are 1 or 5 percent and time frames are weekly or monthly. The VaR is the dollar value associated with a low probability of loss. A weekly 1 percent VaR is the dollar loss that would be expected to occur in 1 out of 100 weeks; a 1 percent monthly VaR would be 1 out 100 months or every 8.3 years.

Suppose a $10 million portfolio has an expected return of 1 percent and standard deviation of 1.5 percent over the next month. You'd expect the portfolio to be $10.1 million after one month. Some months you'd get more than average return; others, less. Figure 5.1 shows the value distribution of the portfolio after one month. The average is $10.1 million; the 1 percent probability level is $9.75 million. The difference between the $10 million

TABLE 5.3 10-Year Performance Statistics: APM Compared to Selected Mutual Funds

Statistic	APM	SLAFX	GMFSX	LZEMX	PASMX	RSNRX	GHAAX	VGPMX
Alpha	18.16	8.23	10.21	3.74	5.95	8.92	7.39	13.65
Beta	0.47	1.30	0.59	1.17	0.90	0.54	0.67	0.62
Mean annual return	21.29	15.01	17.08	10.60	12.25	13.68	13.14	17.18
Sharpe ratio	1.09	0.51	0.94	0.39	0.46	0.52	0.53	0.55
Treynor ratio	33.58	5.57	15.74	2.40	4.97	10.92	8.04	15.04

SLAFX: DWS Latin America Equity S; GMFSX: GMO Foreign Small Companies III; LZEMX: Lazard Emerging Markets Instl; PASMX: Pacific Advisors Small Cap A; RSNRX: RS Global Natural Resources A; GHAAX: Van Eck Global Hard Assets C; VGPMX: Vanguard Precious Metals and Mining

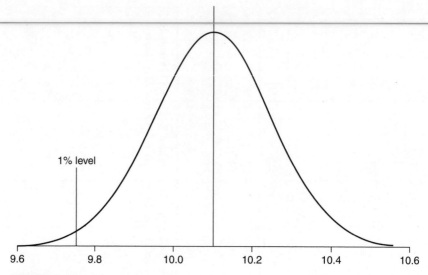

1% level

| 9.6 | 9.8 | 10.0 | 10.2 | 10.4 | 10.6 |

FIGURE 5.1   Value-at-Risk Illustration

original portfolio value and the 1 percent probability level is $250,000 ($10 million less $9.75 million). The VaR is $250,000.

Actually, you'd expect a loss of $250,000 or more every 8.3 years. There really isn't any limit to the lower part, so in theory you could lose everything. VaR doesn't provide any insight into losing it all. It does give some insight into what an "expected" bad loss could be.

A 5 percent weekly VaR gives an idea of a bad loss once every 20 weeks. That's a higher number but more likely to happen. With our $10 million portfolio example, a 5 percent weekly VaR is $147,000.

As mentioned, Michael Brunnquell calculated APM's weekly VaR during April 2007. The portfolio was valued at $1.22 million. The expected return was 0.79 percent, and the standard deviation was 2.29 percent. Michael calculated the probability distribution for each stock in the portfolio and used simulation to come up with the expected portfolio value. The 1 percent weekly VaR was $55,246. Figure 5.2 shows the simulation outcome. The 1 percent level is $1.165 million. The loss from the current value of $1.22 million is $55,246.

One of the advantages of VaR is we can see what an expected loss is, but a disadvantage is that we don't have a benchmark. Using the expected return and standard deviation on the NASDAQ for a $1.2 million portfolio, we found a 1 percent weekly VaR of $59,210. If you invested $1.2 million in a NASDAQ market index, you'd expect a loss of $59,210 or more every

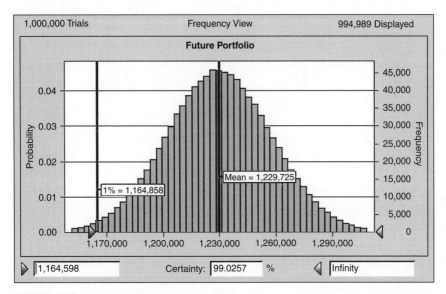

FIGURE 5.2   APM Portfolio Value-at-Risk

8.3 years. APM has a little lower loss expectation, indicating that APM is a little less risky on an absolute basis.

Drawdowns and Semi-Risk

The maximum drawdown (MDD) is the maximum loss that a portfolio has ever incurred during any subperiod of the life of the portfolio. It's the compound return over a peak return to the lowest point after the peak. It's easier to visualize in Figure 5.3. Drawdowns don't necessarily mean long-term losses, but they are a measure of the worst pain that a portfolio has sustained over a period.

The MDD period began in quarter 27, the fourth quarter of 2000, and ended in quarter 36, the fourth quarter of 2002. In the beginning, known as the high-water mark, the drawdown was 47 percent. The ROMAD, return over maximum drawdown, is 1.07. ROMAD is ratio of the compound average return on the portfolio to the drawdown; a higher number is better. It measures how much return to expect for every unit of downside risk. Compared to the drawdowns in the market indices, APM has a better ratio of return to drawdown.

Table 5.4 shows drawdown measures for APM and the big market indices. The maximum drawdown period for everyone began in 2000 and

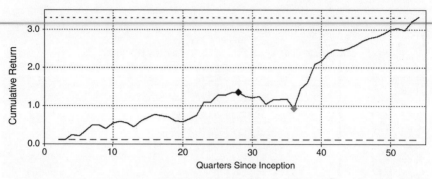

FIGURE 5.3   APM Portfolio Maximum Drawdown

ended in 2002. The Dow Jones Industrial Average (DJIA) picked up before
the rest and before APM. APM's drawdown period started a little after the
others.

The other risk measures in Table 5.4 are related to the idea of semi-
variance. One problem with the general idea of using standard deviation as
risk is it counts big upswings as equally risky to big downswings. Investors
are concerned about losing money, so some argue that portfolio managers
shouldn't be penalized for volatility from the upswings because that's what
we all want. In Table 5.4 we report both the upside deviation and the downside deviation. The Dow and the S&P 500 don't have as much downside
deviation as the APM portfolio or NASDAQ. APM's downside deviation

TABLE 5.4   APM Drawdown and Sortino Measures Compared to Market Indices

	APM	NASDAQ	DJIA	S&P 500
Maximum drawdown	0.43	1.08	0.36	0.55
High-water mark	Q4 2000	Q1 2000	Q1 2000	Q2 2000
End of MDD	Q4 2002	Q4 2002	Q1 2002	Q4 2002
ROMAD	1.2	0.3	0.6	0.5
Minimum acceptable return (%)	5.0	5.0	5.0	5.0
Downside deviation (%)	6.6	14.5	5.4	5.7
Upside deviation (%)	11.4	9.8	4.6	4.9
Standard deviation (%)	13.5	14.5	7.8	7.6
Sortino ratio	2.7	0.3	0.9	0.7
Sharpe ratio	1.3	0.3	0.6	0.5

is lower than its upside, but that is not true for NASDAQ. NASDAQ's downside deviation is large and larger than its upside.

The Sortino ratio looks at returns and the deviation on the downside. The numerator is the portfolio return less a minimum acceptable return. We use the risk-free rate of 5 percent as the minimum acceptable return (MAR). The denominator is the downside deviation. The Sortino ratio is similar to the Sharpe ratio. When the Sharpe ratio is set at the risk-free rate (as we did in this table), we can compare the excess return per unit of downside with total volatility. Most of APM's volatility comes from the upside, not the downside, because the Sortino ratio is better than the Sharpe ratio. We don't get the full picture of the source of volatility just looking at APM's standard deviation, but comparing the upside and downside deviations, we see that there is more upside than downside volatility. Of the market indices, only the S&P 500 has more upside than downside.

SleepWell and SeemsGoood

Over the last decade behavioral finance has become increasingly important. Two risk ideas that have come into play recently seem to have started with the United Kingdom consulting firm Watson Wyatt. It found in a 1999 survey that its investment management clients were concerned not just about the risk numbers but also about two other "soft" risk factors, which at Watson Wyatt called SleepWell and SeemsGood. SleepWell has to do with how comfortable investment managers are with controlling regret. SeemsGood deals with the psychic payoffs; things that really don't produce any financial payoff.[2] For example, investing in a "popular" stock has the psychic payoff of being with the crowd, but popular isn't a good investing criterion.

Regret comes in several forms. Investors regret big losses, they regret not buying early enough, and they regret selling too soon. Everyone likes to avoid regret, but sometimes avoiding regret transfers into inaction. It's easier to buy a popular stock and rationalize it going down since everyone else owned it. In the late 1990s some investors made a lot of money, but now they still are suffering a lot of regret. They held on to their investments as the market tanked, and whatever gains they had evaporated. As we have mentioned, at the beginning of the semester APM students are very reluctant to stray from the crowd and make an independent judgment. Controlling regret aversion is tough, but it's one way to break away from average investing.

---

[2] "The Concept of Investment Efficiency and its Application to Investment Management Structures," T.M. Hodgson, S. Breban, C.L. Ford, M.P. Streatfield, and R.C. Urwin. Presented to the Institute of Actuaries, 28 February 2000.

TABLE 5.5 Categorizing of Behavioral Issues

SleepWell (Regret Risk Control)	SeemsGood (Behavioral Biases)
Loss aversion	Loss aversion
Peer pressure	Overconfidence
Familiarity	Framing
Consensus decision making	Mental accounting
Fiduciary fear	Oversimplification
	Performance myths

Source: T. M. Hodgson, S. Breban, C. L. Ford, M. P. Streatfield, and R. C. Urwin, "The Concept of Investment Efficiency and Its Application to Investment Management Structures," presented to the Institute of Actuaries, 28 February 2000.

A group of Watson Wyatt researchers and some academics have categorized the SleepWell and SeemsGood risks. We show them in Table 5.5. Controlling regret risk is a good thing, but SeemsGood risk is behavioral issues that have no financial payoff. SeemsGood risk captures the investment management biases beyond the financial. In the APM class we need to make sure that we don't fall victim to some of the SeemsGood risks. One SeemsGood risk is overconfidence. Investors can be overconfident in areas where they have some knowledge. Research has shown that confidence isn't related to performance. Perhaps the influx of less confident students every semester helps us from becoming overconfident! Table 5.5 shows some of the SleepWell and SeemsGood issues that all portfolio managers need to be aware of.

No one has come up with a risk measure for these behavioral issues. But being aware and trying to stay free from some of these behavioral risks is just as important, or more important, than focusing on the numbers.

SeemsGood risk also encompasses performance myths. A few of these myths that we should pay attention are:

- Relying too heavily on past numbers
- Seeing patterns in small samples of data where there are none
- Overweighting personal observations
- Failing to recognize mean reversion
- Worrying about short-term results instead of long-term results

A lot of the performance myths can be summarized by short-term "ruler analysis" thinking. We've discussed ruler analysis in earlier chapters, and we will revisit. The risk of using SeemsGood thinking is very common because it's very comfortable for all of us. The trick is not to get too comfortable and to constantly reexamine assumptions.

WRAPPING UP

Large funds spend a lot of time measuring and analyzing performance. We've barely scratched the surface in this chapter. We could break down performance by sector, by industry, or by many other factors. However, the bottom line is: It's absolute returns that matter. It doesn't matter if you beat the market, if the market is down 20 percent. That's a Pyrrhic victory. The second bottom line is: You don't generate returns by measuring them. You generate returns and alpha by staying focused on the investment strategy that you've picked.

Part II is a much more detailed look at how APM picks some of its stocks. We go through the details of writing up a case and coming up with an investment thesis. That's the bottom line to generating alpha.

APPENDIX: RISK AND RETURN CALCULATIONS

Returns: Total, Average, Compound, and Time-weighted

Total return is the ending value less the initial value of an investment net of fees and including any interest or dividends received dividend by the beginning value.

$$Total\,Return$$
$$= \frac{\$\,value_t - \$\,value_0 - fees\,or\,commissions + dividends\,or\,interest}{\$\,value_0}$$

Annual return is the same as total return when the holding period is for one year. Annual average return is the average of a series of annual returns. Investors don't earn average returns if they are invested over a long period. For a long-term average, compound annual returns are more appropriate. Compound returns are the geometric average return. If t is the number of years the investment is held, then

$$Compound\,Annual\,Return = \left(1 + Total\,Return\right)^{1/t} - 1$$

Time-weighted returns are also called geometric returns. They take into account the size and timing of any cash flows into or out of the portfolio. Time-weighted returns can be linked over time to find total return over the evaluation period. Time-weighted returns require a portfolio revaluation every time a cash inflow or outflow occurs. The Modified Dietz approximation is commonly used to estimate monthly or quarterly time-weighted returns to avoid daily recalculation.

Alpha and Beta

Alpha and beta come from the Capital Asset Pricing Model, which is estimated using this regression model:

$$r_i - r_f = \alpha + \beta \left(r_m - r_f\right)$$

α is the intercept. On average, it should be equal to zero. If α is statistically significantly greater than zero, the portfolio is earning excess returns. If α is statistically significantly less than zero, the portfolio is earning less than adequate returns. β is the measure of risk with respect to the market.

Both α and β can change significantly when different market indices and different time periods are used.

Standard Deviation

The ex post standard deviation, s, of a series of returns is calculated as:

$$s = \sqrt{\frac{\sum_{t=1}^{T} \left(return_t - average\ return\right)^2}{T - 1}}$$

The downside deviation is calculated using only $return_t$ values that are less than zero. Upside deviation is calculated using only $return_t$ values that are greater than zero.

Maximum Drawdown

Maximum drawdown is the maximum compound return a portfolio has ever suffered during any subperiod of the life of the portfolio. Current drawdown (time T is today) is defined as:

$$drawdown = max \left[\sum_{t=0}^{T} r_t \right] - r_T$$

The maximum drawdown formula is deceptively simple. To find the maximum drawdown, you need to calculate all subperiod returns and find the minimum over all subperiods:

$$Maximum\ drawdown\,(MDD) = min \left[\sum_{j=1}^{t} r_j \right]$$

The high-water mark is how some hedge funds determine fees and/or managerial compensation. Investors enter a hedge fund at a certain value level called the entering value. If the fund loses money but then makes back that money, investors usually are not required to pay a management fee on any portion of the upside that was below the entering value. At hedge funds, drawdown and high-water marks are very important.

Performance Ratios

$$Treynor\ Ratio = \frac{r_p - r_f}{\beta}$$

$$Sharpe\ Ratio = \frac{r_p - r_f}{s_p}$$

$$Sortino\ Ratio = \frac{r_p - r_f}{downside\ standard\ deviation}$$

Two

Building an Investment Case

In Part I of this book, we provided some historical perspective on how APM has evolved and its performance. We also provided a context on how APM's philosophy fits with other market participants.

In Part II we expand on our philosophy and dig deep into our biggest teaching tool: the case analysis. In a case analysis, we want students to understand where a company has been and then make some reasonable forecasts based on the past and an analysis of where the industry is heading. Forecasting is an art, not an exact science. Outlining each step of how the forecast is built leads to a clear understanding of the company's business. Later, if events unroll differently than expected, it's easy to see and understand the departures from the forecast. We emphasize thorough preparation and clear thinking. We especially want students to avoid ruler analysis and ants on elephants in their cases.

Chapter 6 describes several types of investment philosophies, but we concentrate on our own philosophy and provide an extended example of how one of our long-term holdings, LSB Industries, illustrates this philosophy. Getting close to the information over a long time horizon has helped us realize big gains in this position. However, it wasn't always easy. Lots of people outside APM questioned our thinking when we held on during the bad times.

The rest of the chapters in this part focus on different pieces of researching and writing up a case. In Chapter 7 we discuss the initial preparation for a case. We return to these ideas over and over. If the prep work is lacking, the rest of the case will just be guesswork or conventional wisdom. In Chapter 8 we discuss the actual writing of the case: what to include, what not to include. The most important idea in this chapter is coming up with a preliminary investment thesis based on the preparation in Chapter 7. We also discuss how to describe a company. It seems like it should be easy, but really understanding how a company makes money is more than rephrasing the company's official description. In Chapter 9 we discuss how to put together a pro forma analysis, which should follow easily from the work in Chapters 7 and 8. Finally, in Chapter 10 we put everything together to come up with a final valuation and our target price. That leads to an investment recommendation. Since investing is dynamic, the target price and investment thesis should be examined constantly. We also discuss using the pro forma model to update our thesis and recommendations as new information arrives.

CHAPTER 6

Many Ways to Be a Successful Investor

There are many ways to be a successful investor. Warren Buffett, George Soros, Peter Lynch, John Kornitzer, Jim Chanos, Jim Schier, Tom Laming, Sam Zell, and many others, known and unknown, have been successful over long periods. Each of them has a distinct philosophy. Each has had some rough times, but those rough times have been more than balanced by the prosperous times. In the APM class we try to have a wide variety of speakers talk about their investment philosophies. Not all investment philosophies will work with your view of the world and psychological makeup. It's important to know yourself and know what will work for you as an investor.

APM's early investment philosophy was set by Kent and focused on aggressive event-driven strategies. This was a new way of doing things in 1994. Now a lot of money managers are using this strategy. APM's current investment philosophy is driven by its five guidelines and is influenced by Kent. The portfolio tends to be more contrarian and value-driven. We try to find companies before they become the popular darlings of the investment press and big money managers. To do this we emphasize building an information network and digging into the details of a company.

What is a successful investor? Many fund managers are deemed successful when they outperform their benchmark. It doesn't matter if their benchmark is down 10 percent for the year. If they only lost 5 percent, the marketing machine will beat the drum that they outperformed the benchmarks. One way then to determine successful investors is that they don't lose money very often, and they usually beat market indices. It's very hard to have a long-term record that beats the market in both up years and still makes money in years that the market is down. Lots of people have a great year occasionally. Not very many have consistently good years with some great years thrown in.

Many studies of mutual funds show that most funds do not beat the market. Efficient market theorists hypothesize that those that do are either lucky or incurring extra costs that can't be easily measured. Because there are so many investors, there actually will be quite a few big, lucky winners. The Efficient Market Hypothesis adherents (EMHers) say the good ones are incurring extra costs. If you take those costs into account, then those investors really wouldn't be beating the market. So how do you find long-term investors who are good and not lucky? If you do find some good ones, what are they like? Are they incurring those costs, or can we emulate the strategies that work?

Over the years many great investors with many different philosophies have come to class. Value investors, technical analysts, momentum traders, merger arbitragers, corporate governance activists, and many more. They all have several traits in common. In this chapter we focus mainly on the commonalities and do not describe all of the different strategies. There are lots of other good books that do that, especially Aswath Damodaran's *Investment Philosophies*.[1] We also discuss and illustrate APM's philosophy using LSB Industries as an example.

COMMON TRAITS OF SUCCESSFUL INVESTORS

Extremely successful investors are focused, hardworking, and driven. They are always excited to talk about investments and investing. It's an ever-changing landscape that is endlessly fascinating. They are always looking for the next insight and trying to get another piece of the market puzzle to earn an extra point or 10. A summary of some of the common traits that the class has recognized over the years follows.

- Be honest.
- Read.
- Work hard on the details and the big picture.

Each is covered in detail in the next sections.

Be Honest

To be honest, you've got to keep score. Know where you are with all of your holdings, not just the good ones. Humans tend to remember things that bring

---

[1] Aswath Damodaran, *Investment Philosophies* (Hoboken, NJ: John Wiley & Sons, 2003).

pleasure and forget things that bring regret. It's important to examine both the good and bad outcomes, and determine whether these outcomes were the result of luck or decision making. Sometimes you make the right decision but have a bad outcome. Sometimes you make the wrong decision and get lucky. To become a better decision maker, you have to recognize when luck intervenes.

Being honest is admitting and learning from mistakes. Being honest takes courage. CNBC doesn't invite people to be on their shows to talk about mistakes, but honest investors will learn a lot more from mistakes than from successes. To improve, you've got to figure out what went wrong.

Not everything works, but some things take time to work. Investing is dynamic. The situation changes everyday. It's important to reevaluate your ideas frequently. Make adjustments if necessary. Recognize that some ideas require years to play out. The ideas that take a long time to develop should have the kind of payoff that rewards a patient, long-term investor.

Being honest means knowing yourself. Can you ignore the public clamor and bet against the crowd? If not, then it will be very hard for you to be a contrarian. Most students don't trust their own judgment and analysis. They figure that an analyst who spends lots and lots of time studying a company will make better investment decisions. In many cases, they are right. Yet there are many times when an analyst gets caught up in previous recommendations. A situation might have changed. The analyst understandably doesn't like to admit he or she is wrong. The investors who relied on the analysis aren't always forgiving sorts, but it is better to admit a mistake and move on. Again, as we discussed in Chapter 4, understanding all the participants' motives can give you an edge. Fresh eyes on a situation can lead to new insights and opportunities.

Read

No investment manager ever has come to class and said there was enough time to read. They all want to read more about companies, the world, and just about everything else. We expect students to read about the macroeconomic environment and to read about the companies we're invested in. We all should read authors and ideas that we agree with and, most important, we should read authors and ideas we disagree with.

One APM speaker, Frank Whitsell, director of research at Security Benefit, a mutual fund and financial advisory firm based in Topeka, KS, made the analogy that understanding investments is like a building a wedding cake. Experience really matters. In the first layer of the cake you are forming the base, but you don't have much depth. After a year or two of looking at a company or an industry, you start to understand some things that weren't obvious when you started. Now you are putting on another layer on the cake. Reading about events over the years, understanding your reaction and others' reactions to the same events are all important components to building your cake.

Almost all successful investors are very experienced, but they spend a lot of time reading. Since it's not possible to read everything, it's important to develop a reading routine that is consistent and helpful. Set aside time everyday to read. Multitasking and reading aren't compatible. Block off a quiet hour daily to digest company and world news.

Work Hard on the Details and the Big Picture

Successful investors have a guiding philosophy—the big picture. They are usually eager to discuss, share, and talk about their philosophy. So why aren't we all rich successful investors? Because the devil is in the details. Successful investors spend a lot of time with the hard work of implementing their philosophy. We all like the idea of being a successful investor, but we don't all like the idea of the work it takes and the focus on the details. Surface analysis dooms average investors.

A less common but frequent mistake of new and newly energetic investors is being so engrossed in the details that they lose track of the big picture. In late 2000 it was common to hear people talking about what a great deal certain tech stocks were. Yahoo's price/earnings ratio was "only" 81, down from over 2000 in 1999. People who claimed to be value investors were now saying that Yahoo was a great deal at 81. Historically 81 is still in the stratosphere.

Know what type of investing cycle we're in. Part of keeping an eye on the big picture is recognizing what types of market conditions make it harder for your strategy to produce top results. Value investors didn't give up value investing during the tech bubble, but it was very tough for them to sit and watch the "irrational exuberance" that the momentum investors were enjoying and the big returns they were raking in. Warren Buffett had a bad year during that time, but he didn't abandon his overall philosophy or view of the world.

APM'S PHILOSOPHY

There are two broad categories of investment philosophies: stock picking and indexing. Stock picking typically is viewed as an active strategy. It's also known as security selection. This new and updated name seems more scientific to some managers. Indexing is a passive strategy based on the efficient market idea that you cannot consistently beat the market. One interesting paradox of efficient markets, first written about by Sandy Grossman and Joseph Stiglitz in a 1980 *American Economic Review* article, is the necessity of stock pickers in efficient markets[2]: If there aren't any stock pickers out there scrutinizing the earnings releases and listening to conference calls, then the market can't be efficient. Market efficiency can exist only if there are enough stock pickers making the effort to gain excess returns.

Some flavors of stock pickers are technical analysts, value investors, growth or momentum investors, information traders, arbitrageurs, and market timers. Investors may stick to one style exclusively or use a combination of several stock-picking methods. Most investors don't want to be labeled or categorized unless they are selling something. Part of a successful investor's philosophy may change as market conditions change.

The APM class is a stock picker. If we have to label ourselves, we are primarily contrarian value investors. We are looking for a company at the right price that is misunderstood, out of favor, or overlooked by most market participants. Large U.S. firms tend to be well scrutinized by the market, but sometimes an opportunity will present itself. As mentioned earlier, Berkshire Hathaway was such an opportunity in 2003. Most of the APM portfolio is in smaller companies that don't receive a lot of publicity.

The philosophy is driven both by Kent's belief that most market participants misunderstand certain situations and by Cathy's natural skepticism. We want the students to focus on understanding each company's business well, then judging it relative to other, perhaps better-known comparable companies. The last piece is to understand why the market's view of the situation may be different from what the class's analysis would suggest.

LSB INDUSTRIES

We briefly discussed LSB Industries in Chapter 4. Now it's time to look at it over its history, how it got into the APM portfolio, and where it is now.

LSB Industries was founded in 1961 by its current chief executive, Jack Golsen. The company entered the public equity markets in 1969. Over the years LSB has been a mini-conglomerate. In 1990 it had six divisions: Chemical, Environmental/Climate Controls, Automotive Products, Industrial Products, Engineering Services, and Financial Services. In the early 1990s, the Chemical division was the leading contributor to profits. This

---

[2] Sanford J. Grossman and Joseph E. Stiglitz, "On the Impossibility of Informationally Efficient Markets." *American Economic Review* 70 (1980): 393–408.

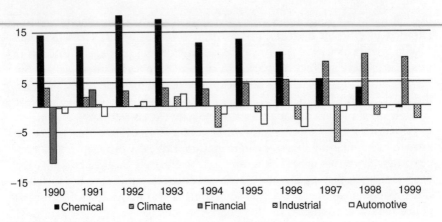

FIGURE 6.1   Operating Profit from LSB's Different Segments

division made acids to use in different industries, ammonium nitrate fertilizer for agriculture, and blasting agents for the mining industry. Figure 6.1
shows the operating profit from each segment in the 1990s. Toward the end
of the decade Industrial and Automotive Products were consistent money
losers, and Chemical's big contribution to profits was eroding. The Chemical
division lost money in 1999. At that time only the Climate Control division
was making money.

Climate Control was actually carrying the rest of the company. The
division went from less than $5 million in operating profit in 1990 to just
about $10 million at the end of 1999. It's a compound annual growth rate
of about 10 percent, but compared to the rest of the company, it was great.
The year 1999 was not a good one for LSB. Overall it lost $49 million
that year.

A combination of causes led to the 1999 losses: the sale of the Automotive business, which had had only two profitable years since 1990, a sale
of a money-losing subsidiary in the chemical division, and the beginning of
some very hard times for the fertilizer business.

When a company sells a division or a subsidiary, it has to take the
division's assets off its balance sheet by recognizing an expense on the income
statement. If the selling price of the division is less than the value of the assets
on the balance sheet, as was the case here, then the company recognizes a
book loss. The company did not actually have a cash outflow of funds from
the transaction, but the loss did reflect the bad outcome from the prior
purchase of the division. The company had already been losing real money
in both of these businesses. In Table 6.1, you can see that the automotive

TABLE 6.1 LSB Industries Divisional Net Operating Profit and Net Income, 1995–2005, in $ millions

	1995	1996	1997	1998	1999	2000	2001	2002	2003	2004	2005
Chemical	13.4	11.0	5.5	3.7	−0.3	1.9	5.9	0.5	3.8	1.9	7.7
Climate	4.6	5.4	8.9	10.5	9.8	11.0	12.5	14.7	11.7	12.9	14.1
Industrial	−1.2	−2.7	−7.3	−1.8	−2.5	0.1					
Automotive	−3.7	−4.1	−1.0	−0.4							
Corporate/Other	−6.6	−3.2	−9.8	−9.4	−8.4	−4.8	−7.4	−6.0	−6.6	−7.8	−6.8
Operating Profit/Loss	6.5	6.3	−3.7	2.5	−1.5	8.1	11.0	9.3	8.9	7.0	15.0
Interest Expense	−10.1	−10.0	−14.7	−17.3	−15.4	−15.4	−13.3	−7.6	−5.6	−6.8	−11.4
Discontinued Operations	0.0	0.0	0.0	0.0	−18.1	−3.1	0.0	−3.5	0.0	0.0	−0.6
Net Income/Loss	−3.7	−3.8	−23.1	−1.9	−49.8	6.2	8.6	0.1	3.1	1.4	5.1

business had lost money every year since 1995. Its last profitable year was 1993. It was actually good news that LSB exited these businesses, but it's a hard spin with an overall loss of $49 million!

Looking forward, you can see that 1999 was the low point for the company. LSB shed assets again in 2000 and started to focus only on two divisions: Chemical and Climate Control. Before we go too far into the future, we need to look at the Chemical business. You can see from Table 6.1 that its profits decreased dramatically from 1995 to 1999; from a $13.4 million profit to a $250,000 loss. What was happening here?

In a letter in the 1999 Annual Report, Jack Golsen outlined a detailed plan to turn the company around. He emphasized for the first time a focus on two core businesses: Chemical and Climate Control. Climate Control had been carrying the company for the last few years, so it's easy to see why that would be a core business. What about Chemical? Mr. Golsen outlined three problems in the business that all hit in 1999: drought, Russian fertilizer dumping, and an unfavorable contract with a supplier. Agricultural conditions will always be a risk for a company doing business in that space. Droughts will happen. Management can't control the weather, but it can mitigate the damage when bad things do happen. We'll discuss how LSB decided to deal with this risk after we discuss the other two related issues.

By 1999 the ammonium nitrate fertilizer industry in the United States had already begun a long-term secular decline.[3] To understand why, we need to understand a few details of the manufacturing process. In making this fertilizer, ammonia needs to be "fixed" with hydrogen. Natural gas is still the most economical and widely used source of hydrogen, and it accounts for 70 to 90 percent of the cost of ammonium nitrate production. In many parts of the world before the mid- to late 1990s, natural gas was a by-product of petroleum production that was "flared" (burned off as a waste product). Beginning in the 1990s, some of that flaring was converted to the production of fertilizer. The biggest cost of production for ammonium nitrate fertilizer was essentially free for many of the new oil-producing countries. Russia, for example, began using most of its natural gas to produce fertilizer. Russian farmers didn't need that much fertilizer, and Russian companies could make it much more cheaply than producers in the United States That's how the dumping started.

In 1999 a large amount of very cheap Russian fertilizer was shipped to the United States. Local producers couldn't compete. Antidumping actions

---

[3] A secular change is a permanent change in an economy or industry. It is distinct from a cyclical change. An example of a secular trend would be the switch from horse-drawn carriages to automobiles after the internal combustion engine became economically viable.

were taken that limited the Russians' ability to undercut U.S. prices, but you can't stop inevitable market forces. It just makes economic sense to have the lowest-cost producers making the product. Protectionism doesn't work. Shipping was the biggest cost for the foreign producers of fertilizer. Before the explosion of low-cost foreign producers, ammonium nitrate fertilizer was produced in regional plants that supplied a relatively small trade area to minimize shipping costs. Now even someone from as far away as Russia could ship to the United States and undercut local producers. The U.S. fertilizer industry was in a secular decline, and dumping was just the latest and most acute symptom of that decline.

Big consolidation was another symptom of the decline of the fertilizer industry. In 2005 Ford West, the president of The Fertilizer Institute, a trade association representing the fertilizer industry, testified before the U.S. Senate about the impact of the price on natural gas on the industry.

> *As a result of the ongoing natural gas crisis in America, 21 nitrogen fertilizer (ammonia) production facilities have closed since FY1998/99 (July 1998–June 1999). Sixteen of those plants have closed permanently, representing a 20 percent drop in total production capacity, while five plants remain idle. Operating rates for the U.S. ammonia industry have also declined significantly from historical levels. The permanent and temporary closures in combination with the drop in operating rates have resulted in a 35 percent decline in U.S. ammonia production from 17.85 million tons of material in FY1998/99 to 11.70 million tons in FY2003/04. U.S. nitrogen imports have increased from 6.11 million tons in FY98/99 to 10.36 million tons in FY2003/04. As a result, U.S. ammonia production fell by over six million tons or 34 percent in only five years. Consequently, the U.S. fertilizer industry, which typically supplied 85 percent of its domestic needs from U.S. based production during the 1990s, now relies on imports for nearly 45 percent of nitrogen supplies.[4]*

Add to the secular decline the agricultural cycle, and LSB's Chemical business was getting hit with a double whammy. Farmers have a very tough job because of the agricultural cycle and fertilizer sales rely on what's happening in this cycle. In a good crop year, crop prices are low and volume

---

[4] Ford B. West, President, The Fertilizer Institute. Testimony before the U.S. Senate Appropriations Interior and Related Agencies Subcommittee regarding the High Price of Natural Gas and Its Impact on the U.S. Fertilizer Industry, October 25, 2005.

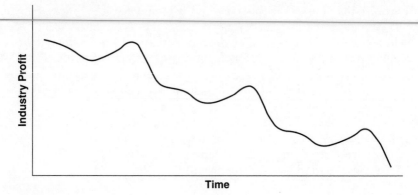

FIGURE 6.2 Industry Profits over Time in a Cyclical Industry with a Secular Decline

is high because there is a lot of supply, usually because of good weather in the growing area. Farmers will have more income and LSB will sell more fertilizer the next year because of the increase in farm income. In a bad year, prices are high, but farmers don't have a lot to sell.

Investing in a cyclical industry can be profitable, if you pick your spots. Figure 6.2 shows what happens to industry profits over time in a cyclical industry that is in a secular decline. The graph shows the view for *industry* profits. Individual firms won't necessarily follow the same path. The weakest will go out of business or be bought by stronger competitors in the same industry. Eventually, though, capacity has to be wrung out. As Mr. West testified, production fell in the fertilizer industry by 34 percent in five years. While once there were a lot of publicly traded fertilizer companies, now there are just a few. Terra Industries, Potash, and Agrium are the three primary North American fertilizer competitors left. Potash and Agrium are Canadian companies.

When an industry is declining, investors move quickly to exit. Companies go out of business or combine with others as production capacity decreases. What determines survival or bankruptcy in this type of situation? It could be luck, scale, or something else. In LSB's case, the something else was the Climate Control business, which really started to earn some money about the time the Chemical business was coming unglued. LSB has never been the biggest heating and air conditioning manufacturer, but it did have a profitable business to tide the firm over through the very toughest times.

You can see in Figure 6.2 that general direction is down in the industry, but some years are cycling up. As some companies leave the industry and

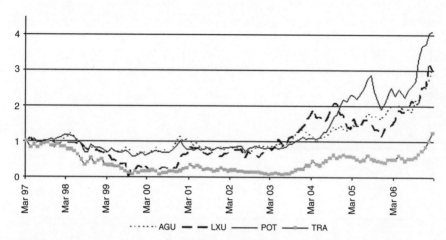

FIGURE 6.3 Returns for Fertilizer Industries Stocks, March 1997–March 2007

plants are taken out of production, that leaves more to go around for the survivors. But investors don't have good feelings for any company in this industry. Stock prices are getting really beat up. When do you want to invest in this type of industry? The idea is to buy low. A few companies in this industry are going to survive. Those survivors will begin to make some money because the weakest will have left the scene and excess capacity has been wrung out of the industry. Figure 6.3 shows the stock chart for the four survivors—LSB, Potash, Agrium, and Terra—from March 1997 to March 2007.

If you invested in any of these companies between 1997 and mid-2003, you would have lost money. Beginning in mid-2003, things started to turn around. By that time excess capacity had been eliminated. Then in 2005 Hurricane Katrina drove natural gas prices through the roof, and the stocks dipped as fertilizer became very expensive to manufacture. Farmers weren't buying—not just because of the prices, but the previous farm season hadn't been great and they were short of cash. Drought and other bad weather dampened planting and agriculture spending. So things didn't get better, even though things were shaping up to get better in the fertilizer business because of new anti-dumping laws and the removal of excess production capacity.

Commodity Prices and Profits

Fast forward to 2007. The year 2006 had been an okay one on the farm. Farm income declined slightly, but crop income was up about 3 percent.

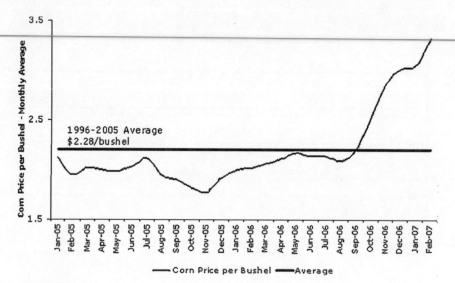

FIGURE 6.4   Monthly Corn Prices, January 2005–February 2007

President Bush pushed corn-based ethanol in his 2007 State of the Union address. Farmers started to receive subsidies for planting corn. Early spring rain was beneficial. The margins on ammonium nitrate fertilizer were the highest in years. Figure 6.3 shows that the market finally was beginning to push the prices of fertilizer stocks up. Increasing crop prices in late 2006 helped. Figure 6.4 shows that corn prices had been lagging their 10-year average over 2005 and the first part of 2006.

In addition to the farmers being able to buy fertilizer, the prices paid to fertilizer manufacturers were getting much stronger. In Figure 6.5 the bars show LSB's margin as the input and selling prices change. This is the margin for LSB's main ammonium nitrate fertilizer plant in El Dorado, Arkansas. El Dorado can produce approximately 250 tons of agricultural fertilizer using ammonia as an input. Making fertilizer is pretty simple economically. The profit formula for the El Dorado plant is:

Profit margin = Ammonium Nitrate Price −

$$((Ammonia\ Price + 25) \times 0.46) - Overhead\ (OH)$$

The solid line in Figure 6.5 is the average weekly selling price of ammonium nitrate in the Southern Plains region (primarily Texas, Oklahoma, and Kansas). The dashed line is the cost of the input to LSB: (Ammonia

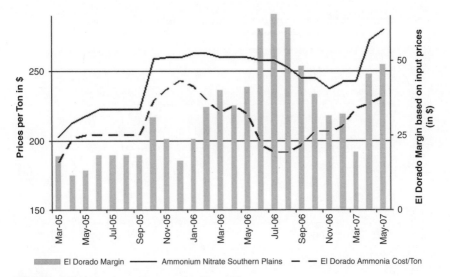

FIGURE 6.5 Fertilizer Input and Selling Prices

Price + 25) × 0.46. The bars are the profit margin calculated using the formula. This profit margin isn't what LSB actually earns because the plant isn't manufacturing at a constant rate over the course of the year, but it does give you an idea of the profit potential when favorable pricing conditions prevail. Most of the fertilizer is sold during the first quarter of the year. In early 2007 fertilizer prices were rising and margins were strong.

The company has two other fertilizer plants: one in Baytown, Texas, and one in Cherokee, Alabama. All of the Baytown plant and most of the Cherokee production is under contract to sell industrial chemicals with a fixed markup over cost. The Cherokee plant can produce 75 tons of product without cutting into its other agriculture production. This plant has a slightly different technology. It has the option of purchasing ammonia and producing at the same margin as El Dorado, or it can purchase natural gas and produce ammonia. If natural gas prices are low relative to ammonia, then the Cherokee plant can produce at higher margins, even though it's a relatively small volume amount.

These fixed-margin industrial chemical contracts were put in place gradually, after the bad year of 1999, to bring some stability and more predictability into the earnings of the LSB chemical side. We estimate that LSB gets approximately $9 million in profit from these agreements. That means the company is giving up any upside when agriculture conditions mean it can sell a lot of fertilizer, such as in 2007. However, conditions haven't been "right" for the last 10 years, so it seems like a pretty good insurance policy.

TABLE 6.2   Overhead Allocation and Profit or Loss

Variable costs	$0.02 per ton
Fixed costs	$100
÷ Capacity	50 tons
Fixed overhead allocation	$2.00 per ton
Total overhead allocation	$2.02 per ton
Actual production	25 tons
Overhead allocated	$50.50
Actual cost	$100.50
Markup over cost	10%
Revenue	$55.55
Cost	$100.50
Profit (Loss)	$(44.95)

One other caveat on these contracts is in calculating overhead. The contracts assume that the company is operating at full capacity. In a good year, it's no problem. In a bad year, when the company doesn't operate at full capacity, the full capacity overhead amount underestimates the cost of overhead.

Why is overhead problematic? Overhead consists of two types of costs, fixed and variable. (Actually there are also semivariable costs, but we can simplify to get the point across.) Suppose a factory has high fixed costs of $100 and low variable cost of $0.02 per ton. If the markup over cost is 10 percent and capacity is 50 tons, Table 6.2 shows how LSB could lose money on these contracts when operating at less than full capacity. When overhead is based on full capacity, the allocation for fixed overhead is the fixed costs divided by capacity, $100 ÷ 50 = $2/ton. For the full overhead allocation, just add the variable cost. Now suppose that production is only 25 tons. The actual costs to produce are $100 of fixed cost plus 50 cents of variable costs, for total cost of $100.50. If overhead cost is allocated at $2.02 per ton, the fixed-cost contracts would assign a cost of $50.50. With a markup of 10 percent, the revenue from the contract would be $50.50 + 5.05, or $55.55. Compared to an actual cost of $100.50, the company would actually lose $44.95.

Figure 6.6 shows that when fixed overhead is very high, a capital-intensive company like LSB needs to operate at close to full capacity for this type of contract to make sense. In this example, LSB would have to produce at 45.4 tons in order to break even. However, once breakeven is reached, profits climb sharply.

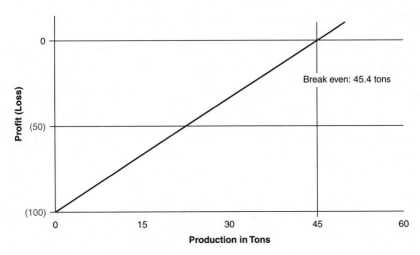

FIGURE 6.6 Profit or Loss and Production

This example illustrates an important point about capital-intensive industries in general and LSB's Chemical division in particular. Paying attention to capacity and production amounts is really important in determining profitability. When demand for fertilizer was low or supply from other sources was high, such as in the late 1990s or early 2000s, profits will decrease dramatically.

Airlines are similar. The fixed costs of running an airplane are very high. When planes aren't flying at full capacity, airlines lose a lot of money. Some airlines go out of business, and the surviving ones begin to fly at near full capacity. They make a ton of money, they add capacity, and the cycle begins again. Investors almost always invest at the wrong time. To buy low and sell high, you need to buy when things are most gloomy and sell when things are going really well. The trick is to remember the cycle. It's easy for us humans to believe "This time it really is different," or "We are entering a new era."

Leverage

LSB has a lot of operating leverage. That's the phenomenon of high fixed costs creating big swings in profit. In addition to the high operating leverage, LSB has had a boatload of debt (aka financial leverage). Table 6.3 shows that in 1999, when the APM class first started buying LSB shares, interest expense was exploding and the EBITDA (earnings before interest, taxes, depreciation, and amortization) to interest expense ratio was at its lowest

TABLE 6.3 LSB Industries Profit, Debt, and Stock Return Measures, 1998–2006

	1998	1999	2000	2001	2002	2003	2004	2005	2006
Operating profit ($M)	2.5	–1.5	8.1	11.0	9.3	8.9	7.0	15.0	27.6
Interest expense ($M)	17.3	15.4	15.4	13.3	7.6	5.6	6.8	11.4	11.9
Long-term debt ($M)	155.7	124.7	93.9	88.0	74.5	71.6	101.7	108.8	86.1
Operating cash flow (EBITDA) ($M)	12.9	8.8	14.0	19.0	15.0	18.0	12.4	23.5	37.2
EBITDA/Interest expense	0.7	0.6	0.9	1.3	2.0	3.2	1.7	2.1	3.1
Common stock price	3.31	1.41	2.44	2.60	2.80	6.38	7.95	6.15	11.58
Annual stock return (%)		–57.6	73.4	6.6	7.7	127.9	24.6	–22.6	88.3

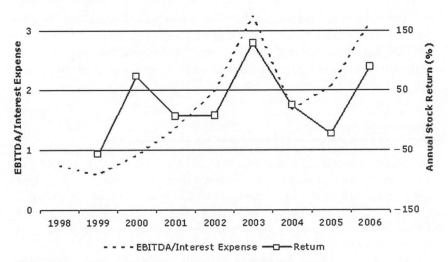

FIGURE 6.7 LSB Stock Returns and EBITDA/Interest Expense

point. All of the company's operating cash and more was going to pay interest on debt. When the ratio is below 1, that's really bad!

When things are going well, financial leverage works like operating leverage for equity holders. All the upside goes to the equity holders. Figure 6.7 shows that the stock returns for LSB correspond pretty well with the EBITDA to interest expense ratio. Higher returns are fueled by higher, better cash flow and lower interest payments. Given the double dose of high operating leverage and high financial leverage, when things go right, the returns are extraordinary. Of course, the flipside is true also.

What Next?

As we write in 2007, we are approaching the golden moment to sell. The chemical plants are running at full capacity, and the Climate Control division has had a couple of extraordinary years with possibly more on the way. The Chemical division should be at the peak of a cycle. What should happen now? If LSB announces a sale of its Chemical division and continues operations as an HVAC company specializing in geothermal heat pumps, we will still be holders of the company. It will really start to look like a growth company. However, if plans to sell the Chemical division don't materialize, it will be time to take a lot of money off the table.

That's a hard thing to do when you've been through a company's trials and tribulations. You know the story, you like the management. Each spring

APM students have been following corn production reports and weather forecasts in the growing areas. It's a great learning experience. Still, sometimes it's good to finally realize your gains. LSB Industries has been a holding that really typifies the APM investment philosophy: Go against the crowd, but really know the name and where the value is coming from.

WRAPPING UP

LSB is only one example of stocks that we've invested in, but it illustrates many of the core principles of the class's investment style. To find these companies, each week the students write up an analysis (which we call a case) on a different company. In the next four chapters we go into much greater detail about how we do a case analysis and how we decide based on that work whether to invest or not.

The case has been a fundamental part of the class since inception. The format changes from time to time, but the bedrock still is properly valuing an investment opportunity, really understanding how the company makes money, and finally, if we invest, evaluating why we think this is an opportunity that the market hasn't fully appreciated.

CHAPTER 7

Prepping for a Case

The case analysis is the basis of the APM class. Each week students work in groups to write a company analysis. We call them cases, real-time cases. They form the basis for deciding whether a company comes or goes in the portfolio. The case covers a stock investment that is going to be discussed by the next speaker. The students get practically immediate feedback on their work. They can adjust any assumptions that they've made after hearing from the speaker. The cases are meant to be thorough analyses of a particular investment. They also are meant to prepare students to be critical consumers of the research reports of sell-side analysts.

Each group's case is three pages of analysis with an attachment containing more detailed information about the group's valuation model. Each case begins with a summary of the investment thesis and its key supporting ideas. The next part is a short description and analysis of the company, its historical operating and financial performance, its position in its industry, and its competitive advantage. The final piece is a valuation and risk analysis. In the valuation, groups come up with future benchmarks that we can use to determine whether the investment thesis still holds.

If each member of the group does a thorough job of prepping for the case, the writing and analysis is much easier. The group can discuss the company based on the facts and come up with an opinion. Without the basic groundwork preparation, cases can become an unrelated collection of facts that don't really have a unifying theme. That makes it hard to form an opinion and then support that opinion.

One part of what it takes to be a successful investor is a disciplined approach to gathering facts and making judgments on those facts. Discipline in case preparation is great for building discipline in fact gathering. Experience in reviewing financial statements, listening to conference calls, and understanding news reports is critical. Taking a long-term, comprehensive view is a hard skill to develop in today's world of sound bites. It's hard to develop in a semester-long class, but if we can build a solid information base, the hope is that good judgment will follow.

Without basic grounding in facts, investing is based on "feelings," "intuition," or what everyone else is saying. That's when investing isn't investing but betting on public opinion. If that's your strategy, you'll never do better than average except by chance.

Getting the facts together and organizing them is the subject of this chapter. In the next chapter we look at analyzing and drawing conclusions from those facts. Both pieces are necessary components of a good investment strategy. Just because you have the facts doesn't mean you'll make the right judgments, but having the facts is necessary condition.

GETTING STARTED

Here's the suggested preliminary case preparation from the syllabus for a weekly case analysis:

- Read the 10-K, most recent 10-Qs, proxy statements, filings with the Securities and Exchange Commission (SEC), and analyst reports.
- Listen to any recent conference calls or presentations on the company's Web site or filing with the SEC.
- Read about industry trends. What is the industry structure? What is the firm's competitive advantage?
- Find other original source material on the company, industry, or pertinent macroeconomic trends.
- Find the operating performance trends over time. How do the company's numbers relate to its competitors now and in the past? Graph revenue, earnings before interest, taxes, and depreciation (EBITDA), net income, and earnings per share (EPS) over time. What other operating metrics are important for this company?
- What are the valuation metrics for the company and competitors: price to earnings (P/E), total enterprise value (TEV)/EBITDA, price to book (P/B), price to sales (P/S)? Have they changed over time?

This is a lot of material to sort through in a short amount of time, but reading the 10-K and listening to conference calls gives students grounding in how the company views itself. They've also got to understand the company's history and see how it has played out through the financial statements. Finally, because they need to see how the market has interpreted the past results, they need to tie past operating results to past market performance.

Where do students find all of this material? First and foremost, the SEC Web site and company Web sites contain all required filings by any company. The SEC's search engine is called EDGAR (Electronic Data Gathering, Analysis, and Retrieval). You can easily find EDGAR from the SEC's home page (www.sec.gov). Companies must file electronically annual reports such as proxy statement and 10-Ks within 60 days of the end of a fiscal year for the largest companies, 75 days for most others, and 90 days for some very small companies. Quarterly reports, 10-Qs, must be filed within 40 days of the end of a quarter, and Section 16 (we'll discuss these soon) filings must be within 2 days.

10-Ks, Other Filings, and Analyst Reports

A 10-K is not the same as a company's annual report. A 10-K can replace an annual report, but an annual report cannot replace a 10-K. Some companies issue a glossy marketing document as their annual report. It usually contains the financial statements, a letter from the chief executive, and lots of nice pictures. Some companies have eliminated the glossy annual report and just have a 10-K, which contains required information. The appendix in this chapter contains a complete list of the items that have to be included in the 10-K. Some of the highlights are complete financial statements including footnotes, management's discussion and analysis of the financial statements, a discussion of the risks facing the company, and information about any lawsuits.

Other SEC filings provide detailed information about company and insider transactions. All press releases have to be filed as 8-Ks with the SEC. Companies will also have those posted on their Web sites. Section 16 filings are called form 4s. They are insider trading forms that let you know who is buying or selling stock. All corporate officers and anyone else who holds 10 percent of a company has to file a Form 4 within 48 hours of a trade.

Investment banks, brokerage firms, and other organizations publish research reports. Students in the APM class have access to many of these reports through a service called Thomson One. Thomson collects analyst reports and analysts estimates of future earnings, revenues, and many other operating metrics. When CNBC or other news stories talk about the Street's expectations, they are referring to the consensus estimate put together by Thomson.

Conference Calls

In August 2000 the SEC adopted a rule called Regulation (Reg FD). FD stands for "fair disclosure." The regulation was adopted to prohibit companies disclosing information to selected individuals and not all investors. Before the rule was adopted, analysts and others from large firms could talk to chief executive and chief financial officers and receive information that wasn't available to the general investing public. Quarterly conference calls in which management discussed the quarter's performance and gave guidance about what they thought would happen in the future was just for a select group of analysts and portfolio managers.

Now anyone can listen live to a company's quarterly call, either on a telephone call or through the Internet. Anyone can ask a question. Reg FD changed the quality and amount of information available to the general investing public virtually overnight. It's amazing that more investors don't take advantage of this opportunity, but it's rare to hear anyone who isn't an investment professional ask a question during conference calls. Company officials get a list of all callers and Internet participants. Based on informal conversations with corporate officers, most of the listeners who don't ask questions are also investment professionals.

Companies leave the calls up on their Web sites or have telephone re-play number for varying periods. Some leave all their quarterly calls up for a year; others, just for a few days. Occasionally the call never makes it to a telephone or Web replay. In most such situations, that is because something bad happened during the quarter and the question-and-answer session didn't go well. That's one reason why listening to the live call can provide some good tidbits. One of Enron's last conference calls in 2001 provides the best example of what can happen during a call. Investors were angry, and management didn't have very good answers. Lots of peo-ple indicated they sold their shares during that call, if they hadn't already done so before. It seemed to be the last straw. The November 13, 2001, press release for this call is a typical example of the press release for a conference call.

Press Release

ENRON CORP. TO HOLD CONFERENCE CALL AND WEBCAST TO PROVIDE INVESTOR UPDATE

FOR IMMEDIATE RELEASE: Tuesday, November 13, 2001

HOUSTON – Enron Corp. (NYSE: ENE) will hold a conference call and webcast to provide an investor update on Wednesday, Nov. 14, 2001 at 9:30 a.m. EST. A live webcast of the call will be available through the "Investors" section of www.enron.com.

Enron is one of the world's leading energy, commodities and services companies. The company markets electricity and natural gas, delivers energy and other physical commodities, and provides financial and risk management services to customers around the world. Enron's Internet address is www.enron.com. The stock is traded under the ticker symbol "ENE."

Another example of how it pays to listen to live calls is an H&R Block call in November 2002. Some context and background to assess the information in the call is useful. On November 6, 2002, a Texas jury awarded a partial summary judgment of $75 million to Ronnie and Nancy Haese. They had filed suit against H&R Block for failing to disclose some fees that were charged when they took out a RAL (refund anticipation loan). Over the period of the suit, H&R Block had received only $3.5 million in total fees. The $75 million judgment was stunning in its size and scope. H&R Block held a conference call soon after the award to discuss the case. The stock dropped from $41 to $35 overnight after the judgment. During the call the next day, management explained that the size of the verdict and the summary judgment (the case didn't go to a jury, the judge decided the outcome) were unprecedented. H&R Block indicated that the company would appeal. After listening to the call, the APM class checked with alumni and friends who were attorneys. Most felt that this was a rogue judge and the judgment would be significantly reduced or thrown out entirely. The class had been thinking about making a purchase, but the stock had been a little pricey. We decided this was the buying opportunity we'd been looking for. We purchased shares on November 14 at $32.90. Management's and the legal team's candid way of addressing the problems they were facing sold the class. If we hadn't been listening to their calls, we probably wouldn't have been able to properly assess the impact of the verdict on the company.

Of course, you can't believe everything you hear. *Verified* trust is always prudent. Things still could have gone south for the company, but investing is always about taking a risk. If you wait until all the uncertainty is cleared up, you'll be buying high and selling low.

Industry Information

Good industry information is usually the hardest thing for students to find. There are two problems. Sometimes it's hard to pinpoint what industry a company is in. A company may compete against divisions of other companies, but there isn't a well-defined industry definition. Garmin is an example of a company with a hard-to-define industry. Originally Garmin was the only public pure play in global positioning systems (GPS). It competed against a lot of different companies or divisions of companies, depending on the segment. Table 7.1 shows how Garmin looks at the competition. In the aviation segment, Avidyne is a private company and the other two competitors are segments of much larger companies. Of all the companies listed in the table, only one other concentrates exclusively on GPS systems as Garmin does, and that is TomTom. The companies compete in only one of the segments, but

TABLE 7.1 Garmin's Competitors

Segment	Competitors	Segment	Competitors
Aviation	Avidyne	Recreational Products	Cobra
	Honeywell Aerospace segment		Lowrance
	Rockwell Collins (government segment)		Magellan
Marine	Furano	Automotive	Magellan
	Lowrance		Navman
	Raymarine		TomTom
	Simrad		

it is one of Garmin's most important segments. Still, if you use TomTom for a comparable analysis, you'd be overlooking the huge margins that Garmin gets from aviation.

Most of the time people use one of the predefined industry classifiers to determine screens for industry. Garmin's Global Industry Classification Standard (GICS) code is 25201010 and its Standard Industry Classification (SIC) code is 3812. Table 7.2 shows the main classifications for GICS codes. Since Garmin begins with 25, it is in the Consumer Discretionary category. The GICS has 10 sectors, 24 industry groups, 67 industries, and 147 subindustries. The system was developed by Morgan Stanley and Standard & Poor's (S&P) for investment professionals.

Garmin's code of 25201010 is broken down as:

25	Consumer Discretionary
2520	Consumer Durables & Apparel
252010	Household Durables
25201010	Consumer Electronics

TABLE 7.2 Global Industry Classification Standard Sectors

10 Energy	35 Health Care
15 Materials	40 Financials
20 Industrials	45 Information Technology
25 Consumer Discretionary	50 Telecommunication Services
30 Consumer Staples	55 Utilities

The description given by MSCI for Consumer Electronics is:

Manufacturers of consumer electronics products including TVs, VCRs, hi-fi equipment, game consoles and related products. Excludes personal home computer manufacturers classified in the Computer Hardware sub-industry, and electric household appliances classified in the Household Appliances sub-industry.

Some of the other companies listed in this code include Cobra Electronics, Emerson Radio, Harmon International, and Koss. None of these companies makes GPS systems.

The other industry classification system is the North American Industry Classification System (NAICS). It was developed by the government to take the place of the SIC, which was in use for many years. Many companies still use SIC codes. The NAICS system is much more detailed and has many more categories. It is the basis for data collection by many government offices. Garmin's NAICS code of 334511 is described as "Search, Detection, Navigation, Guidance, Aeronautical, and Nautical System and Instrument Manufacturing." An entirely different set of companies share Garmin's NAICS code; there is not a single overlapping company. Some of those companies are Flight Safety Technologies, Homeland Security Network Inc, Northrop Grumman Corp., and Orbit International Corp.

Using either NAICS or GICS codes doesn't get you to the correct set of comparables for Garmin. The NAICS may be a little closer, but it's not that great. Most analysts use industry screens based on one of these two systems. So it's important to recognize when a company, such as Garmin, doesn't fit well into the model.

Parts of some companies can be analyzed using industry comparables. For example, the Chemical division of LSB Industries could be compared to NAICS companies with a 325311 code: Nitrogenous Fertilizer Manufacturing. The GICS code 15101030—Fertilizers & Agricultural Chemicals—contains companies that manufacture pesticides, phosphate fertilizers, and any other agricultural chemical. LSB's main GICS code is 15101020—Diversified Chemicals—and its NAICS code is 325188—All Other Basic Inorganic Chemical Manufacturing. Neither of these codes is the same as those of LSB's main competitors, so a screen based on fertilizers wouldn't include LSB. However, LSB's "wild card" component for its Chemical division is the fertilizer business. Understanding how others may categorize the company in the industry and the drivers of the industry are important components in understanding the company's Chemical division.

Usually the best way to compare is to start using the NAICS or GICS code to see what companies are included. See if they make sense. Then ask the investor relations department at the company who it actually competes against. From these various sources, compile your own list of comparables and industry information.

The second problem students have in getting good industry information is cost. Lots of industry consultants and industry organizations compile lots of detailed input pricing, demand, and other very valuable information. Unfortunately, you need to belong to the industry organization or subscribe to the consultant's services to receive that information. For example, a subscription to *Fertilizer Week*, a weekly report on fertilizer input prices, selling prices, and demand, costs $2,660 per year. A competing report costs $1,489 per year. *Green Markets* primarily covers the North American market, and *Fertilizer Week* covers the global market. Both provide fertilizer industry news in addition to pricing information.

Some industry group and government information is freely available, but it can be difficult to track down. Reading analyst industry reports is a good way to get up to speed on an industry. Many times it is a question of finding the right pieces of information, and analyst reports can help provide a broad overview as well as some insight on where to get good numbers.

Finally, since good industry information is not always easy to find, this is the area that students can really add value. A good, thoughtful review of the industry and a company's place in it is hard to find.

Other Information

For background, students also can use any pertinent news articles, macroeconomic trends that affect the industry, or conversations with company officials or with company customers or suppliers. At many companies, the investor relations (IR) department can be a good source. Many times it will provide a little different take on competition or a more accessible version of some of the legalese that is presented in the 10-K.

An example of some unexpected information came when a student group called IR for a midsize oil E&P (exploration and production) company. The students had a question about an item on the income statement. The IR person was very helpful, answering not only their specific question but going on to explain the two different types of accounting that E&P companies could use. He provided a list of competitors and the type of accounting that each used.

Sometimes IR is distinctly *un*helpful: impossible to reach, never returning calls or e-mails. When you do reach them, they won't provide any useful information. They'll say something like "Look in the SEC filings. We don't have anything to add." While this response is frustrating, it does provide useful information. The message the company is sending is: "We don't like to

deal with shareholders. They are a pain." If there are other shareholder un-
friendly actions, such as unclear language in the filings, perhaps the company
has something to hide. Clearly IR doesn't want to help tell the company's
story.

Past Operating Metrics

Once the background has been set by reading company and industry information and listening to conference calls, it's time to see how to relate
to the impression received from the background sources to the financials.
Students need to see how the numbers played out in the past in order to
understand how to forecast the future. They need to answer a big question:
Is the company going to use the same operating strategy in the near future,
or is it going to change? The follow-up is: How will industry and economic
conditions affect results in either case?

First we need to examine the operating numbers over time. Usually
it's easier to get an idea of what's happening by looking at graphs and by
organizing the information in tables. We'll use our portfolio's long-term
holding Jos. A. Bank (NASDAQ: JOSB) as an example because it's relatively
easy to get good comparable information for the retail clothing companies.
After reading some background, it's pretty clear that margins and sales
growth rates are key operating metrics for most retail companies. Actually
those are important numbers for most companies.

Table 7.3 shows Jos. A. Bank sales and earnings before interest, taxes,
depreciation, and amortization numbers and growth for the years 2002
to 2006. EBITDA is important because it measures the results from the
operating portion of the company. If EBITDA isn't there, then net income
won't be either. We'll discuss its importance more in Chapter 9.

The actual sales and EBITDA numbers aren't that meaningful. We need
to put things in perspective over time. One way to provide perspective is
to look at the EBITDA margin (EBITDA divided by Sales). Higher margins

TABLE 7.3   Jos. A. Bank Sales and EBITDA, 2002–2006

	2006	2005	2004	2003	2002
Sales	546.4	464.6	372.5	299.7	243.4
EBITDA	88.9	74.8	52.6	38.1	25.4
EBITDA margin %	16.3	16.1	14.1	12.7	10.4
Sales growth %	17.6	24.7	24.3	23.1	
EBITDA growth %	18.8	42.4	38.0	50.0	

~~mean more profit. Net income can increase through sales growth or through~~
margin expansion. When both happen together, that's the best.

The compound annual growth rates in sales and EBITDA over this period were 22 and 33 percent, respectively. Table 7.3 also shows that margins were increasing over the period and sales were growing in the double digits. That combination leads to the EBITDA growth numbers. You can see in 2004 that sales grew 24 percent and the EBITDA margin went from 12.7 to 14.1 percent, translating into a 38 percent growth in EBITDA.

Figure 7.1 shows how quarterly gross, EBITDA, and profit margins have changed over time and the relation among the three. The figure on the top shows that gross margin is increasing over time. It's harder to see the increase in the figure on the bottom. Profit margin is the bottom line: net income divided by sales. If the profit margin is decreasing, that can mean trouble.

The other big item that jumps out from the graphs is the cyclical pattern. It's not surprising that a retailer has a quarterly pattern. The holiday margins are much higher than the other quarters in the year. That means it is more appropriate to compare a quarter to the previous-year quarter than to the last quarter to see how the company is doing. Another lesson from these two views is that there isn't too much difference in EBITDA margin and profit margin. You take away the same story from either.

Students need to look at a lot of views of the same metrics to figure out which view tells the story the best. For this company, if you want to emphasize margin expansion over time, it's clearer in the top graph. If that's the story you want to communicate in the case write-up, then we'd probably take out either the EBITDA or profit margin line just to clean it up a little. If you want to communicate the gap between gross margin and EBITDA margin, then the top graph would do a better job. The difference between gross and EBITDA margin is selling and administrative expenses. Most retailers have to advertise a lot, so this gap isn't that unusual. If there was a dramatic change in one of the margins over time, then that might be what you want to communicate. Figure 7.2 shows the dramatic drop in LSB Industries profit margin in 1999. Operating or EBIT (earnings before interest and taxes) margins had been down for a few years, but not dramatically compared to the profit margin.

The picture tells us we need to look at what happened between EBIT and profit lines on the balance sheet. In the next chapter we'll discuss in a lot more detail what happens in each part of the income statement and balance sheet. Right now we're just discovering how and where to look.

Through their preparatory readings students should have discovered that inventory is a concern that has been raised by analysts and in news stories. There are a few different inventory metrics. Two useful inventory

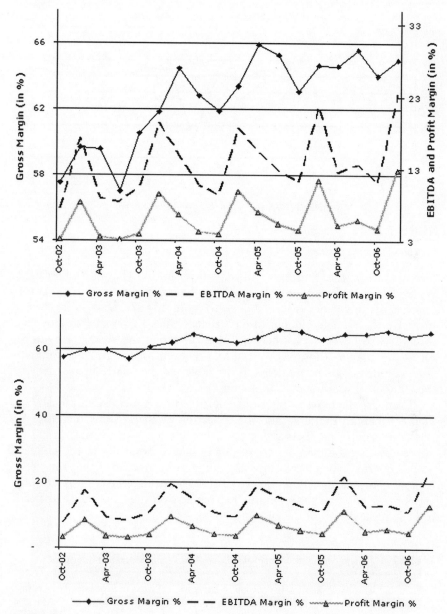

FIGURE 7.1 Two views of Jos. A. Bank Gross, EBITDA, and Profit Margins

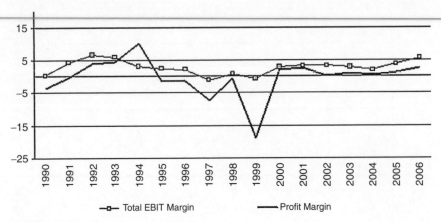

FIGURE 7.2   LSB Margins, 1990–2006

measures are inventory turnover and days in inventory. They measure related concepts, but inventory turnover measures the number of times in a year (or quarter) that inventory is turned over, so more is better. Days in inventory measures the average number of days that it takes a company to move its inventory, so fewer days is better. Table 7.4 shows the average inventory ratios and margin ratios over the last four quarters for Jos. A. Bank and two close competitors. The numbers in the table are the quarterly average for the 2006 fiscal year for each company.

Compare the table to the similar information presented graphically in Figure 7.3. Both the table and the collection of charts show that Jos. A. Bank's inventory numbers are much worse than the competition's. They also show that the margins are generally better, especially in the holiday season quarter. The charts show the comparison over time, but the table is more compact and shows a slice of time. Students need to look at both views to see how things are or aren't changing over time, but they also need to look at the details of the current numbers.

TABLE 7.4   Inventory and Margin Ratios for Jos A. Bank and Competitors

Company	Ticker	Inventory Turnover	Days in Inventory	Gross Margin	Operating Margin	Profit Margin
Jos. A. Bank	JOSB	0.3	1,486	64.8	12.1	7.1
Casual Male	CMRG	0.6	612	45.2	5.2	7.5
Men's Wearhouse	MW	0.6	644	46.6	11.8	7.8

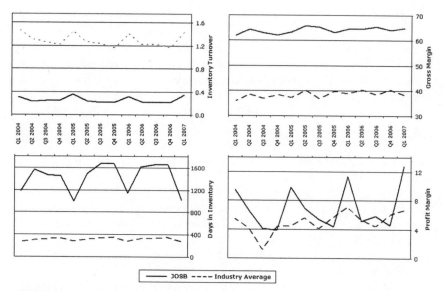

FIGURE 7.3 Inventory and Margin Ratios for Jos. A. Bank and Competitors

Market Metrics and Valuation Ratios

The operating metrics describe the financial performance of a company over time. Other important pieces of information are how the market is assessing a company relative to its peers. There are several seemingly straightforward numbers that students need to calculate. First are market capitalization and TEV. Next are the valuation ratios: P/E, P/B, P/S, and TEV/EBITDA. Some people add price to cash flow, but cash flow can be defined in many ways so it is not as standard or as specific.

Market Metrics: Market Cap Market capitalization (market cap) is the easiest to calculate. It is price times the number of shares outstanding. Just because it's the easiest to calculate doesn't mean there aren't some details that can trip students up. Price is whatever the market says it is, so it's important to specify when it is calculated since price changes frequently. It's customary to using a closing price on a particular day. The number of shares outstanding usually isn't too hard, but there are a few details to pay attention to. The number of shares outstanding also depends on the day because firms can buy back shares or issue new shares.

Finding actual shares outstanding on a particular date can be difficult. Companies don't have to announce that they have repurchased shares. Shares outstanding don't include treasury shares—shares that have been issued and are held by the company, usually because of repurchase. Companies do report the shares outstanding in 10-K and 10-Q filings at the end of each quarter. If there is a major transaction, such as a secondary equity offering, a tender offer, or conversion of a substantial amount of debt or preferred stock, companies will report a total in the filings for the event. The new number is automatically picked up on many of the popular financial Web sites. If a major transaction has occurred, students should verify the shares outstanding.

Earnings per share calculations don't use shares outstanding at the end of a quarter but average shares outstanding. Usually that's not too different from the shares outstanding on a particular date unless there has been a major transaction. A major transaction will affect the share price so that the value of the company reflected by market cap before and after the transaction doesn't change much. For example, as a company issues new shares, the price of one share will decrease unless there is some news accompanying the transaction that the proceeds from the new shares will be used to increase the value of the company.

Another issue with share count is whether to count just the common shares outstanding or use the fully diluted count. Reported shares outstanding don't include fully diluted shares, which usually should be used in EPS calculations. They are shares that could be converted from convertible securities—preferred stock or convertible debt. Fully diluted shares also include possible dilution from executive stock options. Both can add a significant number of shares to common shares outstanding. Table 7.5 shows common shares outstanding at the end of a quarter and the shares used in determining basic and fully diluted EPS for the same quarter for a number of APM portfolio companies. The percent difference from common shares outstanding will be the same percent difference in market capitalization, if those share count numbers were used. A positive percent difference between the basic EPS shares and the common shares outstanding means that the company sold some treasury sold or somehow increased the number of shares outstanding over the quarter. Negative numbers indicate that a share repurchase occurred in the quarter.

Most of the share increases are small on a relative basis. Sometimes companies with executive stock options have to increase the shares by selling treasury stock to exercise the options at expiration. We do see in this quarter that LSB increased the number of shares outstanding by 12.3 percent, a fairly large increase that could represent some dilution to common shareholders. A change this big should be investigated. What happened during this quarter was that LSB made a tender offer to convert a large portion of convertible preferred shares to common. For preferred shareholders like the APM class, this was a very positive development.

TABLE 7.5 Share Counts (in millions) for Selected APM Portfolio Companies

Name	Ticker	Common Shares Outstanding (Shout)	Shares: Basic EPS	Shout % Difference	Shares: Fully Diluted EPS	Shout % Difference
Anheuser-Busch	BUD	766.1	763.5	0.3	773.3	−0.9
Berkshire Hathaway	BRK	1.5	1.5	0.0	1.5	0.0
Brooke Corp.	BXXX	12.6	12.5	0.4	13.9	−9.8
Capitol Federal	CFFN	74.1	72.6	2.1	72.8	1.8
Deere & Co.	DE	226.9	227.2	−0.2	229.8	−1.3
Garmin Ltd.	GRMN	216.1	216.2	−0.1	218.7	−1.2
Jos. A. Bank	JOSB	18.0	18.0	0.1	18.4	−1.7
KS City Southern	KSU	75.9	75.6	0.4	90.3	−16.0
LSB Industries	LXU	19.7	17.5	12.3	21.0	−6.3
NIC Inc.	EGOV	61.8	61.7	0.2	62.0	−0.3
OSI Systems	OSIS	16.8	17.2	−2.6	17.2	−2.6
Plains E&P	PXP	72.4	75.3	−3.8	76.5	−5.3
Scientific Games	SGMS	90.5	92.0	−1.6	95.3	−5.0
Sohu.com	SOHU	36.6	36.7	−0.2	39.0	−6.0
Valero Energy Corp.	VLO	603.8	599.0	0.8	615.0	−1.8

It's good to examine the difference between shares outstanding and the fully diluted shares. If there is a large difference, then common shares outstanding should be adjusted to reflect the possible dilution. Kansas City Southern has a large difference between fully diluted and common shares outstanding primarily because of its Series C convertible preferred stock. Here is the reconciliation the company provides in its 10-K:

	2006	2005	2004
Basic shares	74,593	75,527	62,715
Additional weighted average shares attributable to convertible securities and stock options:			
$9.0 million VAT/Put settlement payment	–	110	–
$47.0 million escrow note	1,667	1,439	–
VAT/Put settlement contingency payment	1,418	918	–
Convertible preferred stock	13,389	13,389	–
Stock options	1,266	1,358	1,268
Nonvested shares	53	6	–
Diluted shares	92,386	92,747	63,983

Since the basic shares are an average of the shares outstanding, it's straightforward to calculate fully diluted shares outstanding by substituting the common shares outstanding for the basic shares.

Brooke Corp. also has some significant potential for dilution. So to calculate market capitalization, students should use fully diluted shares outstanding.

At this point we should probably make a general comment on the level of preparation for a case. We're going through the ideal scenario. At the beginning of the semester, "ideal" can vary a lot from "actual," but this is the point we're hoping that the students reach by the end of the semester. It may seem a little obsessive to worry about seemingly minor details, such as the difference between common shares outstanding, basic EPS shares, and fully diluted shares. Most of the time there is only a minor difference, but when there is a difference, the correct valuation of company hinges on getting the share count right and understanding what's going on.

Market Metrics: Total Enterprise Value   Now that we finished the simple part of market metrics, market capitalization, we can move to calculating total enterprise value. TEV is the all-in market value of a company.

$$TEV = Market\ Cap + Market\ Value\ of\ Debt$$
$$+ Market\ Value\ of\ Preferred - Cash$$

Enterprise value can also be considered as the takeover value of a firm. If you acquire a firm, you acquire its liabilities as well as its assets. You also can use the cash to pay off some of the debt, so sometimes you'll see TEV defined as market cap plus net debt. Net debt is debt less cash. For companies that don't have debt or preferred shares, TEV is easy. It's the same as market cap less cash.

Of course, as with shares outstanding, cash and debt are not always straightforward. "Cash" means any liquid asset that is not meant to be part of operating assets. We discuss this more in the next chapter, but most of the time you can find cash and short-term marketable securities in the current asset section of the balance sheet.

Calculating the "real" market value of debt is a little harder. Again, we'll put off many of the details until the next chapter, but most of the time people use the long-term debt plus the current portion of long term debt that is recorded on the balance sheet as the market value of debt. These entries are "book" values, not market values, but when inflation is low and interest rates aren't changing much, book value is usually fairly close to market value. For firms with publicly traded bonds, you can look up the market value of those bonds. However, even firms with publicly traded bonds may have substantial debt holdings that are not publicly traded.

Another debt consideration is calculating the value of debt-equivalent claims, such as leases and pension liabilities. Including leases is important if you are comparing two companies where one leases a big portion of its assets but the other has purchased its assets. For example, Jos. A. Bank leases almost all of its stores, but a large old-line department store company such as Macy's Department Stores owns more than half of its properties. Leases don't appear on the balance sheet, but the details of the leases must be disclosed in a footnote in the financial statements. A quick glance at the 10-K notes will let you know if you need to make an adjustment.

Valuation Ratios There are four commonly used valuation ratios and quite a few more less common or industry-specific valuation ratios. The common ones are that we'll discuss here are: price to earnings, price to book, price to sales, and TEV/EBITDA.

The P/E ratio is the most widely quoted number for a company after its stock price. It's easy to compute and pretty easy to understand. It is just price per share divided by earnings per share. Of course, the question is which earnings per share number you should use. We've discussed basic and fully diluted EPS, and now we'll throw another one in the mix: forward earnings. Stocks actually trade on forecasted numbers, forward EPS in this case, and not on historical numbers. All of the major financial Web sites

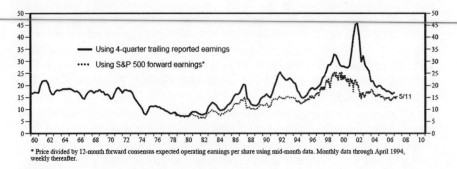

* Price divided by 12-month forward consensus expected operating earnings per share using mid-month data. Monthly data through April 1994, weekly thereafter.

FIGURE 7.4 P/E Ratios for the S&P 500
Source: Yardeni Research, Inc., *Valuation Chart Book* (with Database), May 15, 2007, 1, www.yardeni.com

provide consensus analyst estimates for EPS numbers. For any S&P 500 (large-cap), 400 (mid-cap), or 600 (small-cap) index company, there will be several analysts providing estimates. For smaller companies outside the S&P 1500, there may be only one analyst estimate or sometimes none. For example, LSB Industries didn't have any analyst coverage until 2007. If you are going to be consistent and compare everyone on forward numbers, then you need to forecast your own EPS numbers for companies that don't have them.

Figure 7.4 from Yardeni Research, Inc. shows where P/E ratios have been historically both for reported EPS (trailing numbers) and for forward EPS. You can see that forward P/E ratios have always been lower than trailing P/E ratios. Since 1989 the average forward P/E for the S&P 500 is about 15. It's essential to put any P/E in perspective historically and with respect to comparable companies. Since there is more information available about P/E ratios than any other valuation ratio, it is easier to put this ratio into perspective than the other three ratios.

What's a good P/E? It depends. If you are buying, you'd like to buy what you would consider to be an undervalued stock. You'd like to see a relatively low P/E. Of course, that means the market is assessing the firm's prospects differently than you are. You think that earnings are going to be higher than the market does. Historically, different sectors have different P/E ratios. Higher-growth sectors should have higher P/Es. For example, the technology sector has a higher P/E ratio than the industrials sector. Currently healthcare is in between tech and industrials.

Price to sales ratios are used primarily as an alternative or supplement to P/E ratios. P/S is defined as market cap divided by total revenue or, equivalently, price per share divided by revenue per share. When a company has an operating loss, then its P/E ratio isn't meaningful. P/S ratios were used extensively in the dot-com boom with many of the tech start-up companies. Lots of those small companies didn't have earnings, but they usually had some sales.

Price to book is used primarily for financial institutions because "book value" or balance sheet values are closer to market value than for nonfinancial companies. P/B is defined as market cap divided by book value or price per share divided by book value per share. Financial assets—the main assets of financial institutions—are revalued to market value at regular intervals. In theory, a financial company should trade at least at the value of its financial assets plus a little more for expanded growth or any other opportunities that the market sees. A P/B ratio of 1 means that the company is trading at the value of its assets. The company could be liquidated and shareholders would receive that amount. A P/B of less than 1 means the company is trading at a discount. Most financial institutions trade at P/B ratios between 1.5 and 2.

Our favorite ratio for nonfinancial institutions is TEV/EBITDA. This ratio is informative because of its focus on operating income (EBITDA) and the total value of the company. Capital structure is taken out of the picture so the students can see how operating results support the full value of the company. Figure 7.5 shows the TEV/EBITDA ratios for the current S&P 500 companies from September 2002 to April 2007. The overall average in this period is 11.3, and the median is 10.6.

Table 7.6 presents an overall view of these common ratios. Using the simple average can lead to trouble because a few extreme values can have

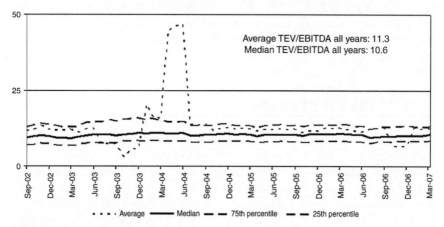

FIGURE 7.5 TEV/EBITDA Ratios for S&P 500, 2002–2007

TABLE 7.6 Valuation Ratios by Capitalization April 2007

	Index	Average	Trimmed Mean	Median
Price/Earnings	S&P 500 (Large cap)	4.3	20.2	19.1
	S&P 400 (Mid cap)	25.7	22.3	20.2
	S&P 600 (Small cap)	20.1	19.2	19.5
	1500 (All)	16.3	20.6	19.6
Price/Sales	S&P 500 (Large cap)	2.5	2.2	1.8
	S&P 400 (Mid cap)	2.3	2.0	1.6
	S&P 600 (Small cap)	2.2	1.8	1.5
	1500 (All)	2.3	2.0	1.6
Price/Book	S&P 500 (Large cap)	2.3	3.5	3.1
	S&P 400 (Mid cap)	3.7	3.0	2.7
	S&P 600 (Small cap)	3.0	2.6	2.3
	1500 (All)	2.9	3.0	2.7
TEV/EBITDA	S&P 500 (Large cap)	12.3	11.0	10.5
	S&P 400 (Mid cap)	11.3	11.0	10.1
	S&P 600 (Small cap)	10.3	11.0	10.4
	1500 (All)	11.2	11.0	10.4

a big effect on the average. You can see that the average P/E for the S&P 500, the large caps, is 4.3, a really low number. It's so low because Public Storage, Inc. (PSA) had a 12-month EPS of −1 cent. With a stock price of $82.95, that gives PSA a P/E of −8,295! When EPS is close to zero, the ratio gets very distorted. The median and trimmed mean aren't affected by extreme values. You can also see in Table 7.6 that valuation ratios vary by market cap.

UNDERSTAND THE BUSINESS

It's not always easy to understand the main way in which a company makes money. There are lots of reasons why students might not be clear on what a company actually does. One reason is that the company might be involved in very specific technical processes that they might not understand. Another more widespread reason is that companies aren't always very good at communicating exactly what they do. The 10-K describes the business of the company in legal terms. The first time many students read the legal definition of a company, they still don't understand how the company makes money. The 10-K mentions all products and services that a company provides, no matter how insignificant they are to the primary business. It doesn't matter that 95% of revenues and profits come from the main business. The 10-K will discuss the 5% portion in almost as much detail. We tell the students that understanding the business means that you can describe what the company does to a bright 10-year-old.

Here's an example of how American Dairy describes its business in the 10-K. It contains a detailed history of the corporation and acquisitions, mentioning these businesses: manufacturing and marketing of medical devices, a nonoperating public company shell, the production and distribution of milk powder and other dairy products, production and supply of processed milk and soybean products, a marketing company, and a walnut-processing plant. It's a good thing that the name of the company has Dairy in it, or you would be into the third paragraph of the description before you could actually figure out what was going on. Still, the name is a little misleading because in the third paragraph, we learn that American Dairy is actually a dairy company in China.

American Dairy (ADY) 10-K Business Description

Item 1. Business.

General

American Dairy, Inc was incorporated under the corporate laws of the State of Utah on December 31, 1985, originally with the corporate name of Gaslight, Inc. It was inactive until March 30, 1988 when it changed its corporate name to Lazarus Industries, Inc. and engaged in the business of manufacturing and marketing medical devices. This line of business was discontinued in 1991, and it became a non-operating public company shell.

Effective May 7, 2003, American Dairy completed the acquisition of 100% of the issued and outstanding capital stock of American Flying Crane Corporation (formerly called American Dairy Holdings, Inc.) ("AFC"), a Delaware corporation. As a result, AFC become a wholly-owned subsidiary of American Dairy. In addition, American Dairy amended its Articles of Incorporation to change its name to "American Dairy, Inc." and completed a one-for-nineteen (1-for-19) reverse split of its Common Stock. For financial reporting purposes, this transaction was treated as a recapitalization of American Flying Crane and the historical figures prior to May 7, 2003 represent the activities of American Flying Crane.

AFC holds 100% of the issued and outstanding capital of Heilongjiang Feihe Dairy Co., Limited ("Feihe Dairy") in The People's Republic of China. The principal activity of Feihe Dairy is the production and distribution of milk powder and other dairy products. Feihe Dairy has one wholly-owned subsidiary, BaiQuan Feihe Dairy Co., Limited, that is engaged in the production and supply of processed milk and soybean products for Feihe Dairy, and has a 95%-owned subsidiary Beijing Feihe Biotechnology Scientific and Commercial Co., which is the marketing company for Feihe Dairy.

American Dairy also has three other wholly-owned subsidiaries, Lang Fang FeiHe, Gan Han FeiHe and Shanxi Feihesantai Biotechnology Scientific and Commercial Co., Limited (the third of which was originally formed to develop and operate a walnut processing plant).

Current Corporate Structure

The following chart reflects the current corporate structure of the American Dairy entities:

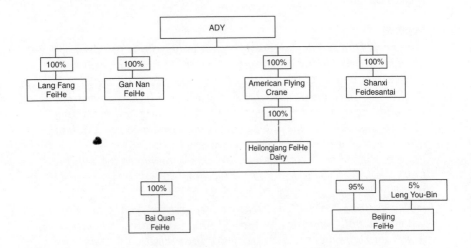

Source: U.S. Securities and Exchange Commission, Washington, DC, 20549, Form 10-K, Commission File Number: 0-27351, American Dairy, Inc. Filed April 2, 2007.

The company does a little better with its Investor Fact Sheet.

American Dairy, Inc. conducts operations in the People's Republic of China ("China") through its wholly owned subsidiary, Feihe Dairy. Founded in 1962, Feihe Dairy is one of the leading producers and distributors of milk powder and soybean products in China. Feihe Dairy is located in Kedong County, China, and has been in operation since 2001. American Dairy also has a milk powder processing plant, Baiquan Feihe Dairy in Kedong County, and also has a milk powder processing plant in the city of Qiqihaer, Heilongjiang Province.

In this description, it's clear the company produces milk. It doesn't mention walnuts, medical devices, or shell companies.

Here's another example—Capitol Federal's business description from its 10-K.

Our principal business consists of attracting deposits from the general public and investing those funds primarily in permanent loans secured by first mortgages on owner-occupied, one- to four-family residences. We also originate consumer loans, loans secured by first mortgages on nonowner-occupied one- to four-family residences, permanent and construction loans secured by one- to four-family residences, commercial real estate loans and multi-family real estate loans. While our primary business is the origination of one- to four-family mortgage loans funded through retail deposits, we also purchase whole loans and invest in certain investment and mortgage-related securities using FHLB advances as an additional funding source.

Cap Fed's description tries to make clear what its primary business is—origination of mortgage loans—but it also mentions all of the other types of business. What isn't that clear is the vast majority of the loans that Capitol Federal originates are on single-family houses. The operating characteristics for two- to four-family mortgages are very different from for single-family houses. Two- to four-family mortgages would be rental properties; the single-family residential mortgage is very different. Even though Capitol Federal's statement of business is quite a bit clearer than American Dairy's, students still need to work to understand what the company's bread and butter is. They will need to focus on the single-family mortgage space. They would explain to the 10-year-old that Cap Fed lends money to people to help them buy a house.

READY TO WRITE THE CASE

Getting all of the information together, reading it, finding comparable companies, calculating the basic metrics, and summarizing the historical numbers seems overwhelming, especially initially. The students have one week for each case. Fortunately, the more they do it, the easier it gets. They also learn where they should focus their attention. The first time they read a business description, it's hard to turn the abstract legalese into a contract business. After writing the case and hearing the CEO talk about the company, it is easier the next time. Building experience is an essential part of the APM class.

In the next chapter we discuss pulling all the information together, forecasting the financials, and getting to the bottom line of recommending whether to buy, sell, or hold the stock for the APM portfolio.

APPENDIX: 10-K REQUIREMENTS

PART I

Item 1. Business
> Item 1A. Risk Factors
>
> Item 1B. Unresolved Staff Comments

Item 2. Properties

Item 3. Legal Proceedings

Item 4. Submission of Matters to a Vote of Security Holders

PART II

Item 5. Market for Registrant's Common Equity, Related Stockholder Matters, and Issuer Purchases of Equity Securities

Item 6. Selected Financial Data

Item 7. Management's Discussion and Analysis of Financial Condition and Results of Operation
> Item 7A. Quantitative and Qualitative Disclosures about Market Risk

Item 8. Financial Statements and Supplementary Data
> (1) A balance sheet as of the end of each of the two most recent fiscal years

(2) Consolidated statements of income, statements of cash flows, and statements of other stockholders' equity for each of the two fiscal years preceding the date of the most recent audited balance sheet being filed

Item 9. Changes in and Disagreements with Accountants on Accounting and Financial Disclosure

Item 9A. Controls and Procedures

PART III

Item 10. Directors, Executive Officers and Corporate Governance

Item 11. Executive Compensation

Item 12. Security Ownership of Certain Beneficial Owners and Management and Related Stockholder

Item 13. Certain Relationships and Related Transactions, and Director Independence

Item 14. Principal Accounting Fees and Services

Item 15. Exhibits, Financial Statement Schedules

CHAPTER 8

Writing a Case

Students yearn for a template. Investors are looking for a guru. All of us want to find the most efficient way to the job done. Procedures and processes in service and manufacturing help companies turn out a consistent product time after time. Some things are a little harder. Doctors have consistent procedures, but it takes years of training both with books and hands-on to learn to how to diagnose and treat diseases. Making good investment decisions takes experience and hard work. It helps to have a consistent approach and way to look at the world. For APM students the case is their procedure. Cases have three parts:

1. Investment thesis and recommendation
2. Analysis and description
3. Valuation, summary, and conclusion

After a proper preparation, the students should be ready to identify the key issues confronting the company and how those issues will affect an investment in it. They should have begun to form a preliminary opinion about the company's valuation, but until they finish a proper valuation that includes preparing pro forma income statements and finding future cash flows, they won't have the full valuation nailed down.

The hardest part of the case is coming up with the investment thesis. That's also the hardest part for all of us in making an investment decision. Many times investors skip this part. Lots of facts, figures, and information are available. How do you boil down all of that information into a few coherent ideas about key drivers of a stock's price? That's the purpose of the case. Investigate, summarize, analyze, but have an opinion based on a thorough investigation.

Initially some students are reluctant to take a stand. Typical statements include: "I can't predict the future so I'm going to assume that things are going to stay the same," or "XYZ analyst really knows what's going on. How can I add anything to what he says?" It's a good thing students realize they are inexperienced and don't know all there is to know about a company, but they actually underestimate how much they know relative to the general public. Besides insiders, usually there are only a few good analysts who have spent enough time to really understand what's going on with a company. That is especially true of small, relatively ignored stocks. APM class is the place for students to get experience, learn from mistakes, and start understanding what's going to drive an investment.

A lot of investors, even analysts, are reluctant to stray too far from a company's history. That's why ruler analysis is so prevalent. That's also why more investment opportunities are available when things are changing with a company. Evaluation of those changes may be hard, but that's also when you can uncover gems. Recovery from bad years, new management, and other inflection points mark changes that are potential opportunities for patient investors.

Students may also assume that all analysts are created equal. It's the analyst's job to research and write about a particular industry or group of companies, an analyst knows what's going on. Many times that is a good assumption, but as in all investment decisions, it's good to examine the incentives. Most analysts don't want to be bold and stray far from the pack. Let's say a stock hasn't done much for a while, and most analysts have a hold rating. Now suppose an analyst really believes that a stock is going up 50 percent. What are the rewards for being so far from consensus? If this analyst is wrong, people will really remember it. He'll be made fun of and the like. If he's right, he would gain in reputation as much from saying the stock is going up 10 percent as from saying it's going up 50 percent. There isn't a lot of upside to being that far away from consensus, but there is a big downside. That's why you don't see a lot of targets that different from the current price. If you examine the model assumptions, you'll find that they are geared toward getting a price in the "right" range: not too high and not too low. Current price anchors a lot of the estimates.

When students make some reasonable assumptions, build a valuation model, and get a price that's very different from the market price, they automatically assume they've made a mistake. Often that's a good assumption, but assuming no mistakes, that's the time to trust your judgment. Reexamine assumptions and check everything. If it still checks out, go with your analysis. If future events don't line up the way you imagine, the benchmarks from your model will let you know where you went astray. Students learn a lot from making bold pronouncements, whether they are right or wrong. That's how experience is built.

CASE FORMAT

The case has three parts, but the three parts aren't necessarily written in order. Part 1 is a summary and should be written last. Part 2 should be written first and Part 3 written second. After the extensive preparation that was described in Chapter 7, Part 2's analysis and description should be relatively easy to write. Part 3's valuation, summary, and conclusion flows from Part 2. Here's a description of the case format from the APM syllabus.

Part 1. Investment Thesis and Recommendation
State your recommendation clearly. It can be buy, sell, or neutral. Provide bullet points that communicate your investment thesis. The thesis should be explained in detail later in the write-up. Provide a summary table containing the most relevant data. The data you provide should contain valuation metrics, performance metrics, and descriptive metrics for the company. Prepare Part 1 last.

Part 2. Analysis and Description
Describe the company. What do they do to make money? Use simple language that anyone can understand. Do not use legalese. Provide historical information on operating and financial performance. What is the company's strategy? What will the revenue growth and margins be for the next several years. Are they changing? Why? Use these forecasts as assumptions in your pro forma statements.

Provide information on the company's place in its industry. What industry or industries does the company operate in? Who is the competition? How do the company's operating metrics compare to others in the industry? What is this company's competitive advantage?

What else is important in understanding the company: insider holdings or trading, special circumstances, mergers or acquisitions, new management, or any other important information?

Make sure you provide an overview of the key drivers in the company, not minor details. These need to be related to your investment thesis.

Part 3. Valuation, Summary, and Conclusion
Provide a summary table of a relative valuation and a summary of a discounted cash flow model, if appropriate. Discuss your model(s), risk, and recommendation. Include a sensitivity analysis on key variables.

This is the "ideal" way to write up a case. What's the reality for the students? In addition to the general instructions, we provide some leading questions designed to help focus their attention on key areas. The questions are supposed to provide some guidance to help students determine what else is important in understanding the company. What tends to happen initially is that many groups split the questions up among the group members. Then they cut and paste their answers together. The valuation assumptions may or may not correspond to the forecasts in part 2.

Why in the world would we want to point out the types of mistakes that students might make? Don't we want to provide an example of the right way to analyze companies and invest? We absolutely want to do this, but we feel that it's very common for beginning investors to be uncomfortable in the sea of information they need to process. When you are working in a group, it's common for the first group task to be to divide up responsibilities. The problem comes in putting the pieces together. How do you come up with an investment thesis, if each member of the group has focused only on a small piece of the picture? It's a little like the poem by John Godfrey Saxe of the Indian legend of the blind men and the elephant. Each man felt only a small piece of the elephant, each of the blind men characterized the elephant differently, and each came away with a totally wrong view of it.

It's not just groups that get in trouble when trying to put all of the pieces together to come up with a coherent picture. Individuals also can have a hard time pulling out the main themes. Synthesizing all the parts into a coherent view is a talent born of experience. It separates good investors from the average. Sometimes it's easier just to focus on a few favorite indicators without looking at the big picture. Groups actually may have an advantage because after some initial floundering, they can discuss their different viewpoints, make sure that they aren't overlooking important points, and analyze the facts that can support their views. Good investment teams work this way.

How should the process work? All the group members should independently review the material discussed in Chapter 7. One person can gather the operating and valuation numbers to share with the others ahead of time. Each person should form a preliminary idea of the investment thesis and key drivers based on the preparation. Each person should also come up with assumptions for the pro forma model based on past performance and potential changes. This type of preliminary work will lead to more productive group meetings. If everyone has a good basis, then coming up with a forecast and a thesis will be based on a discussion of facts rather than feelings.

The next step for the group is to decide what are the investment themes and thesis. They don't necessarily have to decide whether they think it's a buy or a sell at this point, but they should have a pretty strong inclination in one direction or the other. The valuation ratios, the operating performance, and the research that they've already prepared should give them a strong sense of direction for their theme and thesis.

In the rest of this chapter we discuss the details and provide some examples of Part 2, the case analysis and description. This is the first step to building the pro forma model for valuation. It's also where students get in trouble with too much description and not enough analysis. The key is to describe things just enough to set the stage for the valuation.

DESCRIPTION

What's the business? During the preparation for writing the case, the students should have worked out exactly what the company does to make money. Now they need to decide how to communicate the main business and how much of the legal structure is important for an investor. The 10-K description includes quite a bit about the legal structure. Lots of companies are legally "holding companies," or have other complicated legal structures. It can be a tough job to decide how much of that information is relevant to a shareholder. To an investor who is going to buy the whole company or a significant stake in it, this information may be of vital importance. To a small shareholder, it may not matter at all.

Another part of describing a company is describing its past financial and market performance. Again, these things were part of the case preparation. Now the task is to whittle down the numbers and decide how best to tell the company's story. Not every chart or graph is informative. Sometimes putting different pieces of information together tell the story. The insight and imagination that comes from deciding how to put those pieces together are part of understanding what's driving the business.

Brooke Corp.

We'll start with a challenge. Brooke Corp. is a small—$150 million in market cap—company located in Overland Park, Kansas. Figure 8.1 shows a portion of Brooke's Investor Relations Web site (http://invest.brookecorp.com). Notice the Corporate Profile.

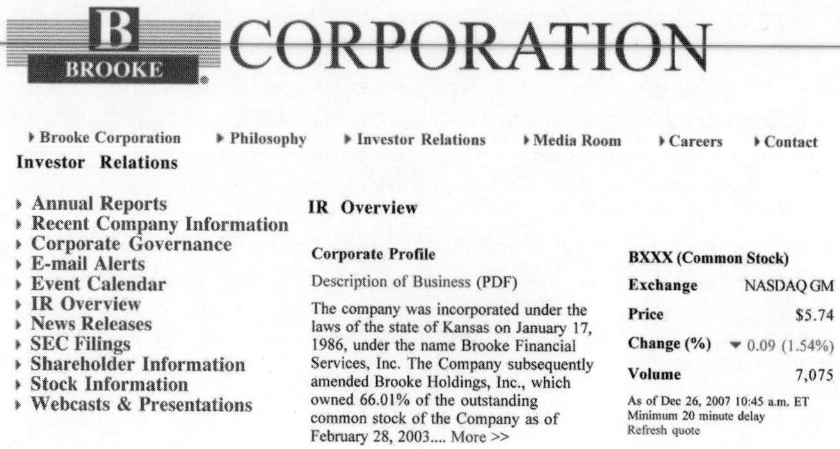

B BROOKE CORPORATION

▸ Brooke Corporation   ▸ Philosophy   ▸ Investor Relations   ▸ Media Room   ▸ Careers   ▸ Contact

Investor Relations

▸ Annual Reports
▸ Recent Company Information
▸ Corporate Governance
▸ E-mail Alerts
▸ Event Calendar
▸ IR Overview
▸ News Releases
▸ SEC Filings
▸ Shareholder Information
▸ Stock Information
▸ Webcasts & Presentations

IR Overview

Corporate Profile

Description of Business (PDF)

The company was incorporated under the laws of the state of Kansas on January 17, 1986, under the name Brooke Financial Services, Inc. The Company subsequently amended Brooke Holdings, Inc., which owned 66.01% of the outstanding common stock of the Company as of February 28, 2003.... More >>

BXXX (Common Stock)

Exchange	NASDAQ GM
Price	$5.74
Change (%)	▼ 0.09 (1.54%)
Volume	7,075

As of Dec 26, 2007 10:45 a.m. ET
Minimum 20 minute delay
Refresh quote

FIGURE 8.1   Brooke Corp. Corporate Profile
Source: Courtesy of Brooke Corp (www.brookeagent.com)

The Description of Business is 17 pages long. You have to click on the link to find that the pdf file begins like this:

DESCRIPTION OF BUSINESS

Nature of the Business

The Company engages primarily in the business of selling insurance and related services through franchisees. More specifically, most of the Company's revenues are currently derived from sales commissions on the sale of property and casualty insurance policies through its franchisees, although an increasing share of revenues are derived from consulting, lending and brokerage services provided to franchisees.

The Corporate Profile is a history of the different steps that Brooke Corp. has taken to be where it is today. The Description of Business is actually a very good and very detailed description of the business, its strategy, and company segments. It also includes the history. However, it isn't featured as prominently on the Web site as the Corporate Profile, so not everyone may find it.

Here are the introductions from the six groups in spring 2007 class. They all started with a description of the company.

Group 1. Brooke Corporation is an insurance holding company that conducts business through three operating subsidiaries: Brooke Franchise, Brooke Credit Corp., and Brooke Brokerage. The three subsidiaries are highly synergized.

Group 2. Brooke Corporation is a franchise business with more than 700 franchise locations in 29 states. These franchises sell property and casualty insurance, and other services to individuals and small businesses. To complement these franchises, Brooke has developed Brooke Credit Corporation to lend to its franchisees in order to fund the acquisition of franchises or the start up of new franchises.

Group 3. Brooke Franchise Corporation franchises property and casualty insurance agencies in the U.S. Franchise products primarily include automotive, homeowners and business owners insurance, while other franchises sell individual health insurance, life insurance, annuities and securities. Franchises are not just associated with an emerging brand identity, but are also offered network access to the products of leading insurance carriers, marketing and business management support, back office assistance and financial management tools.

Group 4. Brooke Corporation, BXXX, is a franchise business that sells property and casualty insurance as well as a few other services to individuals and small businesses. BXXX has five business segments that break down as follows:

Segment % of EBITDA

Franchise Services	Brokerage	Lending Services	Corporate	Intersegment Activity
20.76%	18.45%	63.42%	−2.71%	0.07%

Segment % of Revenue

Franchise Services	Brokerage	Lending Services	Corporate	Intersegment Activity
79.22%	5.99%	14.90%	2.36%	−2.47%

Group 5. Brooke Corporation (BXXX) is a franchising business that focuses on finding entrepreneurs who have experience in insurance sales and the drive to open and run their own branch locally.

BXXX provides franchisees with the support of a large, nation-wide firm and the ability to sell the leading insurance products while having the feel of a small, private office. BXXX believes that to be successful in this industry, relationships and small town feel are extremely important. BXXX has also developed business segments that work together to simplify the process of opening a new franchise. They currently operate in three segments: franchise services business, brokerage business, and lending services business.* With most revenue coming from franchises, it's clear that the more franchises opened the better. The chart below shows the number of franchises operating over the past three years.*

*Brooke Corporation 2006 10-K, p. 2
**Brooke Corporation 2006 10-K, p. 112

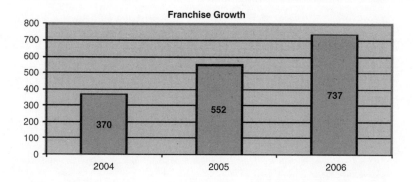

Group 6. Brooke Corporation operates through three subsidiaries, Brooke Franchise Corporation, Brooke Credit Corporation, and Brooke Brokerage Corporation. Brooke Franchise is a franchisor of primarily property and casualty insurance agencies. Brooke Credit lends primarily to small insurance agencies and franchisees, and Brooke Brokerage operates as a wholesale insurance broker to franchisees and other unaffiliated agents.

We think it's useful to look at the possible ways that a company can be described. (We also promise that we won't put every group's work up all the time.) It's a little unfair to look at just the initial description, but most investors have never heard of Brooke Corp. and they need to know right away what the company does. Group 1 provides the bare bones. You know right away that Brooke Corp. is an insurance holding company with three operating business. Groups 2 and 6 focus on the franchise aspect and provide a little information about how the credit company fits. Group 3 provides some information about some of the services offered to the franchisees. Group 4 shows the relative importance of each operating segment in terms of operating profit.[1] Group 5 provides a description of the company but also takes a stand on what is driving the business. The company's revenues are all related to the franchises. So as the group states, "the more franchises opened the better."

Groups 4 and 5 use a chart or a graph to provide some additional, concrete description. Group 4 shows right away that while lending isn't the biggest contributor to the top line, it is the biggest contributor to profit. That clues us in to fact that the brokerage and the lending businesses are more profitable than the direct revenue from the franchises.

Brooke Corp. has a unique business model. Insurance companies usually come in two varieties: independent agents or large companies with commission agents. As the operator of a franchise, Brooke combines some features of each. Independent agents own their own businesses and build up equity over time. They can sell their business and cash out at retirement. They also can deal with a wide variety of insurance companies, finding the best deal for their clients and for themselves, though they do have to bear all of the overhead costs and risks of running a business. Large insurance companies have captive agents who operate on a commission based on the policies sold. The agents don't build any equity in the business, but they don't have to bear a lot of the overhead costs or the risks either. The more successful agents have an incentive to leave the large company to start an independent agency in order to build equity. Some large companies have recognized this problem and have a means to let some agents build equity value in their franchise. However, this isn't a widespread practice.

The Brooke management team came up with another solution to this problem. Franchisees can build equity and offer a wide variety of insurance products, while Brooke provides a cost-effective way to share overhead costs with centralized processes. Economies of scale drive down the overhead cost of running a small business. Franchisees can focus on selling insurance policies and still bear a large part of the operating risk.

Brooke makes money on every policy that the franchisees write. It also makes money by making start-up loans to the franchisees. As Group 4 shows, lending is more profitable than the franchise commissions. However, lending isn't possible without new franchises coming on board.

---

[1] We hate to quibble with what is a really good introduction, but to make it even better, as we were grading the case, we suggested that the group eliminate the last two columns: Corporate and Intersegment Activity. They aren't really business segments of the company. The focus should be on the business segments.

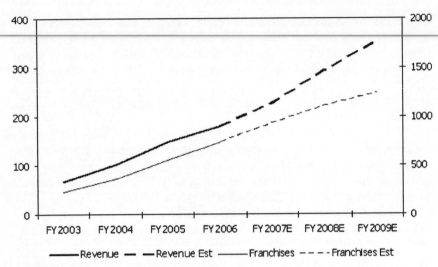

FIGURE 8.2   Spring 2007 Group 6's BXXX Revenue and Franchises Chart

After we know what the company does in simple terms, we need to provide some details on how it is doing and how the industry is doing. Group 6 shows how revenue and the number of franchises have grown together over the last few years. The group uses the graph shown in Figure 8.2 to convey several key ideas. The graph shows the group's estimates for the number of franchises and revenue for the next three years but also shows that the group thinks that some economies of scale are going to be recognized, especially by 2009. The graph shows that revenue is growing faster than franchise growth over 2008 and 2009 because the lines begin to diverge. Before the lines were almost parallel, and revenue growth even dipped in 2006.

Because the graph uses different scales for the two series, it's a little tricky to infer growth rates from it. Table 8.1 shows the annual growth rates that Group 6 used in its model. These numbers confirm the impression that the group is indeed forecasting revenue growth to be significantly higher than franchise growth in 2008 and 2009. The group didn't show the EBITDA numbers in the chart but did show EBITDA information in other charts. From Table 8.1 you can see that group members are very optimistic about EBITDA growing faster than revenue and franchises. The implication is that as Brooke grows, its costs will not grow as fast. Its current fixed cost base will be able to support more franchises.

Tables 8.2, 8.3, and 8.4 are all taken from Group 6's report. They show some additional operating information: EBITDA by segment, return

TABLE 8.1 Brooke Corp. Revenue, Franchise, and EBITDA Growth, 2003–2009

	2003	2004	2005	2006	2007E	2008E	2009E
Revenue	65.1	54.4	42.8	23.6	26.2	29.0	20.6
Franchises	43.6	58.1	49.2	33.5	26.1	18.9	12.0
EBITDA	9.0	15.7	23.2	29.6	32.6	40.2	46.1

on assets (ROA) by segment, and ROA compared to the industry. The group does a nice job of providing key benchmarks by segment and as compared to the industry. Both are important. You want to see how the segments are performing and how the company performs compared to others in the industry. The industry comparison is a little tough since no one else is structured in quite the same way as Brooke Corp. At the same time, it's important to see if the franchise model works.

Group 6 says:

> *From 2004–2006, the overall consolidated ROA has decreased. This can be explained by the increases in assets in the Lending segment returning low rates of assets.*

As we discussed in Chapter 4, the yield curve made 2006 a tough year for many financial institutions. Brooke's lending segment wasn't exempt from the tough lending environment. That is reflected in the lower ROA.

Tables 8.2 and 8.3 together show a fairly common phenomenon. The segment with the highest ROA is actually the smallest segment. High margins and returns are hard to achieve. Lending probably will always be the most variable because that segment is more of a commodity business that depends on the yield curve and market interest rates.

TABLE 8.2 Group 6's EBITDA by Segment*

	Franchise	Brokerage	Lending	Consolidated
2006	3,975	3,533	12,141	19,145
2005	7,672	2,372	10,956	17,398
2004	10,023	545	4,324	12,478

*We made a couple of editing changes to these tables for the book. We added commas to the numbers in Table 8.2 to make things easier to read. We changed the shading (dark blue) and font (light blue) colors. APM students like to use colors to jazz things up. They need to be careful to make sure that when the fancy colors print in black ink, things are still readable.

TABLE 8.3   Group 6's Return on Assets (ROA) by Segment (in Percent)

	Franchise	Brokerage	Lending	Consolidated
2006	3.61%	14.96%	2.58%	3.32%
2005	6.64%	10.77%	5.11%	7.18%
2004	10.26%	1.06%	2.15%	6.17%

Compared to the industry (Table 8.4), Brooke's ROA looks good, not great. The year 2005 was a really good one; 2006, not quite so good, but still respectable. If the predicted economies of scale come to pass, ROA should increase dramatically.

Group 5 also included additional information on revenue sources for the Franchise division. As this group said initially, franchise growth fuels the company since the lending and brokerage segments both rely on franchises for their revenue. Table 8.5 shows how the Franchise Services segment earns its revenues. There are two sources: ongoing revenues and start-up fees. About two-thirds of the franchise segment revenues come from Start-up Services, indicating the importance of new franchises.

Market Metrics: Total Enterprise Value   This case turned out to be a good instructive tool about finding total enterprise value (TEV). In Chapter 7 we said that TEV is:

$$TEV = Market\ Cap + Market\ Value\ of\ Debt$$
$$+ Market\ Value\ of\ Preferred - Cash$$

TABLE 8.4   Group 6's BXX ROA Industry Comparison

	2006	2005	2004
BXXX	3.32%	7.18%	6.17%
ALL	3.17%	1.13%	2.12%
TCHC	6.55%	4.18%	−6.64%
DCAP	2.00%	2.20%	5.00%
PGR	8.46%	7.38%	9.59%

Comparables: All State (ALL), 21st Century Holding Co. (TCHC), DCAP Group (DCAP), and Progressive Corporation (PGR)

TABLE 8.5 Group 5's Franchise Services Revenue Breakdown (in thousands of dollars)

	2004	2005	2006
Share of Ongoing Revenues	10,894	16,257	20,872
Start-up fees:			
Basic services	8,795	19,375	31,770
Buyers' assistance	8,122	10,133	3,137
Consulting fees	5,236	4,916	2,731

Brooke's market cap in April 2007 was $167 million using a fully diluted share count. Debt was $96 million. That gives us a TEV equal to $263.5 before we subtract cash. That's where we have some questions. The students had estimates of TEV from $185 to $263 million. That's a 42 percent difference—quite a wide range. It can make for some wildly different opinions about whether the stock is a buy or a sell!

Here's how we investigated. Cash in the formula just given should include both cash and marketable securities. Marketable securities are just a holding place for a firm's excess cash. If a firm has significant excess cash, we don't want it all to be in a checking account. It should be invested in some short-term investments to earn a higher return.

The problem with identifying the marketable securities comes from the account names on Brooke's balance sheet. Here's a modified portion of the current assets on Brooke's balance sheet from its March 2007 10-Q.

Cash	$19,268
Restricted cash	1,236
Investments	55,496
Securities	81,099
Other current accounts	135,595
Total Current Assets	**$292,694**

Cash should definitely be included, but not restricted cash. What about investments? What about securities? All of the other items are pretty standard working capital accounts, and we wouldn't include any of those. Still, we have potentially $156 million in cash and marketable securities. That's going to make a big difference in TEV.

How do you decide? The first place to look is in the footnotes to the financial statements. Footnote (n) from the 10-Q says:

(n) Securities

The carrying values of securities were $81,099,000 and $50,322,000 at March 31, 2007 and December 31, 2006, *respectively, and consisted primarily of three types of securities (or retained residual assets): interest-only strip receivables in loans sold; retained over-collateralization interests in loans sold and cash reserves. . . . The carrying value for the corresponding marketable securities approximates the fair value as calculated by the Company using reasonable assumptions. . . .*

Footnote (q) explains the Investments entry and says:

(q) Investments

At March 31, 2007 and December 31, 2006, the Company classifies all of its fixed maturity and equity investments as available-for-sale securities and carries them at fair value with unrealized gains and losses, net of applicable income taxes, reported in other comprehensive income. Available-for-sale securities are those that the Company intends to hold for an indefinite period of time, but not necessarily to maturity. Any decision to sell a security classified as available-for-sale would be based on various factors, including significant movements in interest rates, liquidity needs, regulatory capital considerations and other similar factors.

After reading the footnotes, we're still not 100 percent sure. It seems that investments should be included as marketable securities, but securities are assets that are part of ongoing operations. Brooke typically bundles its loans to its franchisees and sells them. The securities seem to fall into that category, so they are part of the regular business of the company and not just a place to park some excess cash. A call to investor relations and a chat with a company representative clarifies that this is indeed the correct interpretation.

Brooke's stock price in early April 2007 was around $12. Table 8.6 provides a breakdown of the enterprise value calculations.

Market Metrics: Valuation Multiples   You can't look at the valuation multiples unless you get the enterprise value right. Group 3's estimate of TEV was $185.4 million, very close. It probably used a lower share price and perhaps included restricted cash. Some Web sites, such as Yahoo!Finance, combine cash and restricted cash. Remember, valuation is an art, not a science. Perhaps we should say it's an art *and* a science. There isn't one number, but there is an acceptable range of values. We hope the range is tight! That's why students and investors love companies with no marketable securities, no debt. There are none of those loose ends to tie down.

TABLE 8.6 Brooke Corp. Total Enterprise Value Calculations, April 2007 (in millions, except for share price)

Shares outstanding	12.6
Fully diluted shares	13.9
Share price	12.00
Market cap—fully diluted	167.0
Debt	
Long-term debt	68.1
Current maturity—long-term debt	28.5
Add total debt	96.6
Cash	19.3
Investments	55.5
Less cash and marketable securities	74.8
TEV—fully diluted	188.8

Group 3 calculated forward ratios using 2008 estimates for Brooke and five comparables from the insurance industry. Here's what the group says:

> *These companies include the DCAP Group, 21st Century Holding Co., Brown & Brown, Inc., to name a few. To ensure the consistency of our three valuations, we calculate the...ratios using 2008 estimates of EBITDA and sales.*
>
> *The median of these multiples can be seen in Table 8.7.*

TABLE 8.7 Group 3's Comparable Valuation Ratios

	TEV/EBITDA*	P/E*	P/S*
DCAP	10.57	N/A	0.45
TCHC	3.48	4.23	0.87
USIH	8.99	12.16	1.37
AJG	6.48	15.77	1.63
BRO	9.43	16.99	3.54
Median	8.99	13.97	1.37

*2008 EBITDA, EPS, and Sales Estimates

Our estimates of Brooks' TEV/EBITDA, forward P/E and P/S multiples are 4.54, 8.00, and .60, respectively. These multiples are *significantly lower than the median of the comparables chosen for our valuation.*

*These multiples were calculated on a fully diluted basis, assuming the conversion of 2006 Perpetual Convertible Preferred and stock options granted.

Insurance Industry Information   The spring 2007 groups all did a good job of describing Brooke with relevant comparisons and choosing good operating metrics. They showed the relative importance of the different segments and what they expect to happen.

Group 4 presented some excellent information from the Insurance Information Institute (www.iii.org). It pointed out that property and casualty insurance is in a current down cycle: a good buying opportunity! Here's what Group 4 adds:

Every insurance market moves in cycles. Periods of increasing premiums correspond to higher profits for insurers. This leads to increased competition and lower profits. Property and casualty is now in the low profitability part of the cycle.

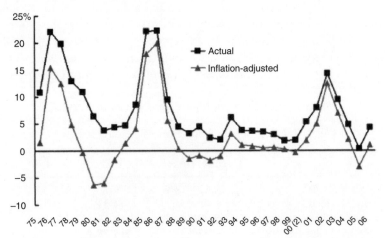

Source: ISO, Insurance Information Institute, Overview & Outlook for the Property/Casualty Insurance Industry, http://www.iii.org/media/presentations/industryoutlook/

In the past 30 years, the down part of the cycle has lasted four years (1979–1982 and 1989–1992). We are in the third year of this down cycle. In 1992 many insurers went out of business due to large claims, but the surviving firms benefited from less competition. A similar bad year may be what it takes to start the up cycle.

INVESTMENT THESIS

After finishing a description of the company, even though we haven't finished a complete valuation, we should have a good idea of how we feel about the company as an investment. Since we'll need to make a lot of assumptions for the valuation and pro forma analysis that we discuss in the next chapter, we need to clearly define our investment thesis.

For Brooke, in April 2007, the spring class had four buys and two holds. Here are a few of the spring 2007 groups' investment theses:

Group 3: Buy
- Brooke Corporation's overlapping segments and relative vertical integration result in synergies similar to those of a large corporation while offering local service.
- Brooke Credit has established itself as a premier lender in its target niche market which will continue to grow and drive this segment that comprises 60 percent of their EBITDA.
- Brooke is currently trading at TEV/EBITDA, forward P/E, and P/S multiples significantly lower than the median values of their comparables suggesting a considerable undervaluation.

Group 4: Buy
- If property and casualty insurance cycles up, Brooke will benefit. We believe we may be at the end of a four-year down cycle.
- Brooke can make attractive franchising offers and consistently succeeds in expanding existing franchises.
- The stock price is suffering from a temporary increase in advertising costs which should produce greater revenue in the future.
- The dividend yield is attractive at 5.9 percent.

Group 6: Hold
- It will be a challenge to sustain franchise growth rates due to market saturation and increased competition.
- To sustain growth, BXXX will have to take on higher-risk franchises, increasing the chance of default.

- BXXX has a strong business model creating a competitive advantage through segment synergy.
- Growth outside the franchise segment creates room to grow that may not have previously existed.

Each of these theses provides an indication of what to look for if we did invest in Brooke. Group 3 thinks we should look for significant multiple expansion. Group 4 thinks there is an industry play from the down cycle in property and casualty and that the advertising should help in the future. Group 6 doesn't think that franchise growth will be very strong.

Your investment thesis should give you a road map to help you determine if your investment is on track. Brooke releases monthly information about the number of total franchises, new franchises, and conversion franchises. If the number of franchises starts to falter, it may turn out that Group 6 is right. However, if we continue to see strong growth numbers, then those recommending a buy could be right. The investment thesis should be concrete and give the investor a way to evaluate the investment now and as more information becomes available. You can't come up with the investment thesis unless you've done a good job of describing the company and considering the pertinent industry or competitive issues.

NEXT STEPS

We've spent a lot of pages on the case analysis, but it is the heart of the APM class, and we discuss it more in the next chapter, where we focus on the last part of the case, the valuation. We go into a lot of detail, but if you've done the prep work, written up a good description and analysis of the company and its place in the industry, the valuation shouldn't be too big of a task.

We mentioned at the beginning of this chapter how students yearn for a template. The case analysis is a broad template. Some students feel there is still too much room for subjective judgment. Others chafe at the confines of case structure. Since we can't please all the people all of the time, we figure we've probably got it right if we have half the class complaining on either side!

CHAPTER 9

Gazing into the Crystal Ball

Pro Forma Statements

So what did the class decide to do with Brooke? We already had a 2 percent position in Brooke since May 2006. We added to our position in October. Again the class was voting, and again we voted to add to our position in April 2007. Figure 9.1 shows Brooke's stock price from June 2005 to June 2007. It lost 17 percent since June 2005 while the NASDAQ climbed 26 percent over the same period. The white diamonds show when APM made purchases with the associated prices.

The figure shows a couple of things. We haven't exactly timed our purchases of Brooke to coincide with low points in the price. However, if Brooke is at $20 in a year, buying at $12.29 versus $11.90 doesn't make that much difference in return. Of course, if we're wrong and the company is at $13 next year, then timing the market better does make a big difference. Where do we think it will go? That's the valuation piece of the case.

Valuation starts with predicting the future by building a pro forma model of a company's cash flow. From the pro formas, groups come up with what they think the share price should be now. Their evaluation is called the intrinsic value. Coming up the intrinsic value can be the easiest part of the case or the hardest. When there has been a thorough job on the preparation, description, and investment thesis, then the pro formas and valuation fall into place easily.

Building your own model or at least understanding someone else's model offers several advantages for investors. The first step in the model is coming up with pro forma financial statements. When you forecast the quarterly numbers, you'll have a benchmark to see how well the company is doing compared to your model. You can update your model and think about whether you still agree with your initial predictions. You'll learn something about the company's guidance, too. Does it have a tendency to underestimate or overestimate in its guidance numbers? Another advantage comes from the

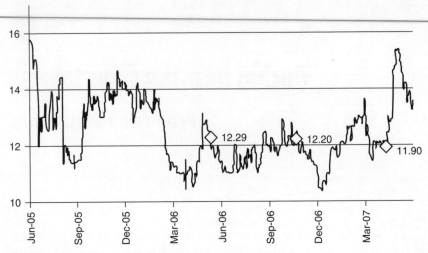

FIGURE 9.1 Brooke Stock Price, June 2005–June 2007

process of building the model. The information that you've developed from prepping the case and describing the company has to be put into the context of the financial statements. You can see the link between results on the factory floor (so to speak) and how they get translated on the statements. That's where digging into the footnotes to understand the details of revenue recognition begins to crystallize the issues involved.

Sometimes students can get too involved in building the model for the model's sake and forget about the prep work, the information they developed for the description and the investment thesis. Valuation then becomes an exercise in ruler analysis. If the growth in the past was 20 percent, they'll make it 20 percent for the next two years and then 3 percent, without any regard to what they've discussed in terms of the product's life, how long a significant competitive advantage will last, or any similar insight they've developed.

Ruler analysis is average investor thinking. Research analysts like to do it, too. They don't have to stray too far from what's happened in the past. No matter that they believe things are changing, whether for good or bad, it's hard to put a big change in a model. The message in the APM class is stick to your convictions. If you think there will be a big move, be bold and predict it, but be grounded by the facts. In this chapter we discuss building a pro forma income statement and predicting free cash flow. These models form the basis for both relative and discounted cash flow (DCF) valuation that we cover in the next chapter.

PRO FORMA FINANCIAL STATEMENTS AND FREE CASH FLOW

According to the *Oxford English Dictionary*, pro forma means "for form's sake; as a matter of form; in the way of formality." There are two common usages. For form's sake can mean perfunctory, something you do just to fill out the forms, or it can mean use a particular format to produce a model. Pro formas in APM fall into both meanings. The ruler analysis pro forma is the perfunctory type. The thoughtful, well-reasoned pro forma uses the format of financial statements based on generally accepted accounting principles (GAAP) to produce a useful model. The form is the accounting form.

Most of the time in class we focus on the income statement. The balance sheet is important, but usually it's enough to model just a few items from the balance sheet without reproducing the whole statement. We take the income statement a step further and calculate free cash flow. Accounting statements are prepared on an accrual basis using what accountants call the matching principle. The idea behind the matching principle is that expenses should be recorded in the period during which the benefit from those expenses is earned. For example, a company may pay for a new plant all at once, but the benefit from that plant will be derived over many, many years. The plant will be expensed on the income statement as depreciation. Most noncash expenses recorded on the income statement arise because of the matching principle. Depreciation and amortization are usually the largest noncash items.

In finance and especially for valuation, we care about the timing of the cash flows. A basic principle in finance is that a dollar today is worth more than a dollar in the future. Other reasons to focus on cash involve some mistrust of accounting earnings. Here's what some financial professionals have to say:

> *It's a lot harder to manipulate cash flow from operations than it is earnings per share.*
> *Cash is fact and accounting profit is opinion.*
> *Unlike some items that can be clouded with financial reporting issues, cash is real, finite, and measurable. Cash is cash.*[1]

We go to some effort to calculate current and forecast future cash flow. We basically undo some of the biggest items in accrual accounting to get to the cash flow. Why don't we just use the statement of cash flow? After

---

[1] Charles W. Mulford and Eugene E. Comiskey, *Creative Cash Flow Reporting* (Hoboken, NJ: John Wiley & Sons, 2005), 1.

all, it's required by GAAP. It would be wonderful to be able to use the statement of cash flow and forget about all the adjustments. The problem is that the statement of cash flow doesn't provide the type of managerial dashboards that the income statement does. Actually, there are two official versions of the statement of cash flow, creatively called the direct method and the indirect method.

The direct method is also called the income statement method. It's exactly what we would like to see:

Cash from Revenue

less Cash Expenses

Operating Cash Flow before Taxes

less Cash Taxes

Cash from Operating Activities

You'd be able to figure out margins based on cash expenses. We could use real operating cash flow instead of earnings before interest, taxes, and depreciation (EBITDA), which only approximates operating cash flow. Unfortunately, one of our esteemed accounting colleagues, Mike Ettredge, estimates that less than 1 percent of firms use the direct method. In fact, we have never seen a firm that uses the direct method. In the indirect method, firms start with net income and calculate operating cash flow based on changes in current asset balance sheet accounts and a few direct adjustments. This method effectively obscures cash revenue and expenses. Companies say that the direct method gives too much information to customers, suppliers, employees, and competitors. So investors and research analysts spend a lot of time trying to reconstruct the information that companies could provide if they chose the direct method.

Free cash flow is only one of many cash flow variants that investors calculate. Before we show how to calculate it, we'll break the income statement and balance sheet into two main decision areas.

AN INDUSTRY CALL FOR DIRECT STATEMENTS OF FREE CASH FLOW

CFO Blog: Commentary and Opinion

Go Direct by Tim Reason   Add the *Financial Times* Lex column [published August 24, 2005] ... to the growing chorus of voices suggesting—strongly—that FASB and the IASB require the direct method be used to compile cash statements. The direct method, notes Lex, is "intuitive and virtually impossible to manipulate—perhaps why many companies dislike it."

A case in point is the floor plan financing that companies with financing arms—such as Harley Davidson, Ford, GM, Caterpillar and others—provided to their dealerships. The SEC recently forced these companies to change the way they recorded the cash flows from those transactions after criticism from accounting professor Charles Mulford of the Georgia Institute of Technology. . . .

In the past, these companies would take back notes receivable instead of accounts receivable for sales. Under the indirect method, this looked like a cash inflow from the dealer that was subsequently invested in the investing section of the cash flow statement. "The appearance is they've made a sale, they've collected the money, and invested the money in notes receivable," Mulford told me back in January. "Under the direct method," Mulford explained at the time, "I'm convinced they could not show it as cash collected from the customer because they have not collected it."

On a somewhat related note, notice that although the SEC did subsequently force these companies to "reclassify" the way they record these transactions (as operating cash flows), it did not require restatements. . . .

Source: August 25, 2005, 04:05 p.m.
(www.cfo.com/blogs/index.cfm/l_detail/4334362)

Financing versus Operating Decisions

Sometimes finance professors talk about the three types of decisions that firm managers have to make as the financing decision, the investment decision, and the dividend decision. The financing decision is whether to use debt or equity financing; the investment decision is what to invest in; and the dividend decision is how much to pay out in dividends. The first two are the big ones, so we focus on those.

In 1930 Irving Fisher developed his separation theorem, which states that the investment decision is independent of the financing decision. This insight is still very relevant today. The investment decision for a firm isn't what stocks to buy, but it's really the most fundamental decision: what business should it be in and what resources should it put in the business. For example, Garmin makes global positioning systems (GPS). Some investment decisions that the company faces are: Should they build a new plant, should they invest in new supply chain software, should they start a new line of business. The investment decision can be called the operating decision, and it is the fundamental basis of what the firm is. The financing decision is how to raise money to be in business. The separation theorem means that those operating decisions should not depend on how Garmin raises the money to accomplish those projects.

Not only should the financing and operating decisions be separate, when we value a firm, we need to separate the operating value from any value that financing provides. This idea underlies the huge activity in private equity: creating value through financing. A company can have a good business that generates lots of cash flow, but earnings might not look that good. If a company is valued on a price/earnings (P/E) basis, then it will look expensive. If it's valued on a cash flow basis, then it will look like a good buy.

Income Statement   The income statement contains information both about the operations of a company and about its financing activities. Revenue, operating costs, cost of goods sold are all operating results. Interest expense is a financing cost. The balance sheet also contains both operating assets and financial assets. Operating assets include working capital, property, plant, and equipment. Marketable securities and other available-for-sale securities are financial assets. The whole Liabilities and Shareholders equity side of the balance sheet, with the exception of some working capital liabilities, is a detailed breakdown of the financing of the company. In order to value a company correctly, we need to separate the two types of information.

Figure 9.2 shows how a typical income statement can be broken into two pieces. The results of the operating decision are usually the first part of

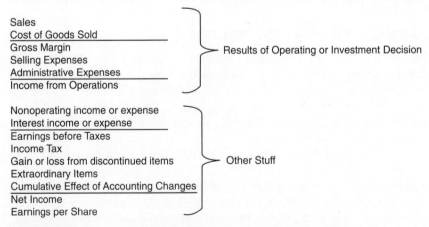

FIGURE 9.2   Income Statement: Operating Information and Other Stuff

TABLE 9.1   Jos. A. Bank Clothiers Income Statement from the 10-K Filed April 17, 2007

	2006
Net sales	546,385
Cost of goods sold	207,947
Gross profit	338,438
Operating expenses:	
Sales and marketing	212,331
General and administrative	52,453
Store opening costs	559
Total operating expenses	265,343
Operating income	73,095
Interest expense, net	938
Income before provision for income taxes	72,157
Provision for income taxes	28,935
Net income	43,222
Per-share information diluted:	
Net income per share	2.36
Diluted weighted average number of shares outstanding	18,342

In thousands, except per share information and stores.

the income statement. Everything else, nonoperating items, is that "Other Stuff."

What you would like to see, quarter after quarter, is that almost all the contribution to net income comes from the top part of the income statement and that not much happens with the bottom part. If, quarter after quarter, there are significant things on the bottom that swamp the operating results, that's the time to be suspicious about what's going on with the company.

Figure 9.2 is an illustration of a "typical" income statement. Of course, there is no "typical" income statement. Every firm gets to come up with its own names. In Hong Kong, sales aren't called revenue but turnover. Here are the income statements for Jos. A Bank (Table 9.1) and Starbucks (Table 9.2) from their 10-K filings. Starbucks gives more detail on the breakdown of revenue and costs. Jos. A Bank has a more stripped-down version with a longer history but still good detail on expenses. We show just the most recent year, but Jos. A. Bank reports 2002 to 2006. Jos. A. Bank has very little going on except in the operating area. No special or extraordinary items, just taxes and interest expense.

Starbucks breaks out its revenue in more detail, and it has one more item below the operating line, the effect of an accounting change. One nice

TABLE 9.2 Starbucks Income Statement from the 10-K Filed December 21, 2006

Fiscal Year Ended	October 1, 2006	% of Revenues
Net revenues:		
Company-operated retail	6,583,098	84.50
Specialty:		
Licensing	860,676	11.10
Foodservice and other	343,168	4.40
Total specialty	1,203,844	15.50
Total net revenues	7,786,942	100.00
Cost of sales including occupancy costs	3,178,791	40.80
Store operating expenses	2,687,815	40.80
Other operating expenses	260,087	21.60
Depreciation and amortization expenses	387,211	5.00
General and administrative expenses	473,023	6.10
Subtotal operating expenses	6,986,927	89.70
Income from equity investees	93,937	1.20
Operating income	893,952	11.50
Interest and other income, net	12,291	0.10
Earnings before income taxes	906,243	11.60
Income taxes	324,770	4.10
Earnings before cumulative effect of change in accounting principle	581,473	7.50
Cumulative effect of accounting change for FIN 47, net of taxes	17,214	0.30
Net earnings	564,259	7.20

feature that is a common size statement that shows the percent of revenue for all of the line items. You can see directly that the operating margin is 11.5 percent and the net margin is 7.2 percent.

Balance Sheet   The assets on the balance sheet generate the results of the income statement. The assets can be operating assets or nonoperating assets such as marketable securities. The Liabilities and Shareholders Equity side of the balance sheet generally shows who owns the assets. Some of the current liabilities are classified as working capital, which is part of the operating side. Figure 9.3 shows a typical balance sheet and identifies which accounts fall in which category. Current assets and current liabilities are broken out in more detail below the full statement.

Assets	Financing or Operating?	Liabilities and Shareholder's Equity	Financing or Operating?
Current assets	Mixed–mostly operating	Current liabilities	Mixed–mostly operating
Long-term investments	Usually operating	Long-term debt	Financing
Property, plant and equipment	Operating	Shareholder's equity	Financing
Intangible assets	Usually operating		
Other assets	Can be either		

Current Assets		Current Liabilities	
Cash and cash equivalents	Special treatment	Accounts payable	Operating
Accounts receivable, net	Operating	Accrued expenses	Operating
Inventories, net	Operating	Deferred tax liability	Operating
Prepaid expenses	Operating	Other short term debt	Can be either
Other current assets	Mixed	Current portion of long-term debt	Financing
Total current assets		Total current liabilities	

FIGURE 9.3 Balance Sheet and Financing or Operating Accounts

We like to see firms that have mostly operating assets. The other assets would be investments such as stocks, bonds, or money market certificates that are being held to finance a new plant, acquisition, or similar. It's fine to hold significant cash or marketable securities if there's a plan for spending it, but a company doesn't need to hold extra cash indefinitely. It should return it to the shareholders in dividends or stock repurchases if it doesn't need it.

John Maynard Keynes, in his *General Theory of Employment, Interest and Money*, outlined three reasons that firms need cash:[2]

1. Speculation
2. Precaution
3. Making transactions

Too much cash for speculation and precaution is a bad thing. Just enough cash for making transactions is okay.

Working Capital   Working capital is easy to define, but the concept is harder to describe. The textbook definition is:

$$Net\ Working\ Capital = Current\ Assets - Current\ Liabilities$$

In APM we modify that slightly to:

$$Net\ Working\ Capital = Current\ Operating\ Assets$$
$$- Current\ Operating\ Liabilities - Cash$$

---

[2] John Maynard Keynes, *The General Theory of Employment, Interest and Money* (London: Macmillan, 1936), Chapter 15, "The Psychological and Business Incentives to Liquidity."

What's the idea behind working capital? Basically, it's the net short-term assets that you need to accomplish the day-to-day operations of the firm. For example, not all sales are cash sales; some are credit sales; that's accounts receivables. A firm doesn't always pay its bills in cash; those are accounts payable.

The change in working capital is the cash increase or decrease from those short-term assets and liabilities. An increase in current operating liabilities means that less cash has left the firm; that's an increase in cash. An increase in current operating assets means that more cash hasn't been collected; that's a decrease in cash. An increase in inventories means a decrease in cash. It can seem counterintuitive, and students initially get lost. Here's the bottom line. If changes in working capital are consistently just as big as EBITDA, that's not a good thing. Most of the time working capital should be a minor detail in the value of the firm. Exceptions could be start-up companies without sufficient capital from debt or equity financing, or companies that are financially distressed and getting close to bankruptcy.

Working capital management can mean a lot of money to large companies. It can mean survival to some small companies. Working capital management can be summarized with the old adage: Slow down payments, speed up collections. For investors, we don't want to worry about a company's working capital. That's management's job. We just trust but verify that they're doing what they should. If a company is growing, then working capital should be growing also. Knowing when to focus on working capital is part of developing a sense of where things should be.

Figure 9.4 shows how Jos. A. Bank's change in working capital relates to its EBITDA, both from a quarterly and from an annual perspective. The figure shows the quarterly changes and EBITDA on the left. There's a lot of variability in the quarters, which is typical of retailers. They build inventory in some quarters and then sell it down. Looking at the quarterly numbers, you might be alarmed. Changes in working capital are just about as big as EBITDA for quite a few quarters. However, if you look at an

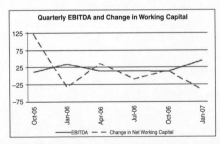
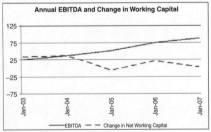

FIGURE 9.4   Working Capital Changes and EBITDA for Jos. A. Bank

annual perspective, the changes are smoothed out. EBITDA is increasing steadily. Changes in working capital are still variable, but EBITDA has clearly outpaced them in the last three years.

BUILDING A PRO FORMA

When we build our pro forma income statement and calculate free cash flow, we want to pay special attention to the operating numbers. If there are significant nonoperating items, we'll need to investigate and model them differently. Following is a bare-bones list of items that can start our model. It's bare bones because each segment's operating income or gross margin should be modeled separately. If selling expenses or something else is really important, then that could be a separate line item also. (See Figure 9.5.)

Free cash flow is the amount of cash that a firm has to divide between the equity holders and the debt holders. Interest payment and dividends haven't been subtracted. You can compare free cash flow across firms because it doesn't matter how the firm is financed. It is the operations that are front and center.

Sales
Cost of Goods Sold
Gross Margin
Gross Margin %
Selling and Administrative Expenses
Depreciation & Amortization
Operating Income

Nonoperating income or expense
Tax Expense
Net Income
Diluted Shares Outstanding
Earnings per Share

EBITDA (Operating Income + Depreciation & Amortization)
− Capital Expenditures
− Cash Taxes
− Change in Net Working Capital
Free Cash Flow

FIGURE 9.5 Pro Forma Income Statement and Free Cash Flow

TABLE 9.3   Taxes Paid and Tax Expense for ConAgra, 2002–2006

	May-06	May-05	May-04	May-03	May-02
Cash income taxes paid	340.0	296.7	315.8	249.0	310.4
Income tax expense	309.7	470.0	427.6	436.0	483.2
% difference	9.8	−36.9	−26.1	−42.9	−35.8
EBITDA	1,475.3	1,762.8	1,840.6	1,948.2	2,292.9
% of EBITDA: cash taxes	23.0	16.8	17.2	12.8	13.5
% of EBITDA: tax expense	21.0	26.7	23.2	22.4	21.1

The base for free cash flow is EBITDA. From that we subtract three cash items: capital expenditures, cash taxes, and the change in net working capital. Capital expenditures are represented on the income statement by depreciation expense, but the actual cash that goes out is what we're after. The capital expenditure amount for each quarter is on the statement of cash flows. Cash taxes aren't the same as tax expense on the income statement. In fact, they can be very different. Cash taxes are reported in the footnotes of the 10-K. Table 9.3 shows the difference for ConAgra. For most years except 2006, the actual taxes paid were anywhere from 26 to 43 percent lower than the tax expense reported on the income statement.

ConAgra Example Pro Forma

Let's see how we would forecast the pro forma numbers for ConAgra. Then we'll discuss presentation. Spreadsheets make it easy to have lots of years and quarters, but when you need to communicate the numbers, you need to make some careful decisions. First, the nuts and bolts.

Here's where you need to know the history and if things are changing with the company. Figure 9.6 shows ConAgra sales and EBITDA over the last 10 years. The chart shows that things haven't gone well since 2002. There has been a precipitous drop in sales and EBITDA. There was a similar decline in net income and earnings per share. The stock price didn't do all that well, either. It lost 28 percent in 2005 alone and was up only 13 percent since the beginning of 1997 versus a NASDAQ increase of 54 percent over the same period. With ruler analysis, things would be trending down!

In 2005 ConAgra hired a new chief executive, Gary Rodkin, from PepsiCo. Rodkin has an aggressive strategy to change the company and add value by introducing supply chain management and coordinating and consolidating brands. He has sold off brands and pledged to increase margin by a minimum of 250 basis points. He hired a new supply chain manager

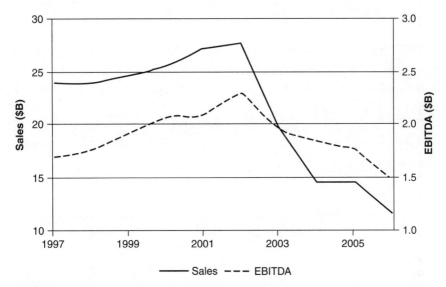

FIGURE 9.6   ConAgra Sales and EBITDA, 1997–2006

from Procter & Gamble as a direct report. If you believe the turn-around story, then you should forecast higher margins.

Table 9.4 shows a ConAgra pro forma. We've only included one year and three quarters of historical data. The sales and EBITDA chart (Figure 9.3) gives a longer-term view of the past. Each of the three quarters in 2007 shows some improvement in both gross and operating margins, giving some evidence that the turn-around has started.

The shaded numbers in Table 9.4 for the fourth quarter of 2007 are the numbers that we need to forecast. The three most important are sales growth, gross margin, and operating margin because the biggest driver of free cash flow is EBITDA. Those three numbers are the most important in determining free cash flow.

We forecast a downturn in sales for the fourth quarter of fiscal year 2007 because ConAgra had a Peter Pan peanut butter recall due to salmonella.[3] We also forecast margins to be off some from the previous two quarters because of the added expense of the recall. Those three numbers give an EBITDA forecast of $380 million for quarter four 2007. Simple addition gives the fiscal year 2007 forecast.

---

[3] Conagra's fiscal year ends in May.

TABLE 9.4 ConAgra Forecast of Free Cash Flow (in $B, except for % as indicated)

	FY 2006	Q1 2007	Q2 2007	Q3 2007	Q4 2007 E	FY 07 E	FY 08 E	FY 09 E	After 08
Sales	11.58	2.69	3.09	2.94	2.92	11.63	11.98	12.34	12.71
Gross profit	3.17	0.76	0.92	0.91	0.76	3.35	3.59	3.70	3.81
Gross margin	27.4%	28.4%	29.7%	31.0%	26.0%	28.8%	30%	30%	30%
EBITDA	1.48	0.35	0.46	0.48	0.38	1.67	2.04	2.22	2.41
Operating margin	12.7%	13.2%	14.7%	16.3%	13.0%	14.3%	17%	18%	19%
Capital expenditures	0.26	0.05	0.09	0.21	0.09	0.43	0.36	0.25	0.25
Income taxes paid	0.34	0.06	0.12	0.09	0.07	0.34	0.41	0.44	0.48
Change in net working capital	(0.13)	(0.19)	0.25	0.04	(0.02)	0.08	0.24	0.25	0.25
Free cash flow	1.00	0.44	(0.01)	0.14	0.24	0.81	1.03	1.28	1.42
Y-O-Y Growth (% change)									
Sales	−20.5	0.6	2.9	2.6	−2			3	3
Gross profit	−9.2	2.3	13.7	13.3				3	
Gross margin	14.2	1.7	10.5	10.4					
EBITDA	−16.3	7.8	28.1	19.4					
Operating margin	5.3	7.2	24.5	16.4					
Free cash flow	115.2	132.2	−443.0	143.2					
OTHER (in %)									
Capital expenditures as % of Sales	2.3	1.7	3.0	7.1	3		3	2	2
Income taxes paid as % of EBITA	23.0	17.4	26.2	19.2	19		20	20	20
Change in net working capital % of sales	9%	16%	5%	5%	8%		2	2	2

For capital expenditures, we use 3 percent of sales, which is higher than 2006 but lower than the large increase in the third quarter. For the change in net working capital, we use a slight increase because when we looked at previous fourth quarters, that quarter usually had a small increase.

For fiscal 2008 and subsequent years, we forecast a revenue increase of 3 percent. Generally, gross domestic product (GDP) has grown at 3 percent, and ConAgra should be able to grow revenue at about the same rate as GDP. Its margins should be much better going forward as the new initiatives take hold.

Presentation Details

There are two pieces to building a model. One is the number crunching, but the other is communicating the model to others and perhaps stepping back to see the big picture yourself. There is trade-off between presenting too much detail and too little. For ease of computation, you need some details in a model that don't really help explain the investment thesis. Too many numbers can overload readers. They might miss the main point because of information overload. Present too little information, and readers tend not to believe the story because they can't see where it's coming from. You need a computational model; then you need to simplify that model for presentation purposes.

Another detail is the number of numbers in the model. Table 9.5 shows ConAgra's total assets for six quarters from November 2005 to February 2007. If you have a large table like this one and you present in millions, you multiply by 1000 the number of numbers that a reader needs to digest. When you're trying to get a big idea across, you need only a couple of significant digits. In the first row, the second and third decimal places are totally irrelevant and only add to the clutter. Even taking those decimals out, that's a lot of number to process. We would use either of the next two rows to present the numbers. If you're only presenting assets, then the third row is fine. If you have other numbers that aren't quite as large, you might need two or even three decimal places. In Table 9.4 we used billions with two decimal places because some of the quarterly numbers weren't meaningful with just one decimal place.

TABLE 9.5 Total Assets for ConAgra, November 2005–February 2007

	Q3Y06	Q2Y06	Q1Y06	Q4Y05	Q3Y05	Q2Y05
In $M	12,280.600	12,356.500	11,993.100	11,970.400	12,383.000	13,308.700
In $B	12.28	12.36	11.99	11.97	12.38	13.31
In $B	12.3	12.4	12.0	12.0	12.4	13.3

Another decision is how many years to forecast and how many years of historical data to include. If you just include the forecast years, readers have a very hard time putting the numbers in context even when the assumptions are included. Sometimes it's a good idea to include the most recent four quarters by quarter with an additional year or two of history for perspective.

We forecast for at least two years. Those two years could include individual quarters until the fiscal year-end, especially when two or three quarters have already reported for the year. The decision about how long to forecast should be based on how long it should take the company to reach a competitive equilibrium. For example, if a company is earning extremely high margins, those margins eventually will attract competition that will cut into the margins. Garmin's initial margins were close to 80 percent. Now there are more competitors, especially in the retail area, and those margins are lower. Still, the Garmin name or technology may help preserve higher margins than for another company.

The product life cycle is also important in determining how long it will take to reach a competitive equilibrium. Figure 9.7 shows a typical product or firm life cycle. In the initial stages, there is very slow growth and the firm may not make any money. In the middle phase, if the product is successful, there will be a strong accelerating growth. Finally the product is mature and growth reaches an equilibrium. The longer a firm can sustain the middle phase, the better.

Since ConAgra is in the food business, we are implicitly assuming in our pro forma that sales growth is in equilibrium when we use the GDP growth rate. Since we think it will take approximately two years to roll out the new management changes that will increase margins, two years is a reasonable horizon in this case before steady state.

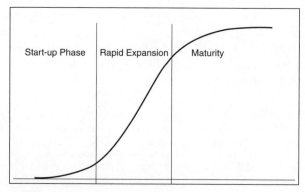

FIGURE 9.7 Product Life Cycle

NEXT STEPS

In the next chapter we use the inputs from a pro forma statement to generate a target price. In building the pro forma, it's critical that we examine anything that might lead to ruler analysis. We need to stay tied to the investment thesis in our projections. It's a fine line because, in some ways, the past can be an important guide to the future. By focusing on what changes management says it will make and assessing the probability of pulling it off, you'll end up with a better model.

Building models takes some practice. It also helps to build a model and update it over time. With every new conference call, press release, or industry update, you can tweak your model and assess the new information. Are things playing out as you thought with the investment thesis? The company might be right on target, but the market may have tanked, taking stock prices with it.

CHAPTER **10**

Valuation

The last step of the case is boiling everything down to one number: a target price based on valuation. We've still got a few details to go over, but we described most of the hard work in the case in Chapters 7, 8, and 9. The preparation work, the investment thesis, and preparing the pro formas all culminate in the intrinsic valuation number.

We'll discuss valuation based on multiples and comparable companies and a discounted cash flow (DCF) valuation. Lots of times groups will do both types. Each type can offer a slightly different insight. If a group does get widely different answers from each method, we ask the group to evaluate which valuation method provides a better view of the company. Groups would much prefer to average the answers since this hedges their bets, but the students need to understand why the two methods might give different answers and to go with the one the fits better. There are probably 50 different valuation methods, but most of them are some variation of the two that we'll discuss.

We observed an extreme example of averaging valuations in a student portfolio competition a few years ago. The student group (not from the University of Kansas) used nine different valuation methods for one company. They obtained all of their valuations from different available canned sources, such as Bloomberg, Quicken.com, and a few other places. They even had a dividend valuation model on a company that didn't pay dividends! Their valuations ranged from $50 to over $200. The stock was selling around $70 or $80. When they averaged all nine, they got a price above the market price, primarily because of a couple of very similar methods that had prices close to $200. Based on their answers to questions from the audience, they didn't really understand any of the details of the models.

Average investors aren't interested in the details. They want a good story without too many numbers. We think you have to know details and know which details are important. In this chapter we go over the details and interpretation of both types of valuation. We cover relative valuation in a little less detail than DCF valuation for a couple of reasons. First, we've already discussed some of the ratios in the previous chapters, and we'll continue to use those in subsequent chapters. Next, relative valuation is easier to understand. A few important details can cause big changes in the bottom line for DCF valuation, so we spend more time discussing the details that make a difference. They include the cost of capital, terminal values, and decisions about the forecast period. Of course, the assumptions in the pro forma analysis can be important variables also.

There are several excellent, comprehensive valuation books that run well over 500 pages. Anyone who is interested in digging into more details should read McKinsey and Company's *Valuation* or one of Aswath Damadoran's valuation books. Both are excellent but a little daunting in their size and scope. A less comprehensive (shorter) but still very good book is *Expectations Investing* by Rappaport and Mauboussin.[1]

No one can do your thinking for you. A valuation is most valuable to investors who build their own model because of the thought that goes into each step of building the model. Students' first models aren't always great. Sometimes they make big mistakes in their assumptions, but it's the process that matters. Students can correct a mistake and learn from it. It's not only students who make mistakes. There are plenty of wrong numbers and outlandish assumptions in professional analysts' research reports, but you'd never know that unless you've done the work yourself.

RELATIVE VALUATION

Most valuation approaches begin with a relative valuation. You look at the price of similar assets in the market and see how companies compare using a standardized price. If you want to buy a car, you're not going to spend $500,000 for a Porsche, even a really nice one, when you can get one for only $90,000 somewhere else. It's the same with housing prices. People fall in love with their houses all the time and want to sell them for lots more than similar houses down the street. Comparable analysis applies to cars, houses, art, and stocks.

---

[1] Aswath Damadoran, *Investment Valuation: Tools and Techniques for Determining the Value of Any Asset* (Hoboken, NJ: John Wiley & Sons, 2002). Tim Koller, Marc Goedhart, and David Wessels, *Valuation: Measuring and Managing the Value of Companies, 4th Edition* (Hoboken, NJ: John Wiley & Sons, 2005). Alfred Rappaport and Michael J. Mauboussin, *Expectations Investing: Reading Stock Prices for Better Returns* (Boston, MA: Harvard Business School Press, 2001).

We've discussed price to earnings (P/E), price to sales (P/S), price to book (P/B), and total enterprise value (TEV) to earnings before interest, taxes, and depreciation (EBITDA). The first three standardize stock prices bases on earnings, sales, and book value per share. The last, TEV/EBITDA, standardizes the value of the firm based on operating cash flow.[2]

Relative valuation is popular because it's not too hard to automatically calculate a lot of ratios and see which companies are highly valued and which are low. You can calculate an average or median ratio and see whether the company you are interested is higher or lower. If it's higher, you might conclude that the company is expensive. Conversely, if it's lower, you might conclude that the company is cheap. Buy low (cheap), sell high (expensive). That's all there is to it.

Originally the Standard & Poor's (S&P) 500 value and growth indices were based on calculating the P/E ratios of all 500 stocks in the index. The lowest 250 were in the value index and the highest 250 were in the growth index. S&P's method is more sophisticated now, but value stocks still are primarily identified by lower valuation ratios.

Of course, if buying low and selling high were that easy, we'd all be rich. There are lots of good reasons why some companies are cheaper than others. The expensive company may have a much higher expected growth rate or other good reasons to sell at a premium relative to the others. Multiples are good starting points, but without some additional knowledge of the company and its comparables, they can be easy to misinterpret or can be used to mislead. For example, a research analyst could pick a group of firms as comparables to make his or her recommendation look good.

To get an idea of how comparables compare, it's a good idea to look at some operating metrics and the variation ratios at the same time. For ConAgra, margins and sales growth are key numbers. Table 10.1 shows ConAgra's numbers and six comparables. All are large caps in the processed food business. Kraft (KFT) and Pilgrim's Pride (PPC) are a little larger and smaller respectively than the others. Their operating numbers, especially Pilgrim's Pride's, are quite a bit different from the others.

If we remove Pilgrim's Pride from the comparables, the return on equity increases, making ConAgra look a little worse. The other operating comparisons are qualitatively unchanged. On a valuation basis ConAgra looks fairly expensive on a trailing P/E basis, and in line with the others on a forward P/E. Based on P/B, P/S, and TEV/EBITDA, ConAgra looks cheap. Earnings per share includes 16 cents per share charge of special items from

---

[2] EBITDA isn't exactly cash flow, but it's a good approximation in a lot of cases.

TABLE 10.1 ConAgra and Comparables Operating and Valuation Metrics

	CAG	Median	Average	CPB	GIS	HNZ	K	KFT	PPC
Market cap	12.7	21.2	25.7	15.2	21.2	15.5	21.4	55.3	2.4
Dividend yield	2.9	2.4	2.2	2.0	2.5	2.2	2.9	3.1	0.3
Profit margin	5.3	9.0	7.5	10.8	9.3	8.6	9.4	7.9	−1.3
EBITDA margin	14.3	17.5	15.6	20.4	21.1	15.7	19.4	14.9	2.3
Return on assets	4.5	6.0	6.3	12.6	6.1	6.0	9.8	4.9	−1.9
Return on equity	11.7	23.4	24.7	52.8	19.2	27.7	46.2	9.6	−7.2
5-year CAGR									
Sales	−15.7	3.1	5.7	2.0	10.5	−1.7	4.3	0.3	18.8
EBITDA	−6.7	−0.2	2.1	0.0	11.2	−0.5	6.0	−3.3	−1.1
Earnings per share	−2.9	5.4	6.7	3.4	5.4	−1.6	16.3	9.7	NA
Price/Earnings	23.5	18.4	11.7	18.0	17.2	25.5	19.4	18.8	−28.8
1-yr forward P/E	18.9	18.9	22.4	20.0	18.7	18.1	18.9	19.5	38.9
2-yr forward P/E	17.4	17.2	17.2	18.7	17.3	16.6	17.2	18.5	10.9
Price/Book	2.7	5.3	5.6	9.4	3.6	7.0	9.4	1.9	2.2
Price/Sales	1.1	1.7	1.6	2.0	1.7	1.7	1.9	1.6	0.4
TEV/EBITDA	8.2	12.0	13.9	13.4	11.4	12.4	11.0	11.6	23.4

CAG: ConAgra Foods Inc.; CPB: Campbell Soup Co.; GIS: General Mills Inc.; HNZ: H J Heinz Co, K: Kellogg Co.; KFT: Kraft Foods Inc.; PPC: Pilgrim's Pride Corp.

discontinued operations. Using EPS from continuing operations, ConAgra's trailing P/E ratio is 17.8, in line with that of the comparables.

What does it mean to be in line? It means that ConAgra's price is neither cheap nor expensive with respect to other companies. It means that ConAgra should earn the same return as the rest of the sector. With a sector P/E of 18 and a S&P 500 P/E of 15, it means that the market expects this sector either to have a higher growth rate or to be less risky than average. Since revenue growth (also called top-line growth) isn't expected to be that high, sector earnings growth can't be high unless the whole sector can find some technology that lowers costs. That's not the case in food processing. By process of elimination, we can conclude that food processing is considered less risky than average, not too startling a conclusion. People always need to eat! The relatively high dividend yield confirms that this sector is pretty steady.

If we look at all of the other valuation measures—P/B, P/S, and TEV/EBITDA—ConAgra looks undervalued with multiples significantly lower than the benchmarks. ConAgra's story is that it wants to expand margins. It thinks it can get up to the industry average. If it can do that, then its EPS would go up faster than the industry. ConAgra would have growth, be in a "safe" industry, and have a good dividend yield. Given those considerations, ConAgra looks like a good buy.

Getting to a Target Price

With relative valuation, you can stop now. You've concluded that the company is a buy based on valuation. We ask the students to go one step further and find an intrinsic or target price or range using the comparable ratios. We call the intrinsic value TEV*(say TEV star) or P* (P star). We use the * (star) to indicate that this is our own valuation of price or enterprise value. The intrinsic price of the whole company is TEV*, and the intrinsic price per share is P*. We compare TEV* to TEV and P* to price (P).

We find TEV* by taking the comparable TEV/EBITDA multiple and multiplying by our forecast of EBITDA. Usually we use a forecast for two years out. For ConAgra, we forecast 2.22 billion in EBITDA for fiscal year (FY) 2009. The comparable's median TEV/EBITDA from Table 10.1 is 12. So our TEV*, is 12 × 2.22, or $26.64 billion. In going to P* from TEV*, we need to consider the same things that we considered in finding TEV in Chapter 7: cash, debt, preferred stock, and number of shares.

Figure 10.1 shows the calculations for ConAgra's enterprise value and P*. The left side shows the actual or market values for ConAgra. The right side shows the intrinsic value starting with the comparable TEV/EBITDA ratio. Four numbers are the same on each side: shares outstanding, debt, preferred, and cash. Three numbers can be compared to see the over- or

Actual Values		Intrinsic Values	
Current Share Price	25.73	Comparable TEV/EBITDA Ratio	12
× Shares Outstanding (Fully Diluted)	502	× 2009 EBITDA Forecast	2,220
Market Capitalization	12,908	TEV*	26,646
− Cash	497	+ Cash	497
+ Debt	3,457	− Debt	3,457
+ Preferred Stock Value	-	− Preferred Stock Value	-
Total Enterprise Value	15,868	Implied Equity Value	23,686
		÷ Shares Outstanding (Fully Diluted)	502
		P*	47.21
% over/undervalued TEV	-40%		
% over/undervalued share price	-46%		
% diffence in TEV/EBITDA ratios	-32%		

FIGURE 10.1 TEV and Intrinsic Value Calculations for ConAgra

undervaluation. First we can compare TEV to TEV*. The intrinsic value is 40 percent less than the market value. Next we can compare market capitalization to the implied equity value or, equivalently, the market share price to P*. The share price is $25.73 and P* is $47.21, a 46 percent discount.

How do our estimates compare to those of the Street? We can check fairly easily. Since ConAgra is a large-cap company, quite a few analysts provide estimates. According to the company's Web site, 12 analysts cover the company. Only four of them have published estimates for FY2009 EBITDA, but the average is $1.8 billion, about 25 percent lower than our estimates. When we use the consensus analyst estimate of EBITDA to calculate the share price with a 12 multiple, P* is $36.45. It is still selling at almost a 30 percent discount to our valuation. Implicitly, we're looking for margin expansion and multiple expansion as the margins expand.

As mentioned, analysts won't come up with a price target so far from the current price. There's too much risk for them if they are wrong. Currently the consensus target price is $26.50. ConAgra is a turnaround story, and analysts as well as the general investing public like to wait and see if the turnaround will indeed occur. Unfortunately, that's the average investor thinking that leads to average results.

Target Price with P/E Ratio

It is much simpler to get a target price with a P/E ratio than with the TEV/EBITDA ratio. All we need is the EPS forecast for two years ahead. But before we calculate our P*, what will we find? We should already know the answer. Since the forward P/E ratio for the comparable companies is slightly lower than the P/E ratio for ConAgra, the only way we'll have a higher target price is with a higher EPS forecast. If we think that ConAgra will continue to trade in line with the other similar companies based on P/E, then we won't see any multiple expansion, only margin expansion. Here's how you find P*:

$$P^* = comparable \; P/E \times EPS \; forecast$$

For ConAgra, we forecast EPS at $1.98, 25 percent above the consensus of $1.58. With a P/E of 17.2, our P* is $33.97. That's significantly below our target using a TEV/EBITDA multiple, but still we'd conclude that ConAgra is selling at a 24 percent discount.

What's important in our analysis is to go back to the prep work and the investment thesis when interpreting the numbers and choosing between which forecast we'll rely on. For ConAgra, we think EPS is messy and harder to forecast because of the product lines the company has bought and sold recently. There will be special items in the upcoming years as the firm exits more lines of business to concentrate on the core. For that reason, we'll rely on the TEV/EBITDA ratio, but we'll take comfort in the fact that the P/E ratio is in line with the industry and the dividend yield is above the industry and above average.

Special Cases for Multiples

There are several instances when multiples are the only way to go. Lots of investors only use multiple valuation. It's always a good idea to make sure you know what the multiple valuation tells you, especially if it's different from a DCF valuation. The special cases for multiples include valuing segments, using the multiples from recently completed acquisitions, and special industry valuations.

For a company with segments in totally unrelated industries, using a different multiple to value each segment is critical. An example that we discussed in Chapter 6 is LSB Industries (LXU). LSB has two distinct businesses—chemical and climate control. The chemical business traditionally sells at a relatively low multiple. Since 2007 has been a record year for earnings, current P/Es aren't representative of historical P/Es. Table 10.2 shows the May 2007 P/E ratios for LXU and several comparables from the fertilizer industry. Current trailing P/Es are almost three times higher than May 2005's ratios and just about twice as high as the forward ratios. LSB looks cheap on a current basis, but in line with the forward ratios.

What's different about LSB that we discussed in detail in Chapter 6 is its climate control segment. A good comparable for that business is WFI Industries, currently trading at 21 times 2008 earnings. We can't use comparables directly to value LSB or any other business with lines in different industries. We need to value the chemical business using the comparables

TABLE 10.2   P/E Ratios for Fertilizer Companies and LSB Industries

	Ticker	Trailing P/E May 2007	Trailing P/E May 2005	FY 2008 Forward P/E
Agrium Inc.	AGU	30.4	11.0	14.8
Mosaic Company	MOS	90.1	31.8	19.0
Terra Industries Inc.	TRA	27.3	8.0	13.5
LSB Industries Inc	LXU	18.4	N/A	15.0

from the fertilizer industry and value the climate control business with that industry's comparables.

Table 10.3 shows a pro forma income statement for LSB that includes both segments. We can use either the operating profit or the EPS numbers. Either way, we need to make some adjustments. If we use the per-share numbers, we need to calculate the weights for the two divisions. If we use the operating profit, we need to allocate the other expenses to the two divisions.

TABLE 10.3   LSB Pro Forma Income Statement for FY 2007–2008

	Actual 2006	Estimate 2007	Estimate 2008
Revenue			
Chemical	260.7	291.9	291.9
Climate Control	221.2	331.7	316.3
Total revenue	492.0	623.7	608.2
Operating profit			
Chemical	10.2	11.7	5.8
Climate	25.4	38.2	36.4
Corporate/Other	−8.1	−9.0	−9.0
Total operating profit	27.6	40.8	33.2
Discontinued operations	−0.3		
Interest expense	−11.9	−9.0	−8.0
Other	0.5	0.0	
Net income before preferred dividend	15.9	31.8	25.2
Preferred dividends	2.6	0.7	0.8
Net income	13.3	31.2	24.4
Shares for basic EPS	14.3	15.0	15.0
Shares for diluted EPS	20.9	22.5	22.0
EPS: Basic	0.93	2.08	1.63
EPS: Fully diluted	0.78	1.39	1.15

Table 10.4 shows how we use P/E ratios for each segment to come up with a stock price. The first column numbers come from the pro forma earnings estimate in Table 10.3. The second column is subjective. There is really no good way to allocate costs. If they could be identified with a specific segment, they would already be reported that way. Subtracting the expenses allocated gives a net earnings for each segment. Divide that by diluted shares and we get per-share segment earnings. The total per share value is the same as the EPS estimate for 2008 in Table 10.3. Now we multiply each segment's per-share value by the appropriate P/E ratio, add those together, and we get P* for the company.

We used a lower P/E multiple for the Chemical segment since it's still a tough industry to be in despite the record earnings in 2007. You can see from the table that we think most of the company's value is coming from the Climate Control business, but this analysis also shows how a reduction in those "Other Expenses" could enhance value. About half of those are corporate expenditures and half is interest expense with a fairly high residual interest rate. Significant savings in interest or corporate could help the share price quite a bit.

Other Specials

We will mention briefly two other special cases before moving to discounted cash flow. APM has been invested in a Mexican tile company called Interceramic, which sells ceramic tiles for households both in the United States and in Mexico. It used to be an American Depository Receipt (ADR) that traded in the United States. After the Sarbanes-Oxley Act passed in 2002, Interceramic didn't want to spend the extra $2 to $5 million every year in added fees. The company delisted and trades only on the Mexican stock exchange now. We still hold Interceramic because of the valuation, and because it is still turning out tiles, profits, and, more important, cash.

Figure 10.2 shows Interceramic's TEV on the left and our valuation on the right. In 2006 EBITDA was $60 million. We forecast only a slight increase in 2007 because of the housing downturn in the United States (not in Mexico) and because the company will have increased costs with a new distribution center in El Paso, Texas. Even forecasting almost no growth, Interceramic is undervalued by 11 percent.

We feel this is a very conservative valuation. The new distribution center should lead to lower costs and increased efficiency in subsequent years. The TEV/EBITDA multiple of 10 is also very conservative. In 2002 Mohawk acquired Dal-Tile. For the acquisition, Mohawk had to file a Prospectus Form 424B3 with the Securities and Exchange Commission (SEC). One requirement is for the company to provide a valuation for the acquisition target.

TABLE 10.4 Calculating P* by Segment

	FY 2008 Estimate	Allocation %	Expense Allocation	Net Segment Earnings	Per-Share Segment Earnings	Segment P/E	Segment Contribution to Price
Chemical	5.8	30%	−5.1	0.7	0.034	10	0.34
Climate Control	36.4	70%	−11.9	24.5	1.112	29	32.26
Other expenses	−17.0			Net EPS	1.146		
Fully diluted shares	22.0					P*	$32.59

Market Cap	450		
Debt	120	EBITDA 2007	62
less cash	18	Dal-Tile Acquisition Multiple	10
TEV	553	TEV*	620

FIGURE 10.2 Interceramic Valuation Using Acquisition Multiple (in millions of US$)

Since Dal-Tile produced only tile and Interceramic is a close competitor, the filing is a chance to get a very good comparable. However, things were selling much more cheaply in 2002. Five years later, we probably would use a slightly higher multiple. Still, we can see that Interceramic isn't fully valued. It is probably discounted since it trades in Mexico. It also has concentrated ownership, which we discuss more fully in Chapter 12.

The other special case concerns industry-specific metrics. We'll just provide one example from the airline industry. A big source of lack of comparability in airline earnings comes from how fleets are financed. Some companies lease, and some companies buy. Because of the very different rules surrounding depreciation and lease expense reporting, analysts look at the EBITDAR: earnings before interest, taxes, depreciation, amortization, and rental expense. Bob McAdoo, a highly respected airline analyst for Prudential Equity Group, has spoken in the APM class. He only uses TEV/EBITDAR to value airlines. He feels that they trade on this multiple, so any other valuation is moot. Bob was ranked number 2 on *Forbes*' top analyst list in 2005 and number 3 in 2006.

DISCOUNTED CASH FLOW VALUATION

Discounted cash flow valuation is the gold standard for valuation. Every finance course begins and ends by teaching that the value of any asset is the net present value (NPV) of its future cash flows. Students spend a lot of time in many finance courses learning about the mathematics of discounting and calculating the proper discount rate. Students learn about the NPV in introductory accounting classes. Even some math classes use NPV examples. We don't want to reinvent the wheel, so in the appendix to this chapter, we provide a very brief review of some of the discounting math. What we do want to focus on is what the important numbers are and how to figure out where to focus. When students have a big spreadsheet full of numbers, it can become just a blur. We know this is going to sound like a broken record, but when you've done the proper preparation and developed an investment thesis, you have a guide to the important numbers. For ConAgra, it's not

~~sales growth, it's margin expansion. For Garmin, it's not margin expansion,~~ it's sales growth.

The issues that we address here are calculating the cost of capital, terminal values, and the forecast horizon. The other inputs to the model come from the pro forma statements discussed in Chapter 9.

Weighted Average Cost of Capital

The weighted average cost of capital (WACC) is the cost that a company would have to pay today for its capital. For debt, it's straightforward; it's the interest rate the company would pay today to the bank or to its bond investors. For equity, it's a little harder to find. Most books tell students to use the Capital Asset Pricing Model (CAPM). That's the place to start, but since there are some problems with implementing CAPM, it's only a starting place and not usually where we end.

Cost of Debt   The cost of debt is usually easy to observe. Companies have to list the terms of their long-term debt in their financial filings with the SEC. If a company has issued bonds recently and interest rates are fairly stable, we probably can use the coupon payment on the recently issued debt as a good indicator of the cost of debt. Companies also can have their debt rated by one of several rating agencies. Bonds traded on exchanges have to be rated. Typically bonds with similar ratings trade at similar yields. The yield can be used as a close proxy for the cost to the company.

Figure 10.3 shows the yield for bonds with different rates. The least risky bonds are Treasury bonds. Treasuries also set the benchmark for all other bonds. The corporate rated debt trades at a spread or premium to the Treasury yield curve. In June 2004 the spread for AAA-rated bonds, the highest-rated corporates, was 22 basis points (bps) for the five-year bonds.[3] The spread was so thin that it's very hard to see in Figure 10.3. BBB-rated bonds are the lowest investment-grade bonds. Many pension funds and other large investment groups are limited to investing in investment-grade bonds. The spread for the five-year BBB bonds is 95 bps; for five-year CCCs, it is 1,400 bps. Still, that's only 4.35 percent for the BBBs and 8.32 percent for the CCCs, historically very low interest rates.

---

[3] Basis points are 1/100th of 1 percent. Twenty-two bps is 0.22 percent. Basis points are commonly used to measure bond spreads and interest rate changes. Traders talk about "bips," or basis points.

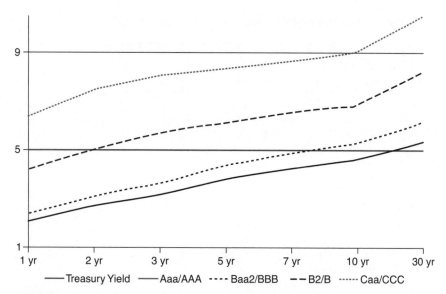

FIGURE 10.3   Treasury and Corporate Yield Curves, June 2004

If a company has a bond listed on an exchange, you can look up the bond and find the current yield to maturity and use that for the cost of debt. For example, at the end of FY 2006, ConAgra had $2.8 billion in senior long-term debt on its balance sheet. It also had $400 million in subordinated debt. Footnote 9 of the 10-K provides all the details of the maturity and current interest rate on ConAgra's note.

In Note 9, which ConAgra filed with the SEC on July 28, 2006, the maturity schedule shows us that 68 percent of ConAgra's debt will mature after 2011, 16 percent matures in five years (2011), and 13 percent matures in 2007. We could do a weighted average of the current yields of the different maturities, but we'll use ConAgra's bond that is publicly traded. It is rated BBB and matures in 2026. On Yahoo!Finance we find that the yield to maturity is 6.33 percent and the coupon rate is 7.125 percent. The 20-year BBB average is 6.8 percent. ConAgra's bonds are yielding less than that, probably because they have an option for early redemption. That option is valuable, so the yield is reduced from the market yield. If ConAgra were to issue straight BBB 20-year debt today, it would have to pay closer to 6.8 percent than 6.3 percent. We conclude that the current cost of debt for ConAgra is 6.8 percent.

9. SENIOR LONG-TERM DEBT, SUBORDINATED DEBT AND LOAN AGREEMENTS

	2006	2005
Senior Debt		
8.25% senior debt due September 2030	300.0	300.0
7.0% senior debt due October 2028	400.0	400.0
6.7% senior debt due August 2027 (redeemable at option of holders in 2009)	300.0	300.0
7.125% senior debt due October 2026 (redeemable at option of holders in 2006)	400.0	400.0
7.875% senior debt due September 2010	500.0	750.0
9.875% senior debt due November 2005	—	100.0
6.0% senior debt due September 2006	—	500.0
6.75% senior debt due September 2011	1,000.0	1,000.0
4.55% to 10.07% lease financing obligations due on various dates through 2024	208.0	232.4
Other	70.7	78.5
Total face value senior debt	3,178.7	4,060.9
Subordinated debt		
9.75% subordinated debt due March 2021	400.0	400.0
Total face value subordinated debt	400.0	400.0
Total debt face value	3,578.7	4,460.9
Unamortized discounts/premiums	(5.8)	(9.1)
Hedged debt adjustment to fair value	3.0	14.6
Less current portion	(421.1)	(117.3)
Total long-term debt	3,154.8	4,349.1

The aggregate minimum principal maturities of the long-term debt for each of the five fiscal years after May 28, 2006, are:

2007	*421.1*
2008	*21.5*
2009	*17.9*
2010	*37.9*
2011	*512.4*

The most restrictive note agreements (the revolving credit facilities and certain privately placed long-term debt) require the Company to repay the debt if consolidated funded debt exceeds 65% of the consolidated capital base, as defined, or if fixed charges coverage, as defined, is less than 1.75 to 1.0, as such terms are defined in applicable agreements. As of the end of fiscal 2006, the Company's consolidated funded debt was approximately 39% of its consolidated capital base and the fixed charges ratio was approximately 3.8 to 1.0.

Net interest expense consists of:

	2006	2005	2004
Long-term debt	$311.9	$349.1	$335.1
Short-term debt	0.4	0.8	7.2
Interest income	(34.9)	(27.0)	(49.6)
Interest included in cost of goods sold	(25.8)	(19.3)	(13.4)
Interest capitalized	(5.0)	(8.6)	(4.4)
	$246.6	$295.0	$274.9

As noted in the above table, interest expense incurred to finance hedged inventories has been reflected in cost of goods sold.

Net interest paid was $304.9 million, $360.3 million, and $334.2 million in fiscal 2006, 2005, and 2004, respectively.

In fiscal 2004, the Company received approximately $134 million from the termination of all of its interest rate swaps (see Note 17). The proceeds are not included in the net interest paid amount for fiscal 2004. The Company's net interest expense was reduced by $11.5 million in fiscal 2006 due to the net impact of previously closed interest rate swap agreements, as compared to $27.5 million in fiscal 2005.

The carrying amount of long-term debt (including current installments) was $3.6 billion and $4.5 billion as of May 28, 2006 and May 29, 2005, respectively. Based on current market rates provided primarily by outside investment bankers, the fair value of this debt at May 28, 2006 and May 29, 2005 was estimated at $3.8 billion and $5.2 billion, respectively.

During fiscal 2006, the Company redeemed $500.0 million of 6% senior debt due in September 2006 and $250 million of 7.875%

senior debt due in September 2010. These early retirements of debt resulted in pre-tax losses of $30.3 million (including $26.3 million recognized in the fourth quarter of fiscal 2006), which are included in selling, general and administrative expenses.

In addition to these early retirements of debt, the Company made scheduled principal payments of debt and payments of lease financing obligations during fiscal 2006, reducing long-term debt by $149.0 million.

The spreads and the shape of the Treasury yield curve changes over time. If you know the company's rating, you can find the cost of debt that it would have if the company issued currently. You'll have to assume a maturity, but 10 years is an average issue and pretty safe to use. If the company's debt is not rated, then you can assess a rating based on the predictability and size of a company's cash flow and the amount of debt.

You can't just use the coupon rate on a company's most recent issue because the shape of the yield curve can change dramatically over time. Figure 10.4 shows the Treasury yield curve in June 2004 and in June 2007. The flatter, higher curve is from 2007. The steeper curve is from

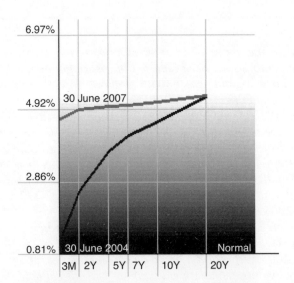

FIGURE 10.4   Treasury Yield Curves, June 2004
and June 2007
Source: Stockcharts.com, Dynamic Yield Curve,
http://stockcharts.com/charts/YieldCurve.html

2004. In June 2007 the spread for 10-year BBB bonds was 127 bps to yield 6.48 percent. The spread was lower and the Treasury rates were lower in 2004.

Cost of Equity   Bond yields provide a floor for finding the cost of equity. Since equity holders are residual claimants, they always have a riskier position than bond holders. That's why understanding the yield curve isn't just for bond investors. Equity investors need to understand where the floor is. In times of low bond yields, we should expect equity returns to be lower than in times of high bond yields.

The textbook way to find the cost of equity is to use the CAPM, which we discussed (in a not very positive light) in Chapter 3. Here's how to find the cost of equity, r_e, using the CAPM. Find beta and estimate the expected return on the market, $E(r_m)$. Use the 10-year Treasury note for the risk-free rate, r_f.

$$r_e = r_f + \beta \times (E(r_m) - r_f).$$

What's the expected return on the market? That's what you expect a broad market index to earn in the next 5 to 10 years on an annualized basis. Table 10.5 and Figure 10.5 help students put market expectations in perspective. These broad market indices give a clue to the "average" market return. The geometric mean is the compound annual average and is the preferred measure.

The Dow Jones Industrial Average (DJIA) has been around longer than the other two major indices, the NASDAQ and the S&P 500. The compound average annual return (or geometric mean) on the DJIA from 1930 to 2002 was 5 percent. Since 1984 it's been higher, at 11 percent. Still, there are extended periods that markets didn't do well. In the 1960s and 1970s the returns were 2 percent and essentially zero for each of those decades, respectively.

No matter what period you look at, the variability as measured by the standard deviation is very high. That means individual years are almost never average. Figure 10.5 shows NASDAQ returns from 2000 to 2006. The average return over the period was −3 percent. The closest annual return was in 2005, when the return was 1 percent, but there were big highs in 2003 and big lows in 2000 to 2002.

So what's our expected return on the market? A lot of people always use 10 percent, perhaps because it's a nice round number. It's higher than the 9 percent long-term average, but many people are optimistic. It also makes the numbers work out better. Remember we said that the cost of equity needs to be higher than the cost of debt because of the risk/return relationship.

TABLE 10.5 DJIA, S&P 500, and NASDAQ Annual Returns

	1930–2006	1951–2006	1972–2006	1930s	1940s	1950s	1960s	1970s	1980s	1990s	2000–2006
DJIA											
Mean	0.07	0.09	0.09	0.05	0.04	0.14	0.03	0.02	0.13	0.16	0.02
Standard deviation	0.19	0.16	0.16	0.37	0.13	0.17	0.15	0.19	0.13	0.12	0.14
Geometric mean	0.05	0.07	0.08	−0.01	0.03	0.13	0.02	0.00	0.13	0.15	0.01
NASDAQ											
Mean			0.12					0.07	0.14	0.28	−0.03
Standard deviation			0.27					0.26	0.14	0.30	0.30
Geometric mean			0.09					0.04	0.13	0.25	−0.07
S&P 500											
Mean	0.09	0.09	0.09			0.14	0.05	0.03	0.13	0.16	0.01
Standard deviation	0.16	0.16	0.17			0.20	0.14	0.19	0.12	0.14	0.17
Geometric mean	0.08	0.08	0.08			0.13	0.04	0.02	0.13	0.15	−0.01

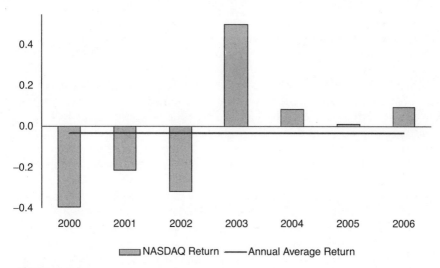

FIGURE 10.5 NASDAQ Annual Returns, 2000–2006

Next we'll provide some examples where the CAPM formula doesn't give a good estimate of the cost of equity and using an expected market return lower than 10 percent provides more problems.

LSB Example One thing that students have always learned how to do by the time they get to the APM class is calculate beta. They've done that in at least one or two classes. What they can't appreciate is that data have been provided by a textbook or a professor. The data are carefully selected so that the output will make sense. In 2001 several student groups had calculated LSB's beta as −0.67. They were happy to see a negative beta stock because they had learned in their investment classes that negative betas are hard to find and that they provide a special sort of diversification for portfolios. At the time the 10-year Treasury bond rate was 5 percent. Let's calculate the cost of equity with these inputs.

$$r_e = r_f + \beta \times (E(r_m) - r_f).$$
$$r_e = 5\% - 0.67 \times (10\% - 5\%) = 1.65\%$$

At this time, LSB was paying approximately 13 percent for its debt financing. If equity is riskier than debt, it doesn't make sense that equity investor would want only a 1.65 percent return on LSB's stock. The cost of equity has to be higher than 13 percent, and it certainly wasn't 1.65 percent!

Other Beta Issues Another quick check on betas that we encourage students to review is the interval estimate of beta. Since betas are estimates, we estimate things with error. Statisticians have long recognized this fact and have come up with the concept of an interval estimate instead of just a point estimate. The interval shows how precisely the data can estimate something. Suppose we estimate beta for two different companies to be 0.8. If one has an interval estimate of 0.75 to 0.85 and the other's interval is 0.5 to 1.3, we conclude very different things about the precision of the estimate. In theory, any estimate in the interval is just as likely as another to be the "true" beta, so we shouldn't be focused on the middle of the interval. We can see that the second interval isn't very precise. In fact, based on the beta estimate, we really can't even tell whether that company is more or less risky than the market, since it contains values above and below 1.

Let's review a few of the APM companies and see if their betas pass the smell test. First, we'll look at Sohu, a Chinese Internet company that IPOed on NASDAQ in July 2000. Sohu earns money by selling advertising on its Web site. It's similar to Google. It also earns money by providing some services to mobile phone users. At one time that part was Sohu's biggest revenue producer, but some changes to the agreement with the mobile phone providers has made that division less profitable.

Figure 10.6 shows how Sohu's beta has changed over time and how it relates to earnings per share. The betas are calculated based on market prices the year prior to the earnings. The index is the NASDAQ. Right after its initial public offering, Sohu wasn't profitable and its beta was high. That makes sense. A new company that isn't making money yet is risky. Beta falls as EPS starts to increase. However, beginning in the second quarter of 2002, Sohu's beta rises as its EPS rises. Once Sohu becomes profitable in the third quarter of 2003, its beta really starts to climb. Look at September 2003. Sohu is now making money; cash flow is strong. Why is beta now at almost 3.5? That implies a required return for investors that is much higher than the previous year when Sohu was losing money! Sohu's stock price was climbing much faster than the market, but it was doing well.

Other companies' betas also have some problems. Table 10.6 compares the beta for four companies, Garmin, LKQ Inc., Jos. A. Bank, and Scientific Games, over time and shows the difference that the market index makes for Scientific Games. We see that Garmin's beta is lower after its IPO in 2000. Beta is high as its financial situation becomes stronger over the last few years. LKQ is similar. It IPOed in 2002, had low beta initially, then ramped up. Jos. A. Bank had a down year in 2006, but it wasn't disastrous. The company still has strong cash flow and is on target with its expansion plans, but beta ramped up for a year.

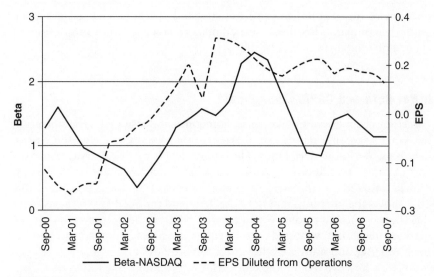

FIGURE 10.6 Sohu's Beta and Earnings per Share, Q3 2000–Q1 2007

We calculated all of the betas with both the NASDAQ index and the S&P 500 index. Scientific Games' beta was the most different depending on the index used. In 2001 and 2007, one beta was greater than 1, but the other wasn't. The last lesson we can learn from this table is how much betas can vary depending on the period when they are calculated and the index used. The cost of equity probably isn't going to change that dramatically from

TABLE 10.6 Betas for Selected Portfolio Companies, 2001 to 2007

| | | | | Scientific Games | |
Ticker	Garmin GRMN	LKQ Inc. LKQX	Jos. A. Bank JOSB	SGMS: SP 500	SGMS: NASDAQ
2001	0.50		0.34	1.02	0.45
2002	0.52		0.39	0.63	0.45
2003	0.86	0.86	0.68	0.93	0.79
2004	1.57	0.78	0.99	1.61	1.05
2005	1.55	1.70	0.98	1.47	1.28
2006	1.77	1.87	1.41	0.94	0.69
2007	1.45	1.02	0.98	1.20	0.99

one year to the next unless some fundamental operating changes are going on in the company. Just because a company's stock gets hot or not doesn't change its fundamental risk profile.

If Not Beta and CAPM, Then What?

Sometimes beta doesn't make sense. Sometimes it doesn't pass the smell test, but what's the alternative? An alternative that we use is called the cost of debt plus. We know two things: The cost of debt is easily observable and the cost of equity should be higher than the cost of debt. We start with the cost of debt and add an equity risk premium of between 3 and 5 percent. Table 10.7 shows the premium that the NASDAQ and the S&P 500 returned over the 10-year Treasury note. We calculated different holding periods for the market indices, but we found that the equity premium is about 3 to 5 percent for NASDAQ and quite a bit lower for the S&P 500.

Here's how we would implement this information. We found that Con-Agra's cost of debt was 6.8 percent. Its cost of equity would be $6.75\% + 3.5\% = 10.25\%$. What part of the range of the equity risk premium you use is subjective. We'll go toward the middle of the range since there's some risk, but not high risk. Let's compare this to what we'd get using the CAPM. Yahoo!Finance currently reports ConAgra's beta as 0.59.

$$r_e = r_f + \beta \times (E(r_m) - r_f)$$
$$r_e = 5\% + 0.59 \times (10\% - 5\%) = 7.95\%$$

Since beta from Yahoo is lower than 1, we get a fairly low cost of equity capital. In fact, it's only 1.15 percent over ConAgra's cost of debt. Still, it makes sense, and whether you go with 7.95 or 10.25 percent is a judgment call.

TABLE 10.7 Equity Premium over the 10-Year Treasury Note for NASDAQ and S&P 500

	5 Year	6 Year	7 Year	8 Year	9 Year	10 Year
NASDAQ	4.89	4.45	4.24	4.08	3.89	3.66
S&P 500	0.70	0.43	0.26	0.26	0.23	0.20

Putting It Together

Once you've got the pieces, putting things together is easy. The formula for the weighted average cost of capital (WACC) is

$$WACC = w_d r_d (1 - \tau) + w_e r_e$$

where

$w =$ Weights for debt and equity

$\tau =$ Effective tax rate

If you've got preferred stock, you'd put a term in for the preferred also. We calculate the weights using enterprise value before subtracting cash. Since the interest payments on debt are tax deductible, the cost of debt is lowered by the tax break. Of course, if a company isn't paying taxes, the tax break doesn't mean much. Here are ConAgra's calculations using (1) the CAPM cost of equity and (2) the debt plus cost of equity.

(1) WACC = 0.21× 6.75%(1 − 0.20) + 0.79 × 7.95% = 7.4%

(2) WACC = 0.21× 6.75%(1 − 0.20) + 0.79 × 10.25% = 9.2%

That's a large difference in the cost of capital, but we've got an upper and lower bound. Based on the preparation that students have finished, they should have a general idea of how risky they feel the company is and what kind of return they require as an equity holder.

We've glossed over lots of details and many ways to estimate each component of WACC, but it all boils down to the central fact that WACC is an estimate that should be in a range that has a floor derived from Treasury securities. That's probably 7 percent for very low risk companies with some leverage to 20 percent plus for a very risky company, probably a start-up or one close to bankruptcy. Academics spend lots of time trying to come up with WACC, but a lot of subjective estimates go into each step. Sometimes it might be more productive to use something simple, such as 8 percent for low-risk companies, 10 percent for average-risk companies, and 12 to 15 percent for higher-risk companies.

That's too easy for some. We attended the annual R.I.S.E. (Redefining Investment Strategy Education) Symposium in Dayton, Ohio. It's a symposium for students involved in portfolio management classes. The symposium has lots of very interesting professional speakers and panels geared toward all aspects of investment management and the profession. In a panel discussion on valuation, one panel member mentioned that her firm used a subjective estimate for the cost of capital. The professors in the audience went wild. They spent the rest of the session lecturing the panel member on the CAPM and didn't she know that she didn't need subjectivity with the CAPM? They were in a frenzy.

I'm not sure how they would resolve the issue of beta estimates that are all over the map. The first case of the spring 2007 semester was Garmin. Almost all of the groups used the CAPM to estimate the cost of capital, but they picked their betas from different sources. The betas ranged from 1 to 1.4 and the WACCs ranged from 10 to 16 percent. Our Garmin mentor, Matt Taylor, told the class, "Make sure that your cost of capital passes the smell test." The higher WACCs didn't pass the smell test. One pseudoscientific way to resolve different estimates is to average everything together. That relieves average investors from thinking and coming up with their own point of view.

Later in this chapter we discuss how to solve for the return that the stock price implies. It's one more way to converge on the intrinsic value of a company. In this case, we'd evaluate whether the implied return is adequate based on our evaluation of the company.

Forecast Horizon

It turns out that the forecast horizon for cash flows is an important driver of the valuation, especially if a company has some type of competitive advantage that allows it to extract higher margins or extra sales. Over time some other companies may figure out how to duplicate that competitive advantage. That's when the margin will start to erode or sales growth will decline.

People have expected Garmin's margins to decrease as more players get into the global positioning system (GPS) business. Garmin's margins have declined, but those declines have been offset by an increase in volume in Garmin's retail segment. Margins in aviation have stayed high because no competitors are on the horizon in that part of the business. How long will high sales growth in the retail division and big margins in aviation last? That's part of the analysis of valuation. Students need to form an opinion based on management's competence and on how well the competition stacks up. The competitive analysis discussed in Chapter 8 provides the underpinnings. If a group thinks that the competitive advantage can last for a decade or more, then the pro forma should reflect that judgment.

It's easy to underestimate the life of a competitive advantage. Microsoft's advantage has lasted much longer than most people thought it would in the 1980s. It's also hard to build a pro forma that forecasts out for many years without some simplifying assumptions. It's okay to use a steady state margin or revenue growth after the first year or two. That could continue for 20 years before making assumptions about the "terminal value."

Terminal Value

We assume that firms don't have a finite life; that they'll continue to generate cash flow for an indefinite period. The terminal value is the shortcut for everything that happens after the explicit forecasts in the pro formas. The terminal value is the present value of a perpetuity.[4] The fewer years in the pro forma, the more important the terminal value is in the valuation.

Because terminal value can be such a big factor in any valuation model, it's important to make conservative estimates for it. There are two parts to the terminal value: the growth rate of the cash flows and the weighted average cost of capital. Since the WACC doesn't change, we'll just consider the continuation growth rate here.

When a company enters a steady state, we can assume that it will grow at the same rate or perhaps slightly lower than the economy. In the United States, the average growth in the economy has been around 3 percent, so lots of people use 3 percent as the steady state. Still, 3 percent is average, and not all industries have grown at the average rate. Some don't grow at all; some grow at 1 or 2 percent. Depending on the evaluation, any number from 0 to 3 percent can be appropriate.

Another method for finding the terminal value is to use a TEV/EBITDA multiple on the last year's EBITDA. We can also use that value to find what the equivalent implied growth rate is. That's a useful check to make sure that all the pieces fit together.

We'll show how to calculate a terminal value for ConAgra using both methods. In Chapter 9, we discussed the horizon for ConAgra's pro formas. Since ConAgra is in a very competitive industry, once it has increased its margins, we're implicitly assuming that it has reached its steady state with a 3 percent revenue growth and margins that are competitive in the industry.

In Chapter 9, ConAgra's pro forma free cash flow for 2010 was $1.42 billion. We assume that the continuing growth rate for free cash flow is 3 percent. Earlier we computed the cost of capital at 9.24 percent. Using those inputs, the terminal value is:

$$\frac{1.42\,(1 + .03)}{0.092 - .03} = \$23.484 \text{ billion}$$

---

[4] The appendix to this chapter has the formulas for the terminal value perpetuities.

Another way to look at this is using the TEV/EBITDA multiple. For that same year we estimated ConAgra's EBITDA at $2.41 billion. Using a conservative TEV/EBITDA of 10 gives us a terminal value of $24.141 billion. That's pretty close to the 3 percent growth rate; it's actually an implied 3.1 percent growth rate. We'll see that this doesn't make a difference in the final intrinsic value, but we can double-check using both ways to make sure we're in the right ball park.

Intrinsic Value

We've got all the pieces in place to find the intrinsic value. In Chapter 9 we calculated the free cash flows, and in this chapter we found the cost of capital and the terminal values. The implied enterprise value is the sum of the cash flows and terminal value discounted at the cost of capital. Since we want the equity value, we subtract debt. We didn't include cash in our free cash flows, so we add that in. Finally we divide by the number of shares to get the intrinsic value of a share of stock. Table 10.8 shows how this works for ConAgra using a discount rate of 9.2 percent. With these inputs our intrinsic share price is $39. The stock is selling at $26.25, a 32 percent discount to intrinsic value.

We can also use the current share price and solve for the discount rate. That will give us an implied return given our cash flow assumptions. We find that the implied weighted average cost of capital is 11.7 percent and the implied return for equity holders is 13 percent.

We can say the same thing in lots of ways. We can compare based on enterprise value, share price, or return to equity holders. They are equivalent ways of saying the same thing. As long as we focus on the important pieces—doing the preparation, nailing down an investment thesis, constructing the pro forma based on preparation, and understanding the company and the industry—the calculations will be minor details.

Sensitivity Analysis

What if we're wrong? We should also value the company to see what the downside is if we're wrong. For ConAgra the downside is that margins don't get up to the industry average. Where does that leave us? Table 10.9 shows a sensitivity analysis for two key inputs, the WACC and the operating margin in 2008. In the worst cast, the cost of capital is actually higher than we estimated, but the margin is lower. If margins are as low as 15 percent and the cost of capital is 10.5 percent, then the intrinsic value is about where the current shares are prices.

TABLE 10.8 ConAgra's Discounted Cash Flows and Intrinsic Value (in $millions except per share values)

	FY 07	FY 08	FY 09	FY 10	Terminal Value 1
Free Cash Flow	807	1,030	1,283	1,423	23,484
Discounted FCF	807	943	1,075	19,105	
	Intrinsic Value 1	**Intrinsic Value 2**			**Terminal Value 2**
Implied Enterprise Value	21,931	22,435			2,414
less Debt	3,457	3,457	EBITDA multiple		10
plus Cash	497	497			
					24,141
Implied Equity Value	18,971	19,475			
Shares outstanding	490	490			
P*	$38.72	$39.75			
Current Price	26.25	26.25			
Premium/discount	−32%	−34%			

TABLE 10.9   Sensitivity Analysis for ConAgra Intrinsic Value

		Cost of Capital		
		9.5%	10.0%	10.5%
Margin	15.0%	30.96	28.38	26.15
	16.0%	33.97	31.18	28.76
	17.0%	36.97	33.97	31.37

We probably feel more comfortable with the cost of capital numbers than the margin assumptions. The margin assumptions are more aggressive than conservative, so there is a bigger risk in not making the margin assumptions. That means as the company goes into 2008, we'll listen very carefully and focus on those numbers.

INVESTING IS DYNAMIC

You don't build a model, put it on the shelf, and forget about it. You build a model and constantly reexamine the inputs, the industry, and the market. Have Treasury rates changed? Then your cost of capital is changing. Has the company made new announcements? Time to update the pro forma. Is there an earnings release and a conference call? See how you did with your assumptions. Reevaluate and refine.

In May 2007 the APM class visited ConAgra headquarters in Omaha. Management's message was: This is a new company. Don't judge us on the past. The heads of the two major divisions, Consumer Foods and Commercial Products, made presentations, as did the head of Product Supply. The heads of Consumer Foods and Commercial Products have been with ConAgra for many years. The head of Product Supply was new. We also toured the trading floor and spoke with the director of trading operations. It can be easy to believe what you hear. You have to not be wooed but maintain objectivity. How can the company be new when the two main divisions are headed up by the same people? The key is the new chief executive pulling off the trick of getting the supply chain in place.

The APM students felt that it was a good bet. He may not pull it off, but we bought the stock and are willing to give him some time to see if he can work through everything that it will take to turn things around. We'll be watching every quarter to listen to the company's message and see if they make the progress we expect.

APPENDIX: DISCOUNTED CASH FLOW FORMULAS

The value of any asset is the present value of all future cash flows. Since a firm doesn't have a finite life, we assume that the value of a firm is perpetuity. There are three possibilities for the perpetuity: no growth, constant growth, nonconstant growth. We are interested in three variables: the discount rate, r; the cash flows, CF; and the growth rate for the cash flows, g. We will use V for the value. V_0 is the value today.

The simplest model is a no-growth model. We assume that the cash flow will remain the same in perpetuity. Real estate is often valued with this model. The equation is

$$V_0 = CF/r$$

The constant growth model assumes that cash flow will grow at a constant rate in perpetuity. The growth rate has to be smaller than the discount rate for this model to make sense. The equation is

$$V_0 = CF_1/(r - g)$$

We frequently use the constant growth model for the terminal value.

The nonconstant growth model is the most general model. (Any time someone uses a "general model," that means the most complicated but the most flexible.) A variation on this is the model that is used most often for discounted cash flow valuation:

$$V_0 = CF_1/(1 + r) + CF_2/(1 + r)^2 + CF_3/(1 + r)^3 \ldots$$

Since we can't practically forecast cash flow to infinity, we make the simplifying assumption that after some point, the cash flows will either disappear because of bankruptcy or grow at a constant rate. The adjusted model is

$$V_0 = \frac{CF_1}{(1 + r)} + \frac{CF_2}{(1 + r)^2} + \cdots + \frac{CF_n}{(1 + r)^n} + \frac{CF_n (1 + g)/(r - g)}{(1 + r)^n}$$

The last term is the discounted terminal value. To use this model, forecast cash flows over the appropriate time horizon, n. Then forecast the terminal growth rate.

Dividend Models

Dividend discount models are a special case of discounted cash flow models. Dividends are assumed to be the only cash flows to the equity holders.

For the dividend models, the discount rate is the cost of equity capital. The cash flows are the dividends per share, Div.

No Growth in Dividends

$$P_0^* = \frac{Div}{cost\ of\ equity, r_e}$$

Constant Growth in Dividends

$$P_0^* = \frac{Div_1}{r_e - g}$$

Problems with Dividend Discount Model   For most equity investors, capital appreciation is usually a more significant source of value than dividends. Many stocks do not pay dividends, or the dividends are not significant enough to make the dividend discount model (DDM) viable. Another problem with the DDM is that it does not account for share repurchases.

The DDM is useful for companies that pay significant a portion of earnings out as dividends. Master Limited Partnerships (MLPs) and Real Estate Investment Trusts (REITs) are required to pay approximately 90 percent of their earnings out as dividends in exchange for tax breaks. The DDM is a good model to use to value those firms.

Discounted Free Cash Flow Models

Here we summarize the steps for a discounted cash flow (DCF) model. Compare total enterprise value (TEV) to an intrinsic total enterprise value (TEV*) that is calculated based on pro forma income statements and the discounted value of forecasts of free cash flow:

1. Find TEV. Add market capitalization, long-term debt, preferred stock; subtract cash and marketable securities.
2. Find TEV*. Forecast revenue, EBITDA, and free cash flow (FCF) by forecasting pro forma income statements. The model for TEV* is:

$$TEV_0^* = \frac{FCF_1}{(1 + WACC)^1} + \frac{FCF_2}{(1 + WACC)^2} + \cdots + \frac{FCF_n}{(1 + WACC)^n}$$
$$+ Terminal\ Value$$

FCF is calculated as:

$$Free\ Cash\ Flow = EBITDA - \Delta\ Working\ Capital$$
$$- Capital\ Expenditures - Taxes$$

3. Calculate the intrinsic share price from TEV*

$$P^* = \frac{(TEV^* - Debt + Cash)}{Shares\ Outstanding}$$

Terminal Value Terminal value can be estimated as the present value of a constant growth perpetuity or using a TEV/EBITDA multiple. The first model is:

$$Terminal\ Value_n = \frac{FCF_n(1+g)}{WACC - g}$$
$$Terminal\ Value_0 = \frac{FCF_n(1+g)}{WACC - g} \Big/ (1 + WACC)^n$$

The second way is

$$Terminal\ Value_n = EBITDA_n \times \frac{TEV}{EBITDA}$$

Three

Class Specials

In this part we provide examples of the companies and issues that we tackle in class. Once students get up to speed and have learned how to research and write the cases, the real fun begins: finding new ideas and evaluating our current holdings. Several themes have emerged over the last few years in our investments. Those themes are the topic of this final section.

In Chapter 11 we discuss China and Chinese investments. Currently, almost 17 percent of the APM portfolio is invested in Chinese stocks. Although they've been a mainstay of our portfolio for many years, China and Chinese investments are commonly misunderstood. We have another 10 percent of our portfolio in other international stocks, for a total of 27 percent of the portfolio in non-U.S. companies. In Chapter 12 we discuss other international investments, including the world energy markets. Another theme in the portfolio is our investment with local companies. We address local investing and possible biases in Chapter 13.

In Chapter 14 we switch away from location themes to corporate governance. Class members have been corporate activists in several semesters. They engaged in letter-writing campaigns to boards and corporate officers to urge them to institute changes that would benefit shareholders.

Chapter 15 recaps the performance of the recent classes. We also review the contribution of the teaching assistants and, most especially, the speakers. All of these individuals have worked together to build a powerful information network for the class.

CHAPTER 11

Investing in China

The APM class has been investing in China since 1994. Kent was one of the first big U.S. investors in China during his years at Goldman. When he came to teach at the University of Kansas, he introduced the class to a very different way of thinking about that country. Investors are just now starting to realize that a Chinese communist government doesn't preclude the possibility of thriving market economy.

China's economy is unlike that of the former Soviet Union. Communism and a market economy may seem like a contradiction, but it's probably because we in the United States typically think of Soviet-style communism. At the end of the Cultural Revolution in the 1970s, China began experimenting with different approaches to expand the economy. In the early 1980s Deng Xiaoping went to the city of Shenzhen in Guangzhou Province in southern China. He declared: "To get rich is glorious." That speech and the establishment of special economic zones unleashed an entrepreneurial zeal that has always been present in the Chinese people. What began as a trickle of markets far from Beijing is now a flood of free markets over much of the country. The unleashing of the market economy has made China the manufacturing center of the world. U.S. companies are the largest group of foreign direct investors in China.

It's not surprising that China's market economy reemerged in the southern part of the country. Shenzhen is just up the Pearl River from Hong Kong, one of the world's largest trading economies. Guangzhou is the area that the Qing dynasty set aside for as the only area foreign traders were allowed to visit in the seventeenth century. There foreigners could set up warehouses for their goods, and government-appointed Chinese emissaries would buy and sell foreign goods. Now Shenzhen is the home of the China's newest stock exchange.

Hong Kong was ceded back to the China in 1997. Hong Kong's addition to China has provided special economic and financial benefits to the country. Hong Kong and the Guangdong (Canton) region have been a major trading and financial center since the Tang dynasty in tenth century. Hong Kong is one of the top three or four world financial centers. While China has a thriving market economy, Hong Kong is really the only well-developed financial center in the country.

In this chapter we provide a brief overview of the Chinese financial system and discuss this dichotomy. Then we briefly discuss the different stock markets before we discuss APM's investment strategy in China. We provide an extended example of a food processor called China Green.

FINANCIAL SYSTEMS IN CHINA

A well-functioning financial system efficiently allocates capital from capital providers to those that will provide the highest return on that capital. Equity markets are only one part of a financial system. Traditionally, equity markets have been the last piece to be added in a financial system. Traditional sources of capital for entrepreneurs begin with friends and family. Governments are the next piece that have arisen historically as capital providers (think of Queen Isabella and Christopher Columbus), followed by banks and commodity markets. Public debt markets started before equity markets.

Financial systems have to have good information to make good capital allocation decisions. Friends and families know who's hardworking, honest, and smart. When the technologies are in place to spread that type of information to a larger group of people, financial systems have a broader range of options, financial markets get deeper and more efficient, and money flows more freely.

In addition to the initial capital allocation decision, capital providers monitor their investments to make sure that they get repaid. Family and friends can make it hard on deadbeats, and relatives generally don't like to leave their loved ones in the lurch. Governments have lots of ways to make life difficult for deadbeats, and they have lots of ways to keep tabs on those to whom they lent money. Modern bankers monitor their loans using financial statements. They usually require periodic payments. In the United States and other well-developed financial systems, credit reporting and monitoring systems are well established. People or companies that don't pay have a hard time getting capital from any other source. The final resort for banks in the United States and countries that are part of the Organisation for Economic Co-operation and Development (OECD) is the judicial system. Public debt investors rely on credit rating agencies that provide information about the probability of getting repaid and on the legal system as a last resort. Public equity holders rely on "efficient markets," analysts, their own research based on audited financial statements, and again, the legal system. It's easiest for equity holders to vote with their feet and sell their shares, if they sense any problems.

In China the two primary sources of capital have been the government and friends and family. Some of the first publicly traded non-SOE (state-owned enterprises) companies evolved from village or township enterprises, funded by pooling local resources. The other large economic institutions in the late twentieth century were the SOEs. That's family, friends, and government funding. We'd expect that banks would be the next evolutionary step, if China is to proceed as other financial systems have.

Big Four Chinese Banks

Until very recently all banks in China were SOEs. Not only were they SOEs, but they weren't run as traditional banks. They were run as government transfer agencies. As a transfer agency they were primarily responsible for transferring central government funds to economic development projects or industrial SOEs around China. About 88 percent of official Chinese financial assets are held in this banking system. In the United States, banks hold only about a quarter of financial assets. In China, however, the traditional source of capital for SOEs has been one of the four national banks: Agricultural Bank of China (ABC), Bank of China (BOC), China Construction Bank (CCB), and Industrial and Commercial Bank of China (ICBC). In addition to funding large projects, these "Big Four" also fund many small "loans" to rural areas.

Traditionally the Big Four have not relied on creditworthiness as a means to allocate capital. Instead they have allocated capital based on social and developmental needs. Nor have the Chinese banks provided the same type of monitoring that is in the United States and other developed economies. In many ways Chinese banks are not functioning like banks; rather they are functioning like wealth transfer mechanisms and development tools. If we think of these banks as subsidy programs instead of financial institutions, then their financial performance isn't quite so dismal.

Figure 11.1 shows the percentage of nonperforming loans from several different world banks. The bottom four are China's national banks.

In early 2004 the BOC and CCB were recapitalized in anticipation of their initial public offerings. They had been recapitalized several times before, but this time may be different. New managers have come in, and there has been an attempt to institute state-of-the-art lending practices. In the past, the lending rate was set by the central bank. In 2004 the banks

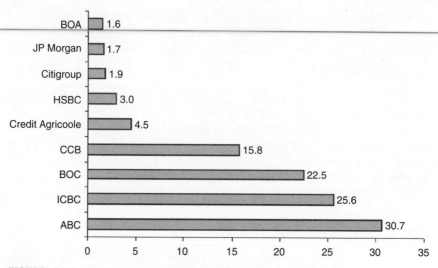

FIGURE 11.1 Percentage of Nonperforming Loans in 2002
Source: Dr. Ziyun He, presentation at the School of Finance and Banking,
University of International Business and Economics, Beijing, 2005

could charge from 0.9 to 1.7 times benchmark rates set by the central bank.
Now there is an attempt to let rates charged to borrowers reflect their risk
profile. Profitability incentives also have been instituted. Still, there is a lot
of risk involved in transforming these wealth transfer agencies into modern
financial institutions. Management has hired armies of top consultants and
academics from premier institutions to advise on the process. The biggest
problem is not with senior management's understanding how to run a financial institution but in building the financial infrastructure needed to make
the necessary changes.

One big change that needs to happen to make the financial system work
better is to transition from a primarily relationship-based credit system to
a data-driven system. Credit reporting agencies and better mechanisms to
judge risk quickly across a large population will allow banks to make better
credit allocation decisions. When the APM students visited China in 2005,
several recognized the business opportunity of a credit reporting agency.
Information isn't aggregated and disseminated or as easily available in China
as in many other countries.

Although credit scoring and credit information systems are limited in
China, the biggest obstacle may be retraining the scores of middle managers
who worked under the old system. It's hard to erase decades of inertia in a

TABLE 11.1   Big Four Banks IPO 2004 Schedule and Actual IPO

Bank	2004 IPO Timetable	Actual IPO
CCB	2004	Oct. 2005
BOC	2005	May 2006
ICBC	2006	Oct. 2006
ABC	2007	Has not occurred. 2012 latest estimate

short time. Still, the Chinese may be more capable than others of taking on such an undertaking.

The bank IPOs were late getting started. It wasn't until 2005 that the first of these IPOs occurred. In October 2005 CCB raised approximately $9.4 billion in its offering. BOC went public in May 2006 and raised somewhere between $9.7 and $11 billion. Both IPOs were significantly oversubscribed. Table 11.1 shows the initially scheduled IPOs for the Big Four and the dates that they actually IPOed. They were about a year off the schedule, except for ABC, which has been postponed for quite a while.

RAISING EQUITY IN CHINA

China has three stock exchanges: Shanghai (SSE), Shenzhen (SzSE), and Hong Kong (HKSE). Hong Kong's stock market is much older and very different from the other two. Well-functioning stock exchanges usually are preceded by well-functioning banks and other parts of the financial system. Banks provide capital for firms to expand, but they also provide a monitoring service that is useful for investors. A company that has been capitalized with bank loans has been reviewed and vetted by any number of bankers to make sure it will be able to repay loans. When that company raises money in the equity market, many times it's the company's bankers who want to get in and get a piece of the equity action. Even if they aren't equity investors, they still don't want a bankruptcy. Even if they are repaid and recover every penny of interest owed to them, it's much better to have a customer who is expanding and needs working capital and additional bank services.

Hong Kong has been a world banking center for centuries, so it's not unexpected that the city's equity market is also one of the most vibrant in the world. That market has always ranked as having the highest degree of shareholder protection. The World Bank rankings rate countries based on

TABLE 11.2 Top 10 Rankings for Investor Protection

Region or Economy	Rank	Disclosure Index	Director Liability Index	Shareholder Suits Index	Investor Protection Index
New Zealand	1	10	9	10	9.7
Singapore	2	10	9	9	9.3
Hong Kong	3	10	8	9	9
Malaysia	4	10	9	7	8.7
Canada	5	8	9	8	8.3
Ireland	6	10	6	9	8.3
Israel	7	7	9	9	8.3
United States	8	7	9	9	8.3
South Africa	9	8	8	8	8
UK	9	10	7	7	8
China	83	10	1	4	5

Source: World Bank and IFC Doing Business Web site, www.doingbusiness.org/ExploreTopics/ProtectingInvestors/

the strength of the measures that protect "against misuse of corporate assets by directors for their personal gain." They look at

- Transparency of transactions (Extent of Disclosure Index)
- Liability for self-dealing (Extent of Director Liability Index)
- Shareholders' ability to sue officers and directors for misconduct (Ease of Shareholder Suit Index)
- Strength of Investor Protection Index (the average of the three indexes)[1]

Table 11.2 shows the top 10 markets ranked in terms of the Investor Protection Index plus China. The World Bank ranks 174 world markets. Hong Kong is ranked number 3, ahead of the United States, which is ranked number 8. China is ranked number 83, slightly below the median ranking. The lowest-ranked countries are Afghanistan at 173 and Mauritania at 174.

China is tied for eighty-third with these countries: Armenia, Bosnia/Herzegovina, Comoros, Congo, Czech Republic, Equatorial Guinea, Germany, Iceland, Italy, Lebanon, Macedonia, Mozambique, Nicaragua, Spain, and Uruguay.

---

[1] *Source:* www.doingbusiness.org/ExploreTopics/ProtectingInvestors/.

The reputation for maintaining a well-run and investor-friendly stock exchanges attracts companies wanting to list on reputable exchanges. Companies typically can raise more money and receive a higher valuation if they are considered to be following shareholder-friendly practices. Many Chinese companies that aren't state-owned enterprises have issued shares in Hong Kong. They trade there instead of on the Shanghai and Shenzhen stock exchanges.

Other Chinese companies have listed directly on NASDAQ and other U.S. stock exchanges. In 1999 a Chinese Internet company called chinadotcom was one of the first Chinese companies to list directly on NASDAQ. Many people are surprised when they realize that quite a few Chinese companies are listed in the United States. The surprise comes from two sources. They are surprised that a communist government would let companies list outside China and think that companies are closely controlled by the government. The second surprise is that the shares that are traded aren't ADRs (American Depository Receipts) or ADSs (American Depository Shares).

Most foreign companies listed on U.S. exchanges are listed as ADRs. They have a primary exchange in their home country, and a large money-center bank converts the shares to dollars and bundles them to trade in the United States. Reporting requirements for ADRs depend on whether they are sponsored or nonsponsored. Nonsponsored ADRs don't have to file with the Securities and Exchange Commission (SEC) because the company doesn't have any official role in the ADR. Usually nonsponsored ADRs trade on the Pink Sheets or bulletin board services. Sponsored ADRs and foreign companies listed on U.S. exchanges have to file reports with the SEC. If they don't have any place of business in the United States, they file annual 20-F reports instead of 10-Ks. They do not have to file 10-Qs, although many voluntarily do file quarterly reports. They also have to follow the Sarbanes-Oxley reporting provisions.

Chinese companies that trade in the United States typically have much higher price/earnings (P/E) ratios than those that trade only in China or Hong Kong. Why? There are quite a few reasons. First, it's not easy for an individual U.S. investor to trade Hong Kong or Chinese shares. Many U.S brokers won't bother with foreign markets. If they do, they usually work with London and perhaps a few other western European or Japan or Canada exchanges. It's a hassle for brokers to deal with foreign exchanges. Usually there aren't a lot of customers banging down the doors to make those investments, so why bother? This fact is a significant barrier to individual investors who want to invest in markets outside the United States. The gray market (described in the box) is the only way for many investors to enter foreign markets, but the lack of regulation is troubling.

GRAY MARKETS

Another type of listing that confuses investors is the gray market listing. This listing has nothing to do with the company. It is a tracking symbol that U.S. brokers use to make a market in a foreign security. Sometimes it is more convenient for U.S. brokers to trade a foreign security in dollars among themselves than to put trades through on the security's home exchange. Gray market quotes are picked up by the Pink Sheets or the OTC Bulletin Board (OTCBB). The Pink Sheets and the OTCBB are central quote services that collect and publish quotes from market makers for a variety of securities that are not listed on exchanges. They are called over-the-counter securities. Neither service is a member of the National Association of Securities Dealers (NASD), the main regulatory body for most brokers, nor are they regulated by the SEC.

The gray market is a collection of securities that aren't listed, traded, or quoted on any stock exchange, the OTCBB, or the Pink Sheets. These trades are reported by brokers to self-regulatory organizations (SROs), and the SRO distributes the data to the data vendors and financial Web sites. Investors can see a price and a volume number, but since the numbers are reported and compiled only once a day, they can't be relied on as trading guides. Since other OTC securities are not traded or quoted on an exchange or in a broker's quotation system, bids and offers are not collected in a central spot. There may be a bid outstanding but no offer.

High, low, close, and volume numbers for gray market quotes are posted to the public only after the close of the market each day. Individual trades are never published. There isn't any regulatory requirement to withhold or to post this information; rather it is just a voluntary practice. There are no regulations by the SEC governing these trades.

Many of the Hong Kong stocks that U.S. shareholders want to own are available on the gray market. You can tell when you are trading a foreign gray market tracking symbol because its symbol has five letters and ends in the letter "F." For example, the APM class bought China Green on the Hong Kong exchange in 2004. The ticker symbol in Hong Kong is the number 0904 since ticker symbols in Hong Kong are always numbers. When we trade now, our broker is likely to use the gray market, where the symbol is CIGEF.

We keep track of the difference in prices when the Pink Sheets are updated around 5:00 p.m. central time daily. The Hong Kong market closes at 2:00 a.m. central, so we usually can predict whether the gray market quote at the end of the same day will be higher or lower when it is published. Usually there is about a 2 cent difference between the gray market quote and the HK close, which reflects the additional charge to trade directly overseas. Most online brokers use gray market quotes and usually won't place direct orders in the home country.

The table shows tickers and quotes in both markets for three Chinese stocks listed in Hong Kong.

Comparison of Gray Market Quotes and HK Close on July 12, 2007

	HK Ticker	Gray Market Ticker	HK Close $USD	Gray Market Quote
China Green	0904	CIGEF	0.91	0.89
Golden Meditech	8180	GMDTF	0.51	0.54
Launch Tech	8196	LHTCF	0.23	0.22

We in APM are lucky to have A. G. Edwards as our stockbroker. A. G. Edwards has got to be the most customer-friendly stockbroker in the nation. Whenever we have a question about a trade, want to get something quickly or get special reports, they're totally helpful. Our stockbroker is Al Simmons in Kansas City. He's the best. The account was originally set up with Al and Gene Diederich. Gene was in the first APM class and was Kent's fraternity brother at KU. Gene is now at the A. G. Edwards headquarters in St. Louis. The class has visited the headquarters several times for tours of the trading floors. We've talked to the traders at the foreign desk who handle our orders. It's a great group of people, and it's been a boon to the APM class when we switched our accounts there in 2002. We digress; back to other reasons why P/E ratios are different depending on trading venue.

Probably the biggest reason that the P/E ratios are higher for Chinese companies traded in the United States is that investors think the company has been given a de facto seal of approval. If Chinese companies are trading here, they must be financially strong, well-managed, good companies, or else they wouldn't be approved to trade in the this country. In fact, however, while there are listing requirements for NASDAQ and other U.S. exchanges, those requirements are actually less stringent than the listing requirements in Hong Kong and in China. There, to get listed, you actually have to have a history of revenue and profits. That isn't the case in the United States. Plenty of U.S.-traded companies have never had a profit; some don't have revenue yet.

The biggest difference between the companies traded in the United States and those traded in China may be the financial market sophistication of management. That doesn't mean that the Chinese management team isn't as good or the business itself isn't as good. It does mean that perhaps management doesn't have the foreign contacts or other resources to navigate the U.S. legal and regulatory maze. Perhaps they don't want to spend the money. It is cheaper to list in China and Hong Kong.

Table 11.3 shows that the Chinese exchanges are still very small compared to many of the world's stock markets. Together Shanghai and Shenzhen are only about half as big as Hong Kong in terms of total market value. Hong Kong is only 15 percent of the London Stock Exchange and 4 percent of the New York Stock Exchange (NYSE). Despite the smaller size in terms of share volume, the average daily value traded in terms of dollars and shares is quite high. It's higher than London and 35 percent of the value traded on the NYSE. What really stands out in the Chinese markets is the annual turnover of almost 800 percent and 500 percent in Shenzhen and Shanghai, respectively. Someone is doing a lot of trading in the stocks that are available on the Chinese markets! Each share is getting traded multiple times per year. Not a lot of buy-and-hold people are investing in China.

China's Shanghai and Shenzhen exchanges traditionally have been the home of the publicly traded state-owned enterprises. The SOEs may be large companies in terms of employees or revenue, but the number of available shares to trade can be extremely limited. Many of the shares were either owned by the state or by employees who had been given bonus grants of shares. In some shares the free float is pretty limited. That means the shares that are available are in high demand.

COMPANY EXAMPLE: CHINA GREEN

China Green began largely as a producer of fresh fruits and vegetables for the highly selective Japanese market, supplying fresh produce from its cultivation base in Fujian during the Japanese winter. Japanese produce consumers are notoriously picky. They demand the highest quality in the world for their fruits and vegetables. The appearance and taste have to be unblemished. China Green's longstanding relationship is a testament to its operational excellence and technological advancement. From this base, it

TABLE 11.3 World Stock Exchange 2004 Comparative Statistics

	Shenzhen	Shanghai	Total China	Hong Kong	NASDAQ	NYSE	London	Frankfurt
Total market value (billions $US)	133	313	446	869	3,703	20,000	6,055	1,053
Total trade value 2004 (billions $US)	197	926	1,123	516	8,800	10,787	2,300	1,033
Average daily trade value billions $US)	8	5	13	16	35	46	9	4
Average daily share volume (millions of shares)	1,053	1,485	2,538	16,000	1,800	1,460	3,496	n/a
Annual turnover	792%	474%		59%	238%	54%	38%	98%
Listed securities	536	966	1,502	1,096	3,250	2,800	2,916	5,390

has expanded to domestic sales in China (now over half its revenues) as well as other Asian markets. It also has expanded its product line to include a broader range of food and beverage products. The core cultivation business remains a very profitable and growing source of cash flow. The company has been classified by both the buy- and sell-side analysts as a boring agricultural producer. That misclassification led to a big undervaluation.

We bought China Green for three reasons:

1. The stock was fundamentally cheap.
2. The company's growth potential was underestimated by the market.
3. The company was misunderstood and misclassified.

Figure 11.2 shows China Green price since 2004 when APM initiated its position in July. We bought 12,000 shares at an average price of 1.64 HKD(Hong Kong dollars) or 21 cents U.S. We added 170,000 shares to our position in the fall of 2004 through January prices of around 1.80 HKD. In May 2007 we sold 102,000 at an average price of 6.80 HKD for a realized annual compound rate of return of 35 percent.

Fundamentally Cheap

The primary reason that China Green traded at a cheap P/E ratio (a P/E of approximately 3.5× when adjusted for significant cash in mid-2004) and still trades well below the market multiple today is that it is classified as an agricultural stock. Although the company is in the food business, the details of the business aren't well understood, and most analysts, especially in 2004, overlooked some critical facts. The company is highly profitable with gross margins well over 50 percent. It has an attractive working capital position. There is no inventory risk. Its inventory is mostly seeds, and they are planted only when the product is presold. Chinese buyers pay cash on delivery. There is the usual agriculture risk of bad weather, but the company has several geographically unrelated growing areas in China that have usually moderate weather. Another reason for its strong working capital position is that it is not capital intensive. Cultivation bases are leased so the amount of capital needed is limited. Land costs are variable costs, not the capital costs of most agricultural growers. Finally, China Green generates a lot of free cash flow, all of which has been reinvested to take advantage of growth opportunities. The result has been top-line growth in excess of 40 percent and bottom-line growth almost as high. Table 11.4 shows China Green's historical and pro forma income and free cash flows.

The valuation discount was also caused by the lack of sell-side analyst coverage or institutional sponsorship. There isn't a lot of news in the United

TABLE 11.4 China Green Income Statement and Free Cash Flows

Year	2003	2004	2005	2006	2007E	2008E	2009E	2010E	2011E
Sales	258.5	375.4	470.5	686.6	947.5	1,279.1	1,707.7	2,266.1	2,606.0
Sales growth		45%	25%	46%	38%	35%	34%	33%	15%
Gross profit	161.1	210.2	254.5	354.4	480.4	662.6	891.4	1,189.7	1,303.0
Gross margin	62%	56%	54%	52%	51%	52%	52%	53%	50%
Selling & administrative expense	26.8	37.9	58.0	103.8	151.6	191.9	256.1	339.9	397.4
Operating profit	132.8	184.1	207.7	268.0	354.5	466.6	629.8	842.5	897.2
Operating margin	51%	49%	44%	39%	37%	36%	37%	37%	34%
Net interest	–	–	0.0	5.7	(4.7)	12.8	17.1	22.7	26.1
Taxes	15.8	33.5	24.4	(9.0)	–	23.3	75.6	101.1	107.7
Net income	117.0	150.6	183.3	271.3	359.3	430.5	537.1	718.8	763.5
Growth in net income		29%	22%	48%	32%	20%	25%	34%	6%
Operating profit	132.8	184.1	207.7	268.0	354.5	466.6	629.8	842.5	897.2
Depreciation	15.6	23.1	33.6	53.1	77.3	109.5	147.7	190.2	222.2
EBITDA	148.4	207.2	241.3	321.1	431.9	576.1	777.5	1032.7	1119.4
Less Δ working capital	27.8	25.9	15.6	-32.2	17.4	44.8	59.8	79.3	91.2
Less capital expenditures	85.5	62.3	185.1	257.1	249.5	288.6	374.3	485.9	553.9
Free cash flow	35.1	119.0	40.6	96.3	164.9	242.8	343.5	467.5	474.3
Growth in cash flow		239%	-66%	137%	71%	47%	41%	36%	1%

States or even in Hong Kong about China Green. The news flow is still mostly limited to interim and annual results releases. This is evident by the stock's trading pattern; it is range bound for long periods of time and then trades up fairly rapidly when the company releases results showing continued strong growth and profitability. The consistency of results and management's execution on expansion has helped to draw attention to China Green. JP Morgan initiated coverage in the spring of 2007 with a buy rating and a target price of HK$7.55.

A few analysts have come to some of the same conclusions as us about the potential of this stock. As a result of this new spotlight on China Green, the share price surged in February 2007. Four Asia-based analysts currently provide coverage. We are just starting to enjoy the rewards of being early into a stock that was overlooked and underestimated. Despite strong returns in 2007, we still believe that China Green is undervalued due to the next two factors.

Underestimated Growth Potential

China Green was viewed by most investment professionals as a boring business for a couple of key reasons:

1. Agriculture was not seen as a growth industry.
2. Gross margins of more than 50 percent and operating margins exceeding 30 percent were unsustainable in their view.

While the agricultural sector in China may not be growing very fast, that isn't true for the China Green's growth prospects. China Green is able to capitalize on the fragmented and inefficient methods used in farming in China. The company has aggregated large plots of land under long-term leases. This is a relatively new development in China; only a few commercial farms employ modern farming techniques. Small subsistence farmers with low productivity dominate the rural economy. It will take a long time for this situation to change due to the sheer number of people still living off the land in China and the socioeconomic implications of such dramatic shift in the lives of most of the population.

China Green, as well as its commercial competitors, will be able to increase land under cultivation at a rapid rate while still remaining a small portion of the agricultural economy. These companies do not compete with each other but rather with small, inefficient farmers. That said, the barriers to commercial competition are actually higher than they might seem. Relatively few Chinese companies have the local expertise and capital to acquire land under long-term leases or the ability to manage such an undertaking in an efficient manner. China Green is also able to find incremental profits by increasing the efficiency of its distribution channel. These are all critical factors in the growth and sustainability of the China Green business model.

But China Green has gone even further to accelerate growth and create additional competitive advantage. Specifically, it has moved downstream into processed and packaged foods. It started off with rice products and canned vegetables and is expanding into noodles and beverages. This vertical integration has multiple positive implications. Through additional product channels China Green can increase its cultivation area and actually use more of the end product. (For example, some slightly damaged produce may not be able to be sold as fresh but can be used in processed products.) China Green is also in the early stages of building house brands, particularly focused on rice, noodle, and beverage products. This is a new and exciting phenomenon in China and one that will create lasting franchise value (and ensuing profits) for companies successful in building brand recognition and loyalty. Based on early indications, China Green is succeeding.

Given that background, we expect China Green to achieve sales growth of almost 40 percent for the fiscal year ending April 2007. Due to the company's high free cash flow, we expect growth to continue at a high level while maintaining excellent margins. Even with recent strong stock price performance, the stock trades under 11 times forward earnings and less than 9 times when adjusted for the significant cash on the balance sheet. The valuation is still very cheap on an absolute basis and even more so when compared to the company's growth rate.

Table 11.5 shows the enterprise value calculations and the valuation statistics based on the pro forma numbers from the Table 11.4.

Misunderstood and Erroneously Categorized

The market views and values China Green as an agricultural company. Both the view and the valuation are wrong. First, China Green is not just an ordinary agricultural company; it actually is a "green" agricultural company. This label is not a hollow one. The company works hard to grow its produce using environmentally acceptable methods, and its long-term relationship with Japanese buyers helps the company succeed at this. The produce is not "organic" in the purest sense of the term. However, they are of high quality and produced in a manner that would meet environmentalists' approval. Worldwide there is a growing premium on and demand in the market for companies that are "green." The growth of supermarkets like Whole Foods and the increasing sales of organic produce in stores like Wal-Mart are examples in the United States. The increasingly sophisticated and health/environmentally conscious Chinese consumer is not far behind

TABLE 11.5   Enterprise Value Calculations for China Green

Equity value (HK$)

Shares outstanding	735.0
Convertible debt shares	118.6
Diluted shares outstanding	853.7
Stock price: April 2007	7.3
Market cap	5,329.0
Adjusted market cap (assuming conversion)	6,189.2
Balance sheet data (RMB) as of 4/30/06 FYE	
Bank balances and cash	852.9
Convertible bonds (book value)	310.8
Net debt (debt − cash)	(542.1)

	HKD	USD
Market cap	6,189.2	793.5
Total enterprise value (assuming conversion)	5,310.3	680.8

Valuation Statistics

	2007E	2008E	2009E	2010E	2011E
TEV/Sales	5.6	4.2	3.1	2.3	2.0
TEV/EBITDA	15.0	11.4	8.4	6.3	5.9
TEV/FCF	32.2	21.9	15.5	11.4	11.2
P/E (cash-adjusted)	14.8	12.3	9.9	7.4	7.0
P/E	16.7	14.0	11.2	8.4	7.9

this curve. So far analysts and investors have not classified China Green among the "green" companies. Should investors realize that this company is one, demand will surely increase, and the stock is likely to command a premium over regular agricultural stocks. But then again, we have already made the argument that being an agricultural company in China can be very profitable for a very long time. Being green will be more of a good thing.

Second, the company is evolving toward being a food and beverage company. China Green now derives a significant portion of revenues from processed foods and beverages under its own brand names. A recent JP Morgan report acknowledges this evolution, yet its target price indicates that it values China Green as a low-growth agricultural stock. Branded food and beverage companies in China, however, are seen as "consumer plays" and trade at an average P/E of 35× consensus forward estimates.

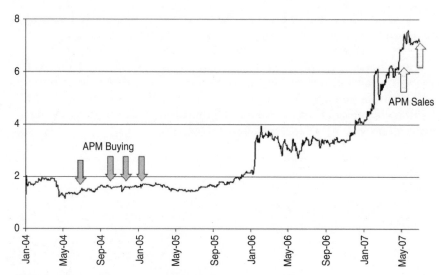

FIGURE 11.2 China Green Stock Price in $HK, 2004–2007

China Green deserves a multiple in line with its true peers, especially given the evolution of its business and high growth rates. But any expansion in valuation multiple when combined with earnings growth of 35 percent or more will lead to continued strong performance in the stock price.

WRAPPING UP

Clearly it's hard to do justice to the topic of "investing in China" in one chapter. During the summer of 2004 APM students visited China with Cathy, stopping at several branches and headquarters of our holdings. We also visited U.S. and other multinational companies and government ministries in the country. The students came away with a totally new view of investing in China. Most had been a little skeptical, but after their visit they realized that China was the fastest-growing economy in the world and likely would remain so for a long time. They realized that the government isn't the monolith that it seems when viewed from afar. The government couldn't and wouldn't suddenly shut down the economic engine fueling the country's rapid push to modernization. The Chinese government can be very supportive of private enterprise, as long as companies do not stray into sensitive political areas. China still needs to address many issues, including consumer protection, pollution, and intellectual property rights.

U.S. investors tend to focus on the negatives coming out of China and to downplay the tremendous opportunities. However, now that the Chinese markets have risen stratospherically, analysts, portfolio managers, the media, and investors are jumping on the bandwagon. The rides probably won't be over for a while, but picking the right companies will be more important than ever. Large state-owned enterprises aren't going to be the most profitable companies in China. Smaller, well-managed, underrecognized companies will provide better investment opportunities.

CHAPTER 12

It's a Big World (After All)

Some investors argue that you can be internationally diversified just by investing in U.S. companies since they derive a large portion of their profits from the rest of the world. Since the end of 2003, both the Standard & Poor's (S&P) World Index and the S&P Emerging Market Index have outperformed the U.S. market (see Figure 12.1). The compound annual rate of return in emerging markets has been 13 percent since the beginning of 2000 compared to 4 percent for the United States and 6 percent for the world. The rate of return on the China index since 2000 is 30 percent. While it's probably possible to earn the same return in the United States by picking the right stocks, why not just go with the best world stocks?

In this chapter we review a couple of prominent world trends that have played an important role in this decade's returns: energy and commodities. In this decade a large portion of the world, especially in Asia, has seen big increases in their standard of living. With those increases has come strong demand for goods and strong energy demands. Oil reserves and discoveries aren't increasing as rapidly as the demand, so oil prices have risen dramatically. With increased manufacturing to supply the new world middle class, other commodities such as steel, copper, zinc, aluminum, and many others used in manufacturing are booming, too.

Students and speakers in class have recognized these trends. Since 2003 the class has had a good percentage of its assets invested in energy and ancillary companies. It has bought several international companies based partly on these trends, but also because the companies were good solid ones and good values. In this chapter we feature one of our long-term holdings, Internacional de Ceramica, a Mexican tile company. Interceramic traded in the United States as an American Depository Receipts (ADR), but after the Sarbanes-Oxley Act of 2002, the company delisted and now trades solely in Mexico. It flies under the radar most of the time, but "smart" money has invested heavily.

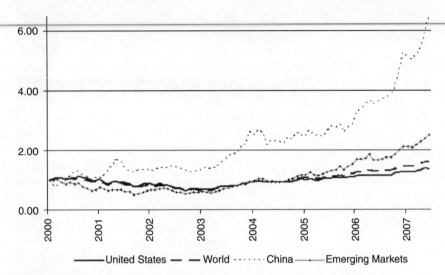

FIGURE 12.1   U.S., World, and Emerging Market Returns, 2000–2007

We also take a quick look at the world oil and gas market and focus on refining capacity. Most of the oil and gas companies that we've bought are American, but they fit into a global trend so we discuss them in this chapter. We feature Valero (VLO), but we also mention Plains Exploration and Production (PXP), Quicksilver Resources (KWK), Companhia Vale do Rio Doce (RIO), Diageo (DEO), and Yanzhou Coal Mining (YZC).

INTERCERAMIC

Internacional de Ceramica is one of the largest North American manufacturer of ceramic tiles. It has manufacturing plants in Mexico and in Garland, Texas. It started operating in 1979 with a plant in Chihuahua and opened the Garland plant in 1995. The company has traded on the Mexican Stock Exchange, the Bolsa de Valores, since 1987. In December 1994 Interceramic listed an ADR on the New York Stock Exchange (NYSE). It started trading in the United States at $21.73. Almost immediately after the listing the Mexican peso was devalued. To make matters worse, the company had financed its Garland plant earlier that year in U.S. dollars. Half of the operating revenue was in the devalued pesos.

In 1994, total long-term debt increased from $92 million U.S. equivalent to $179 million. Most of that increase was $118 million in dollar-denominated loans. The kicker was the revaluation of the Mexican peso, which went from 3.1 \$/MXN in 1993 and most of 1994 to 5.2 virtually overnight at the end of 1994. The currency revaluation hurt Interceramic because of debt payments, but it also caused big disruptions in the Mexican economy. Of course, the U.S. investing public was spooked. Investors weren't going to touch a highly levered Mexican company under these conditions.

As it turned out, the Mexican recession lasted only about 10 months. The country was helped by a U.S. bailout and the beginning of the North American Free Trade Agreement (NAFTA). Between 1995 and 1997 sales increased over 50 percent each year. Sales weren't a big problem; expenses, especially interest expense, were shooting through the roof. In 1994 and 1995 the company lost money and had trouble paying on its debt. What did the class see in a troubled Mexican tile company?

First, hard times don't last forever. Hard times present buying opportunities. Mexicans buy a lot of tile, and Interceramic was firmly entrenched as one of the largest producers in Mexico with a good sales network and factories. The company had begun expanding more rapidly in the United States, especially in the Southwest, where big population growth had started. Accompanying the population growth were many new homes, which were likely to include more and more tile. Mexican influence was strong and the southwestern style was extremely popular. Besides, it made more sense to use tile in the hot Southwest than carpeting. Floors, walls, and countertops were all being tiled. Finally, tile is very much like a commodity. The inputs are dirt and natural gas. Anyone can make tiles, and in fact, lots of people do. The Chinese are starting to make tiles in a big way. However, tiles weigh a lot, and transportation costs make a big difference in the gross margin. Interceramic's plants were in the middle of the largest sales area, giving the company a competitive advantage in terms of transportation costs.

The class bought its first shares of Interceramic in April 1995 and sold again in May, then bought and sold again in July of that year. In 1998 and through 2003 the class started accumulating a substantial position. Figure 12.2 shows the share price and the times when APM was buying and selling. At that time Interceramic's TEV/EBITDA ratio ranged from 2 to 4. There was still the hangover from the tech stock run-up. No one cared about a dodgy Mexican tile company. Sales grew in double digits (see Table 12.1), and income grew even faster.

In 2001 the carpet company Mohawk acquired Interceramic's largest North American competitor, Dal-Tile, at a TEV/EBITDA multiple of 9.7. Interceramic's multiple was 3. Its earnings and revenue growth were also stronger than those of Dal-Tile. Interceramic and Dal-Tile are still two of the largest North American producers of ceramic tile. They have exchanged

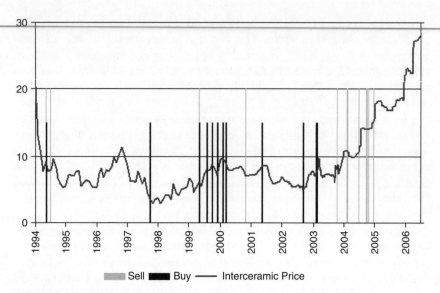

FIGURE 12.2 Interceramic Share Price, 1994–June 2007
Note: Share price has been adjusted to allow for comparability between ADR and the Mexican listing.

the top spot a couple of times. It's a little harder to find as much detailed information about Dal-Tile now that they are a subsidiary of Mohawk and don't have to file independent 10-Ks and Qs.

Table 12.1 shows the financial statements, operating metrics, and the TEV/EBITDA ratio for Interceramic from 2001 to 2006. Currently Mohawk is trading at a 2008 TEV/EBITDA of 9.3. Since tile has grown considerably faster and is forecast to do better than carpeting, 9.3 can be considered a floor for Interceramic.

What are the risks associated with Interceramic? The big risk in 1995 was bankruptcy. With the Mexican devaluation and then the Asian crisis, there was probably a 30 percent chance of bankruptcy. The high debt was a drag on company earnings until 2001. Then, in 2001, the recession dampened demand. Since then and despite the difficult operating environment, the company has been able to expand its distribution network, add a state-of-the-art manufacturing plant, integrate a new supply chain management system, and persevere in bad economic times and good. The risk of bankruptcy is now a remote memory.

A bigger risk now is liquidity risk. Just a few shareholders own a large percentage of the shares. The float is low, and the shares don't trade every day. The concentrated ownership includes the chief executive officer and

TABLE 12.1   Interceramic Income Statement, 2001–2006

	2001	2002	2003	2004	2005	2006
Sales: USD	294.4	293.4	304.7	350.4	418.0	474.3
Gross profit	123.7	123.7	123.7	123.7	123.7	171.5
Gross margin %	42.0	41.9	39.8	35.7	36.1	36.2
SG&A	76.3	81.0	85.3	101.5	119.8	135.5
Operating income	33.2	27.5	20.4	23.5	31.1	36.0
Operating margin	11.3	9.4	6.7	6.7	7.4	7.6
Financial cost	10.8	−6.0	−3.6	−1.2	−0.1	6.8
Net income	18.9	8.4	2.9	19.6	29.4	24.5
Net debt	103.6	107.6	100.3	75.2	108.9	102.6
EBITDA	47.3	41.9	36.0	41.0	52.3	60.5
Sales growth	11.1	−0.3	3.8	15.0	19.3	13.5
Income growth	36.5	−55.9	−65.7	582.1	50.4	−16.8
TEV/EBITDA	3.1	3.5	3.8	4.4	6.9	9.3

his former banker. When the banker left the bank that had been lending Interceramic money, he personally became a major shareholder. There are a couple of other large, nonfamily shareholders. When shares are concentrated, it's good to see others besides family owning large blocks. Those shareholders have a big stake in making sure that the owner doesn't buy too many corporate jets or vacation homes using the company's money. Small shareholders can't necessarily exit the stock at the listed price unless they are willing to be patient.

APM has realized a compound annual return on Interceramic of just over 40 percent per year since initially investing in 1995. Most of that return came in 2004 and 2005. However, there is still upside to Interceramic. With another new factory coming on line in 2008, production costs compared to competitors should be low. The biggest input cost in making tile is fuel. Most factories use natural gas. The cost of the fuel is important, but managing the cost is more important since all producers are faced with the same fuel price. Interceramic has been aggressively reducing its cost of production.

WORLD COMMODITIES

Recently lots of small investors have jumped on the commodity bandwagon. In the late 1990 commodities markets weren't thought of as an investment asset class, but they were used by producers and manufacturers to take out

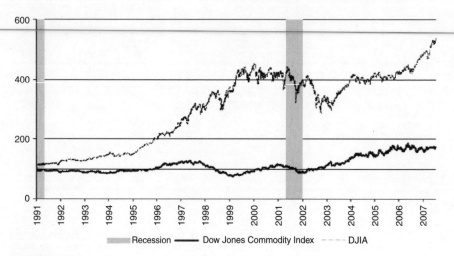

FIGURE 12.3 Dow Jones Commodity Index, 1991–2007

some of their business risk. Farmers would sell their wheat in the wheat futures market to lock in a price. General Mills would buy the wheat to lock in costs. Of course, some specialist traders were trading for investment accounts, but it wasn't a big part of commodity markets. Since 2002 things have changed. Figure 12.3 shows that an investment in the commodity index wouldn't have made much money until the end of 1995. The compound annual rate of return since 1991 is only 3 percent—about the same as inflation. However, since 2002, commodities generally have been on a tear. The index is up 13 percent at a compounded rate compared to the Dow, which is up 6 percent through mid-2007.

Commodity exchanges such as the New York Mercantile Exchange (NYMEX), the Chicago Board of Trade (CBOT), and others may also have been looking to drum up a little business. More trades make more money for the exchanges! More liquidity is better for those trying to hedge positions. The advent of commodity exchange traded funds (ETFs) has also helped pump up volume and visibility. These funds also needed investors. The marketing engines for the exchanges and others jumped into gear. Commodities became an "asset class" that investors needed to be in—the next big thing.

The APM class decided that we didn't have the expertise to be commodity traders. We do understand marketing, we understand how changes in markets affect companies on the top line and their margins, and we also understand commodity businesses. Oil companies are commodity businesses. It's pretty simple how they make money. Their revenues are determined by

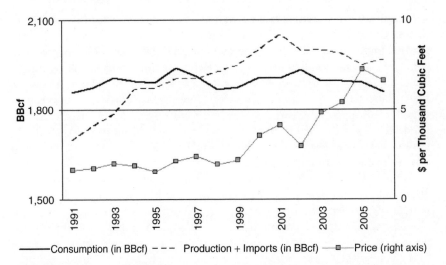

FIGURE 12.4   U.S. Natural Gas Production, Consumption and Prices, 1991–2006

the price of oil, which is set in a world marketplace and by the number of barrels they produce. Costs are determined by the drilling costs on properties they hold and by transportation costs. It costs more to get oil out of the ground in Alaska or in the Gulf of Mexico than it does in Saudi Arabia.

Oil and Gas

Oil and gas prices have made big headlines over the past five to six years. We've fought wars, presumably, to secure our oil supply. Since 2002 oil prices have increased steadily (see Figure 12.4). Several alums and friends of the class have spent their careers as analysts in the oil and gas industry. Beginning in 2002, they independently began recommending more energy or energy-derivative positions, such as refining, to the class.

Brad Shoup is a University of Kansas alumnus who went to work for T. Boone Pickens at Mesa Petroleum in the 1980s as a financial analyst. Mesa Petroleum was Pickens's oil and gas exploration and production company. David H. Batchelder was president of Mesa at the time. During this period Mesa and Pickens became famous corporate raiders. They made several large active investments and unsolicited acquisition offers in major oil companies, including Phillips Petroleum, Unocal, and Diamond Shamrock. Mesa was a pioneer in corporate activism.

Brad left Mesa with David Batchelder to become a founding partner in several related investment management and corporate finance advisory entities, including Batchelder & Partners Inc., DHB Partners LP, Girard Partners LP, and Relational Investors LLC. Relational Investors is an investment management firm with over $1 billion under management. The firm was the first to specialize in corporate activism. We discuss corporate activism in Chapter 14. Since 1999 Brad has worked with a variety of private equity, hedge funds, and specialty funds. He's always stayed on top of the oil and gas markets that he started in with Mesa. When he comes to class, it's with a wealth of institutional knowledge.

One of the lessons he's taught the class about commodities is that it's all about supply and demand. When you understand the supply and demand, you can see where the prices are going. Another lesson is how local and global markets affect a commodity. For example, natural gas is difficult to transport, so the price in the United States is quite different from the price in the rest of the world. For quite a while, natural gas was a waste product in many countries. You couldn't give it away so it was burned off into the atmosphere at oil drilling sites.

In the United States, natural gas has become one of the biggest suppliers of residential heating fuel and a source of energy in many production processes. Figure 12.4 shows the steep increase in natural gas prices since 2001. That increase was mostly responsible for the drop in Interceramic's gross margins since 2001 (see Table 12.1). As we said before, tile is mostly dirt and the fuel to fire the tiles. As the cost of fuel has gone up, Interceramic's margins have dropped.

The other thing you can see about natural gas is that consumption has remained relatively constant, while U.S. production peaked in 2001. Imports have made up a steadily increasing portion of U.S. supply. In 1991, imports were 9 percent of supply. In 2006 they were 18 percent of supply.

The APM class is invested in Quicksilver Resources (KWK), a primarily natural gas exploration and production (E&P) company. Its reserves are 98 percent gas and just 2 percent oil. Quicksilver specializes in developing unconventional gas fields. The primary growth area is the newly discovered Barnett Shale formation in the Fort Worth Basin, near Fort Worth, Texas.

Our investment thesis for Quicksilver is primarily one of relative prices between oil and natural gas. Since 6 metric cubic feet of natural gas is equivalent to 1 barrel of crude oil, crude oil should be priced roughly six times natural gas. The futures prices in Table 12.2 show that crude oil is currently priced at more than eight times natural gas. Either natural gas prices will rise or crude oil will fall so that the ratio will return to 6:1.

We think gas prices will rise for both supply and demand reasons. A large portion of natural gas demand is inelastic. Residential heating systems can't

TABLE 12.2   Crude Oil to Natural Gas Ratio

	NYMEX Henry Hub Natural Gas Futures Price	NYMEX Crude Oil (Light) Futures Price	Ratio
Dec-07	8.44	74.80	8.86
Jun-08	8.19	73.58	8.98
Dec-08	9.42	72.30	7.68
Jun-09	8.20	72.21	8.81
Dec-09	9.18	71.07	7.74
Jun-10	7.68	73.44	9.57
Dec-10	8.80	71.54	8.13
Jun-11	7.33	64.34	8.77
Dec-11	8.29	71.52	8.62
Average	8.39	71.64	8.57

be changed easily, nor can production facilities. The supply and reserves of natural gas aren't increasing. Imports may increase, but transportation and port costs will remain high and increase. It is more difficult to ship natural gas than it is to ship oil. According to the Energy Information Administration of the Department of Energy, LNG (liquefied natural gas) projects are just about the most expensive energy projects. Although prices are declining, it is still difficult to find ports that have the facilities to accept LNG and regasification plants. Security and cost considerations make ports reluctant to take on more big facility additions.

The other side of the coin is that crude oil prices could decrease to rebalance the ratio at 6:1. Many experts don't think that crude oil prices will come down significantly unless there is a technological breakthrough in an alternative energy source. Some well-respected experts think that world oil supply peaked in 2001. Although still a controversial position, it does argue against an oil price decrease. Regardless of whether supply has peaked or not, supply isn't increasing as rapidly as demand, so prices won't be coming down.

The other piece of the investment thesis is that Quicksilver is a well-run company with very good natural gas assets. In terms of valuation, it doesn't look extremely cheap, but we expect above-average top-line and bottom-line growth. Table 12.3 shows the valuation metrics using analyst consensus estimates for EBITDA and net income.

Valero   APM bought Valero (VLO) in May 2002 at the recommendation of fall 1998 APM alumnus Robert Tracy. At the time Valero was upside down

TABLE 12.3   Quicksilver Resources Valuation Metrics

	At Purchase 2006	FY07	FY08	FY09
EBITDA	253.0	344.6	420.7	444.4
Net Income	93.7	112.8	134.4	183.8
TEV/EBITDA	12.0	13.4	10.9	10.4
Price/Earnings	27.1	29.0	24.4	17.8

with its crack spread. Refineries were thought to be a terrible business, but worse, they were boring. The crack spread is the difference between the selling prices and the input costs. Refiners crack oil into several different products, such as gasoline and heating oil. When the crack spread is upside down, refiners lose money on every gallon of gasoline sold. At the time the price/earnings (P/E) ratio was 3.8. Oil was cheap, but gasoline was abundant and even cheaper. SUVs were king! Figure 12.5 compares West Texas sweet crude oil (WTI) prices to the crack spread. In 2002 the spreads were below their long-run average of 6.6 percent. In 2002 Valero profits were 84 percent lower than in 2001, even with revenue growth of 80 percent. That's what happens with commodity businesses. They are price takers; they have no power over the input price or the selling price. They make money in times

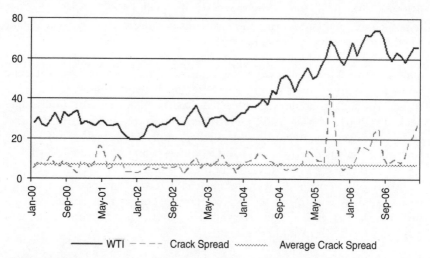

FIGURE 12.5   West Texas Crude and NYMEX321 Crack Spreads, 2000–2006

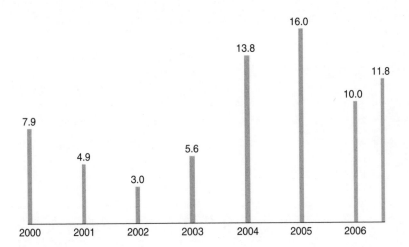

FIGURE 12.6 Per-Barrel Price Difference between Sweet and Sour Crude Oil, 2000–June 2007
Source: Energy Information Administration, Department of Energy

when supply is tight and demand is high. They lose money when supply is abundant and demand is low. They can fiddle at the edges with some cost-cutting or capacity expansion, but most commodity businesses are very competitive.

Valero did have a few things going for it that other companies did not. Not all crude oil is created equal. Some crude has more sulfur, making it harder and more expensive to refine. High-sulfur crude is called sour crude, and low-sulfur crude is called sweet. News reports that quote the price of a barrel of oil refer to sweet crude. WTI is sweet crude. Valero developed an expertise in refining sour crude when most other refiners were limited in the amount of sour crude they could handle. In 2004 that expertise paid off in a big way. The price differential between sweet and sour widened from $5.60 per barrel to $13.80 (see Figure 12.6). One reason that the spreads were increasing was production was declining in sweet crude at the same time more sour crude was being pumped. The average sweet/sour spread in the 1990s had been $6.60 per barrel, so the spread was very low in the early 2000s by historical standards.

The second advantage that Valero had was in refining capacity. There has not been a new refinery built in the United States since 1976. Refineries are smelly, messy, and expensive to build, not to mention the big problems that might happen with an accident. This is the NIMBY (not in my back yard) problem.

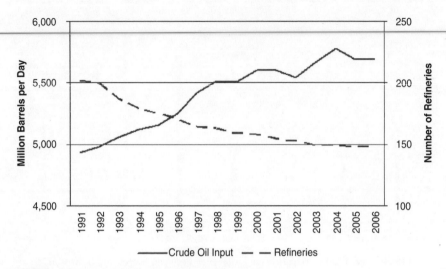

FIGURE 12.7 U.S. Refining Capacity, 1991–2006
Source: Energy Information Administration, Department of Energy

The number of refineries in the United States has been gradually decreasing over the last 25 years as older refineries were taken off line (see Figure 12.7). At the same time, demand for gasoline and other petroleum products was and is still increasing. That means existing refiners, including Valero, were producing more in each plant. They were adding capacity by upgrading technology to their current plants. Valero was especially foresighted. Not only did it add capacity to its plants, it added additional specialized capacity to refine sour crude and to make cleaner California-grade gasoline. Most other refiners were still doing the same old, same old. There was a shortage of specialty gasolines. Valero was selling everything it could produce at a very good price. For a while it was selling almost all of the wholesale gasoline in California.

The other key driver behind Valero's value is related to U.S. refining capacity: international capacity. U.S. refiners were declining partly because more international refiners were coming on line. World refining capacity has grown at a compound rate of only 1.7 percent per year since 1970. Growth has slowed considerably in the Organisation for Economic Cooperation and Development (OECD) countries after a run-up in 1982. Non-OECD growth, primarily Russia, the Middle East, and China, have increased capacity more steadily. Figure 12.8 shows refining capacity in millions of barrels per day. Table 12.4 shows the annual growth rates in capacity for different subperiods. Valero's refining capacity is 3.26 million barrels per

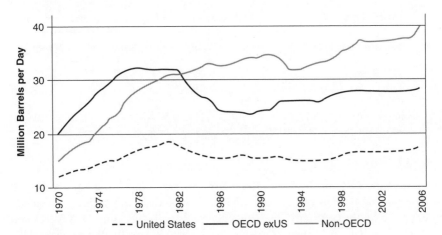

FIGURE 12.8 World Crude Oil Refining Capacity, 1970–2006
Source: Energy Information Administration, Department of Energy

day, or almost 19 percent of the U.S. capacity and 4 percent of the world's capacity.

During the last few years while cash flow has been especially strong, Valero has acquired more refineries. It is now the largest U.S. refiner and has a presence in other countries as well. In 2006 the company announced that the bulk of its acquisition strategy has been accomplished. During 2006 and 2007 it will buy back shares and increase dividends to increase shareholder value.

We've included pro forma statements and enterprise value calculations in the appendix to this chapter. Based on the pro forma numbers for 2007 to 2009, we calculate the valuation statistics shown in Table 12.5. In June 2007 Valero's share price was close to $74 with a forward P/E of 8. Comparable companies are trading in the 9 to 10 P/E range.

TABLE 12.4 Compound Annual Growth in Refining Capacity in the United States, OECD, and non-OECD Countries

Dates	U.S.	OECD ex US	Non-OECD	Total
1970 to 1975	4.5	7.6	8.6	7.2
1975 to 1985	0.5	−1.0	4.0	1.2
1985 to 1995	−0.1	−0.1	−0.1	−0.1
1995 to 2005	1.0	0.7	1.4	1.1
1970 to 2006	1.0	0.9	2.8	1.7

TABLE 12.5 Valero's Valuation Statistics and Implied Price

Valuation statistics	2007E	2008E	2009E
TEV/sales	0.45	0.43	0.41
TEV/operating profit	9.09	8.66	8.25
P/E	8.5	8.1	7.7
Implied Price with P/E = 9	78.27	82.18	86.30

Quick Notes

Companhia Vale do Rio Doce ADR   Keeping tracking of the name of Companhia Vale do Rio Doce (ticker: RIO) may be the hardest thing about understanding the company. The press generally calls the company CVRD, but its ticker is RIO; not to be confused with its competitor Rio Tinto with a U.S. ticker RPT, but RIO in Germany, Great Britain, and Australia. CVRD is a commodity play. In May 2006 Group 8 members Shiheng Cai, Carlos Lock, Anvita Mishra, Paul O'Connell, and Shae Spence recommended that the class buy CVRD. The company is the largest seaborne exporter of iron ore with 33 percent of global market share. Its primary base of operations is in Brazil. Why this company and not another? The group outlined these reasons:

- Plentiful supply of low-impurity-level iron ore
- Lower processing costs
- Mines, mills, and ports located in Minas Gerais or close to the ocean
- Lowest capital expenditures per ton in the industry

Because of the built-in transportation advantage, CVRD's cost to produce should remain lower than that of other competitors. We bought the stock at $46.33. Soon after there was a 2:1 split. It currently trades in the postsplit in the mid-50s—a double in just about one year.

Group 8 members are from China, Peru, India and the United States. Carlos was familiar with the company since he was from Lima, and Shiheng could attest to China's appetite for iron ore. All strong students, they looked for an edge associated with their backgrounds and found it with CVRD.

Yanzhou Coal Mining Co. Ltd.   Yanzhou Coal (ticker: YZC) wasn't a long-term holding or one of our success stories. The class bought ADRs of Yanzhou Coal in 2001 for $22.00. We sold a year later at $21.10. We received a $0.60 per-share dividend, so we almost broke even. At the end of 2006, the ADR price was close to $40, and that was after a weak performance in 2006. Now it's trading near $90.

Yanzhou Coal mines coal and provides coal railway transportation. It brings most of the coal to Beijing, where coal is the primary power source. A former state-owned enterprise, Yanzhou has good assets and decent management. After we sold, the company began overseas expansion by acquiring mines in Australia and in more Chinese provinces.

Why did we sell? There were two main reasons. First, we had two consecutive semesters with no Chinese-speaking students. The annual and interim reports were in Chinese, so we had no one to translate for the class. The second reason had to do with the fact that a substantial portion of the class felt uncomfortable owning a company that helped pollute Beijing.

WRAPPING UP

It's getting harder and harder to be a solely domestic investor. Most U.S. companies source or sell at least some of their products outside the country. Yet many U.S. investors don't understand foreign markets, international accounting rules, or how foreign sensitivities may affect U.S. companies and markets. In APM it's all about digging beneath the surface and going beyond the sound bite to sort through the real story. Of course, he (or she) who has the best information and understanding reaps the highest returns.

APPENDIX

Valero's Numbers

TABLE 12.6 Valero's Enterprise Value Calculations (in $millions except per share and ratios)

Equity Value		Balance Sheet Data as of	31-Mar-07
Shares outstanding	549	Bank balances and cash	1,727
Convertible and stock option	16	Total debt at book value	4,649
Diluted shares outstanding	565	Net debt	2,922
Stock price: June 2007	73.86		
Market cap	40,548	Market cap	40,548
Adjusted market cap	40,548	Enterprise value	43,470
Fiscal year-end	Dec		

TABLE 12.7 Valero's Historical and Pro Forma Income Statement and Margins

	FY 2001	FY 2002	FY 2003	FY 2004	FY 2005	FY 2006	2007E	2008E	2009E
Sales	14,988	26,976	37,969	53,919	81,362	91,051	95,604	100,384	105,403
Sales growth	2.2	80.0	40.7	42.0	50.9	11.9	5.0	5.0	5.0
Gross profit	1,304	1,742	2,585	4,507	7,311	10,258	9,560	10,038	10,540
Gross margin %	8.7	6.5	6.8	8.4	9.0	11.3	10.0	10.0	10.0
EBITDA	1,139	812	1,617	3,423	6,082	8,857	7,170	7,529	7,905
Operating profit	1,001	471	1,248	2,979	5,484	8,006	4,780	5,019	5,270
Operating margin %	6.7	1.7	3.3	5.5	6.7	8.8	5.0	5.0	5.0
Income taxes	331	58	365	906	1,697	2,726	1,577	1,707	1,792
Net income	564	92	617	1,791	1,684	2,724	4,774	5,013	5,264
Net margin	3.8	0.3	1.6	3.3	2.1	3.0	5.0	5.0	5.0
Net income growth	66.2	(83.8)	574.5	190.2	(6.0)	61.8	175.3	105.0	105.0
Diluted EPS*	2.208	0.208	1.273	3.265	6.100	8.640	8.696	9.132	9.589
Earnings growth	57.7	(90.6)	513.3	156.6	86.8	41.6	0.7	5.0	5.0

*Including extra items and discount opportunities

CHAPTER 13

Local Biases

Besides having an international focus, the APM class unquestionably also has a local bias. We've looked pretty carefully at many of the publicly traded companies that have headquarters in the area, primarily Kansas City and Topeka. We've discussed two local companies in some detail, Brooke Corp. and Capitol Federal. In this chapter we look at six current or past holdings. We won't go into quite as much depth in terms of numbers as we have for some companies. We'll focus on the stories, what we've learned, and how we learned it. Here's a list of the companies that we discuss in this chapter.

- American Italian Pasta (PLB)
- Novastar Financial (NFI)
- Inergy, L.P. (NRGY) and Inergy Holdings (NRGP)
- Tortoise Capital
- Garmin (GRMN)
- Kansas City Southern (KSU)

Here are the other area companies we've owned or seriously considered owning:

- Entertainment Properties Trust (EOP)
- Westar Energy (WR)
- Protection One (PONE)
- H&R Block (HRB)
- Applebee's (APPB)
- Payless Cashways (PCS)
- Cerner (CERN)
- NIC, Inc. (EGOV)
- Sprint Corp. (FON)
- YRC Worldwide (YRC)

Executives from local companies usually are willing to visit class, to discuss corporate strategy and provide investor presentations. We've also gone on site visits and attended annual shareholder meetings at quite a few of these companies. The students have gotten a good idea of what analysts do when they go on site visits, and they've listened to a lot of investor presentations. This exposure helps them understand not just one company, but it helps them know what to look for and ask about with other companies also.

AMERICAN ITALIAN PASTA

American Italian Pasta (PLB) is the largest producer of dry pasta products in the United States. The company's headquarters is in Kansas City, Missouri. APM initially invested in American Italian Pasta in the fall of 2000 and held the position until February 2005. The company's then–chief executive officer (CEO), Tim Webster, visited the class three times between 2000 and the end of 2004. He was a very entertaining speaker, and the class always enjoyed his visits. The university has a campus in northeastern Italy close to one of American Italian Pasta manufacturing plants in Verolanuova. The company hosted many students at plant tours in Italy. It manufactured the same pasta in Italy as it did in the United States, but it could charge premium prices because the gourmet market loved the "made in Italy" stamp. The company's annual meetings were always a big hit with students because they were held in the Crown Center Hyatt Regency Hotel, a very nice venue, and the meeting always concluded with a gourmet pasta lunch. The company's chefs outdid themselves coming up with new and exciting dishes for the meeting.

From 1996 to September 2003, at the end of the company's fiscal year, company officers were very proud that earnings had increased every quarter. The compound annual growth rate was 33 percent over that period. When APM bought shares in August 2000, the tech boom was going strong. Even though the earnings had been strong, no one cared about a small pasta company. The price/earnings (P/E) ratio was 11 and TEV/EBITDA (total enterprise value before interest, taxes, and depreciation) was 7× (times), nothing like the lofty valuations that tech companies enjoyed at the time (see Table 13.1). When the tech boom was over, American Italian Pasta was exactly the type of company shareholders were looking for: great earnings and a good basic, easy-to-understand business. In 2001 the P/E ratio was 29, APM took some money off the table. Figure 13.1 shows the share price and the timing of APM's buys and sells.

Unfortunately, a new nonfinancial trend started in 2002–2003. The Atkins diet was hot, pasta wasn't. Earnings took a big hit in September 2004,

TABLE 13.1   American Italian Pasta Valuation, 1999–2004

	Sep-04	Sep-03	Sep-02	Sep-01	Sep-00	Sep-99
Market capitalization ($M)	473.5	698.0	643.2	759.6	323.6	17.5
Total enterprise value ($M)	758.0	994.9	897.4	992.7	456.9	97.0
Net income ($M)	3.0	42.6	41.3	26.3	27.5	23.5
EBITDA ($M)	48.3	101.7	85.2	74.1	63.6	53.0
P/E	158.4	16.4	15.6	28.8	11.8	0.7
TEV/EBITDA	15.7	9.8	10.5	13.4	7.2	1.8

dropping by 93 percent from $2.31 to 16 cents. Before the beginning of the 2004, there were a few signs that pasta sales were dropping, but the quarter ending in June 2004 was bad and September was worse. After the June board meeting, the company announced it would restructure, "right-size," initially by closing a Wisconsin plant. Earlier in the year an executive vice president had resigned; most didn't associate that with operating problems, but now it seemed like a warning. APM sold in February 2005 with decreasing earnings. We didn't see much coming out of the restructuring plan from the previous year, and we had some better opportunities.

Our timing turned out to be okay. By the end of the year another executive vice president, the chairman of the board, and the CEO had all

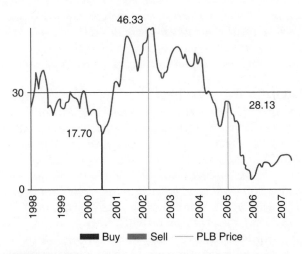

FIGURE 13.1   American Italian Pasta Share Price, 1997–2006

resigned under a cloud. The board retained a forensic accounting firm, Alvarez and Marsal, to sort through financial statements. No charges have been filed, but no financial statements have been filed with the Securities and Exchange Commission (SEC) since May 11, 2005, for the second quarter of FY 2005. At the end of 2006 the company was delisted from the New York Stock Exchange (NYSE) because of failure to file and started trading on the Pink Sheets under the ticker symbol AITP. On May 18, 2007, the company released this press release:

American Italian Pasta Company Updates Restatement Process

KANSAS CITY, Mo., May 18 /PRNewswire-FirstCall/— American Italian Pasta Company (OTC: AITP), the largest producer and marketer of dry pasta in North America, today provided an update to the status of the restatement of its historical financial statements.

As previously announced, the Company has been evaluating the timetable for completion and filing of its audited financial statements and annual reports on Form 10-K for its fiscal year ended September 30, 2005 and for its fiscal year ended September 29, 2006. Based on its evaluation of the timetable, the Company now anticipates making these filings concurrently in the last half of August 2007. "We recognize that this has been an extended process and has taken longer than originally anticipated," said Jim Fogarty, Chief Executive Officer. "We look forward to completing this extensive review and our restatement process."

The date the Company estimates for completing the filing of its financial statements is subject to change based on a number of factors, including the ongoing investigations in which the Company is cooperating, and the review of and continued analysis of issues by the Company and its independent registered public accounting firm.

ABOUT AIPC

Founded in 1988 and based in Kansas City, Missouri, American Italian Pasta Company is the largest producer and marketer of dry pasta in North America. The Company has four plants that are located in Excelsior Springs, Missouri; Columbia, South Carolina; Tolleson, Arizona and Verolanuova, Italy. The Company has approximately 600 employees located in the United States and Italy.

When used in this release, the words "anticipate," "believe," "estimate," and "expect" and similar expressions are intended to identify forward-looking statements, but are not the exclusive means of identifying these statements. The statements by the Company regarding the timing of filing its audited financial statements and annual reports on Form 10-K for fiscal 2005 and fiscal 2006, are forward-looking. Actual results or events could differ materially. The differences could be caused by a number of factors, including, but not limited to, the completion and findings of the Audit Committee investigation, the Company's review of its financial statements, a review and/or audit of the Company's financial statements by its independent registered public accounting firm, the SEC staff review, and the conclusions reached regarding financial reporting. The Company will not update any forward-looking statements in this press release to reflect future events. Contact:

Source: American Italian Pasta Company, 05/18/2007
www.prnewswire.com

We earned a compound annual average return of 31.5 percent over the time we held American Italian Pasta. We learned much more than just the return we received. The moral of the story is that no matter how good the CEO sounds or what the results seem to be, trust and goodwill are primary. Our entire financial system is based on the presumed accuracy of financial reports and executives telling the truth. Bad things don't just happen in China or in Houston. Stuff happens in our own backyard, to the good old midwestern, apple-pie, and American-dream folks, too. Trust but verify. It can happen anywhere.

NOVASTAR FINANCIAL

The APM class owned shares of Novastar Financial (NFI) over pretty much the same period as we owned American Italian Pasta. We initiated our holding in April 2001 and held shares until April 2005. Novastar was a slightly larger company in terms of market cap and TEV in 2004. In 2003 both companies were about the same size with $1 billion in enterprise value. Scott Hartman was and is the CEO of Novastar; Mike Bamberg, the chief investment officer. Both are KU graduates. Scott presented to quite a few APM classes during the time we owned shares and even after we sold.

Students were always very impressed with Scott's investor presentations. Novastar wasn't an easy company to understand. The company has two main pieces: a mortgage lending operation and a portfolio management division that repackaged and resold mortgage loans. Both of these businesses were wrapped in a corporate structure called a REIT (real estate investment trust). REITs are a tax-favored structure that eliminates the double taxation on dividends. A REIT is required to distribute at least 90 percent of taxable

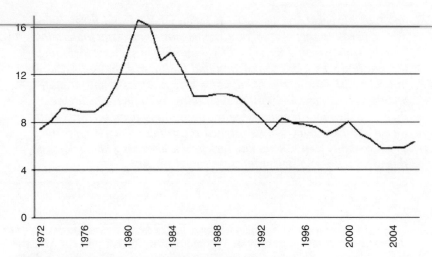

FIGURE 13.2 Interest Rates for Fixed-Rate First Mortgages, 1972–2006
Data Source: www.federalreserve.gov/releases/h16/data.html

income to shareholders. In doing so, they aren't required to pay regular income taxes.

The bottom line was that Novastar was in the mortgage business, but it was making more money on its financial engineering operations. Although the financial statements were hard to read and figure out and we were new to financial engineering, it wasn't too hard to figure out was that interest rates, and mortgage rates along with them, were dropping. Figure 13.2 shows the rates on fixed rate mortgages from 1972 to 2006. In 2002, they dropped to a 30-year low. Adjustable rates were even lower. When rates drop, mortgages are more affordable and demand increases. When the volume in mortgages ramps up, specialty companies such as Novastar start making money on mortgage volume.

Along with the rate drops and increased conventional demand both for new mortgages and refinancing, credit standards were being relaxed. Lots of people who didn't qualify for a mortgage earlier began to qualify. Lots of new mortgage originators started up. It was very profitable to sign people up with lower credit standards, add on some private mortgage insurance (PMI), and pocket the points and associated fees. No one held mortgages anymore; they were repackaged and sold to pension funds, insurance companies, hedge funds, and more. Due to the magic of financial engineering, these CMOs (collateralized mortgage obligations) and ABSs (asset-backed securities) were rated higher than the underlying mortgages. The theory is that one mortgage might go bad, but not all at once, and besides, there's the insurance.

TABLE 13.2 Novastar Segment Revenue and Income, 2001 to 2006

	2006	2005	2004	2003	2002	2001
Portfolio Management (PM)						
Revenue	303.6	196.4	143.0	109.5	73.4	38.3
Net income	105.8	163.7	115.7	99.0	61.0	26.0
Net margin	34.8	83.3	80.9	90.4	83.1	68.0
Mortgage Lending & Servicing (ML)						
Revenue	191.3	124.3	83.8	60.9	33.7	19.7
Net income	−20.7	−23.3	10.1	9.9	−13.6	5.5
Net margin	−10.8	−18.7	12.1	16.3	−40.4	28.0
Total Revenue	566.3	435.1	478.3	352.3	171.8	118.5
Net Income	66.3	132.5	109.1	112.0	48.8	32.3
PM % of Revenue	53.6	45.1	29.9	31.1	42.7	32.3
ML % of Revenue	33.8	28.6	17.5	17.3	19.6	16.6
PM % of Net Income	159.6	123.5	106.0	88.4	125.1	80.6
ML % of Net Income	−31.2	−17.6	9.3	8.9	−28.0	17.0

In 2001 Novastar wasn't doing a big business in mortgage originations, but that started to change as subprime and Alt-A (those with less documentation than a traditional loan) mortgages became commonplace. Novastar began a push to pick up more of its own business as a mortgage originator. Still, its primary business was and still is buying mortgages and packaging up the CMOs. Table 13.2 shows that in most years, the portfolio management segment of the business contributes more than 100 percent to the bottom line. Figure 13.3 from Novastar's 2003 10-K is the company's attempt to show how all the pieces work together.

The APM class bought the stock because of the financing business and because of the rich dividend payout. Mortgage REITs became the new income vehicle for investors. They paid generous dividends. By the fall of 2003, many other had joined the mortgage REIT community, but Novastar outclassed everyone. Group 2 from the fall 2003 class provided the information in Table 13.3.

Group 2 also notes: "The average Mortgage REIT dividend yield, excluding NFI, is 9.79%. NFI's dividend yield is about 13.5 %. The other Mortgage REITs with market capitalization of over $1 billion are SFI, NLY, FBR and TMA."

In 2004 ominous rumblings about Novastar began. A *Wall Street Journal* article said that Novastar failed to comply with some state licensing rules; Herb Greenberg, columnist with TheStreet.com and MarketWatch,

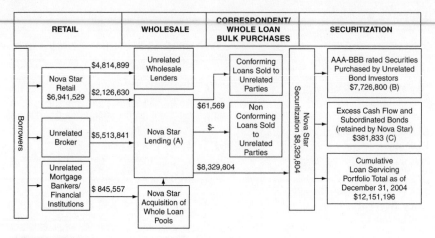

FIGURE 13.3 2003 Novastar Operations Diagram
(A) A portion of the loans securitized or sold to unrelated parties as of December 31, 2003 originated prior to 2003, but due to timing were not yet securitized or sold at the end of 2002. Loans originated in 2003 that we have not securitized or sold to unrelated parties as of December 31, 2003 are included in our mortgage loans held-for-sale.
Source: Novastar Form 10-K for the Fiscal Year Ended December 31, 2003, filed March 5, 2004

TABLE 13.3 Mortgage REIT Yields 2003

Ticker	Mortgage REIT	Yields
AHMH	American Home Mortgage Holdings, Inc.	9.44
ANH	Anworth Mortgage Asset Corporation	11.70
AHR	Anthracite Capital, Inc.	11.20
AMC	American Mortgage Acceptance Company	9.45
FBR	Friedman, Billings, Ramsey	6.52
IMH	Impac Mortgage Holdings, Inc.	13.03
MFA	MFA Mortgage Investments, Inc.	11.57
NFI	**NovaStar Financial, Inc.**	**13.34**
NLY	Annaly Mortgage Management, Inc.	12.79
RAS	RAIT Investment Trust	10.42
RWT	Redwood Trust, Inc.	5.05
SFI	iStar Financial, Inc.	6.95
TMA	Thornburg Mortgage, Inc.	9.35

Source: Group 2 Fall 2003: Jeff Arroyo, David Iliff, Jon Blumb, Pravin Kedia

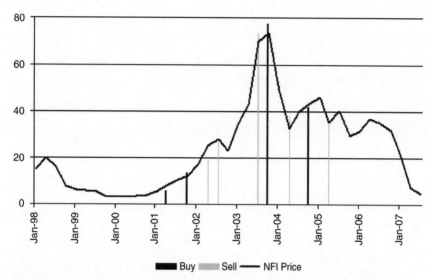

FIGURE 13.4   Novastar Stock Price and APM Trades, 1998–June 2007

began writing stinging commentary; and to top it off, the SEC began an informal inquiry into "certain business practices" as a result of the *Wall Street Journal* article. In February 2005, at the end of Novastar's fourth-quarter conference call, the chief financial officer, Greg Metz, didn't realize he was still live. He said to investor relations (IR) chief Jeff Gentle, "Thank you, Jeffrey. He's the man. He doesn't let anybody get on we don't want to take questions from." After another comment—it is not clear from whom—Metz said: "There was one dickhead who was being pretty much of a dickhead." Certainly not the type of PR that a company is looking for!

APM sold its last shares not too long afterward. The dividend yield was great, but it seemed like more bad news was coming out every day. We had made an average compound annual return of 212 percent over the four years we owned Novastar. APM earned more than half of its return from dividends. Figure 13.4 shows the timing of the class's buys and sells.

The upside was more limited in early 2005, but there was a lot of downside. It was pretty tough to sell because a lot of people were saying, "things are great, the dividend is secure." All of the charges are trivial and will come to nothing. Still, in terms of valuation, the price to book (P/B) ratio that we used for financial institutions was at the highest level ever at 3.5. In 2001 when we bought, P/B was 0.4. The average for other specialty finance companies was 1.9. Time to sell.

Fast forward to 2007. We look pretty smart. The subprime mortgage business is imploding. Novastar is struggling to survive. It has secured enough financing so it won't go out of business this year, but the business will be dramatically changed. It still has legal difficulties in addition to plain old business problems. In early 2005 we didn't foresee subprime mortgage difficulties of this magnitude coming down the pike. But we breathe a sigh of relief that we missed most of the excitement.

INERGY, L.P. AND INERGY HOLDINGS, L.P.

Inergy, L.P. (NRGY) sells retail propane. That sounds simple enough. A sizable minority in the United States rely on propane for heating. They aren't on a natural gas pipeline or in a fuel oil area, but propane can be delivered to their door (think Hank on *King of the Hill*). It's much cheaper than electric heat.

The class purchased Inergy partnership units after a visit from CEO John Sherman in April 2003. The company had IPOed in July 2001. An APM student from fall 1998, Hsulin Peng, worked on the initial public offering (IPO) with the investment banking division of A. G. Edwards. About six months after the IPO, Inergy hired her away to work in its corporate finance area. She stopped by to visit and helped arrange for John Sherman to present to the class. The story was compelling. Sherman had been in the propane business for many years and wanted to run a company his way. There was a lot of potential for consolidation in the industry, and he and his team were the ones to do it. Figure 13.5 from Inergy's investor presentation shows that 61 percent of the propane (LPG) market consists of small independent retailers. In 2005 it was 64 percent. Inergy has grown by consolidating some of the mom-and-pop retailers as well as some of the larger companies.

Inergy is a master limited partnership (MLP). An MLP is another type of tax-favored corporate structure similar to a REIT, but it's for companies in natural resources. It is an income pass-through that eliminates double taxation on dividends. The trade-off is that at least 90 percent of income must be distributed to the MLP holders. The terminology, the accounting, and the structure are complicated. To complicate matters more, Inergy is controlled by another publicly traded limited partnership, called Inergy Holdings, L.P. (NRGP). NRGP is called the general partner. Inergy Holdings didn't IPO until 2005.

Besides being a complicated structure, MLPs seem problematic to a few older investors because of residual overhang from some scandals in the 1970s. Those problems are fading, and a larger drawback to MLP investing comes from some tax issues that arise with institutional ownership, effectively making MLPs an investment vehicle solely for individual investors. That leaves a huge chunk of the market out of the game.

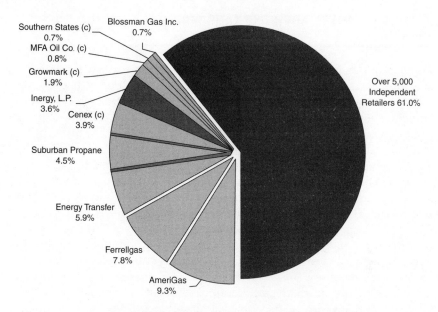

Top 10 Propane Retailers Control ~39% of Market Share [b]

FIGURE 13.5 Domestic Retail Market for LPG, March 2007[a]
(a) January 2007 American Petroleum Institute Report; (b) February 2007
LPGas Magazine; (c) Cooperatives
Source: Inergy Holdings Presentation at A. G. Edwards MLP Conference, March
2007

Still, APM took a look at the existing and potential dividends and the
61 percent of the market that could be added. We thought propane and
Inergy looked like a good buy. The annual growth in dividends had been
57 percent per year. That's not sustainable, but we figured that 5 percent
growth was. We estimated that the cost of capital was 8 percent with a
current annual dividend of $1.43; we had a valuation of $47. NRGY was
selling at $31 with a dividend yield of 4.6 percent.

When NRGP was instituted, we reevaluated our position. Should we
hold NRGP or NRGY or both? We concluded that there was more upside
in the general partner, NRGP, because the general partner receives incentive
distribution rights at increasing percentages up to 48 percent. While there
was upside in the operating company, the general partner had a better claim
on the distributions. We sold NRGY and bought NRGP. To date we've
realized an 11 percent compound annual return on the combination of the
two positions with the dividends. With price appreciation, our realized and
unrealized return is just over 50 percent.

TORTOISE CAPITAL ADVISORS (AND MORE ABOUT INERGY)

Through our contacts at Inergy, we found out about Tortoise Capital. We invited one of the founders to class during the spring 2005, a few months before Inergy Holdings went public. Tortoise Capital operates closed-end mutual funds that primarily invest in MLPs. The founders saw that the MLP universe was exploding, but that universe was closed to institutional investors because of some arcane tax laws. David Schulte of Kansas City Equity Partners had led a private financing from some growth MLPs. He saw the potential. As an attorney, he figured he could find a solution to the institutional investor problem. He won approval from the SEC and pioneered the structure at Tortoise. He opened the Tortoise Energy Infrastructure Corp. (NYSE: TYG), a closed-end mutual fund, in March 2004. If imitation is the sincerest form of flattery, then Schulte and Tortoise should be enormously flattered. By the end of the year three other funds had copied the idea.

In 2007 there are four Tortoise funds. All of them invest primarily in midstream and downstream oil and gas infrastructure companies. The original idea of investing in the publicly traded shares of MLPs has expanded to provide additional private placement financing, both equity and debt. The four funds and inception dates are:

1. Tortoise Energy Infrastructure Corp. (TYG), March 2, 2004
2. Tortoise Energy Capital Corp. (NYSE: TYY), March 26, 2005
3. Tortoise North American Energy Corp. (NYSE: TYN), October 28, 2005
4. Tortoise Capital Resources Corp. (NYSE: TTO), February 2, 2007

Tortoise North American specializes in Canadian resource companies and the Canadian equivalent of MLPs. Unfortunately, a couple of months after inception, the Canadian government changed its tax laws, and the fund hasn't done well. The newest fund specializes in small companies. The APM class currently holds TTO and TYY.

Tortoise (through TYG and TYY) has a large position in Inergy and Inergy Holdings. APM found out about Inergy Holdings from Jamie Melzer, who was in the spring 2005 class. She went to work for Tortoise as a summer intern in 2005 and came back as an APM teaching assistant during the fall 2005 class. Inergy Partners hadn't yet paid any dividends, but she pointed out the upside with the incentive distribution rights and the holdings in the operating company.

Jamie got her job as a summer intern because she was part of a group that represented the class at a portfolio competition at New York University (NYU) in April 2005. Jamie, along with Peggy Cameron, Marcelo Moreiro, and Elizabeth White, traveled to New York to present Inergy at the competition sponsored by NYU's investing club. The student organizers of the competition were very happy to point out that they were from New York and knew a lot more than anyone else because of the wonderful opportunities that the city afforded them and because they, as New Yorkers, were used to the fast pace of the world. We, slow people from the rest of the world, just couldn't compete.

Here's an excerpt from a newsletter article the group wrote on the experience:

... the KU group gave a polished presentation of an APM portfolio stock, Inergy, L.P. (Nasdaq:NRGY), at the investment competition at the Summit. The overall winners of the competition were from the Walton School of Business at the University of Arkansas. Their stock recommendation was Wellpoint Inc (NYSE:WLP). Unofficially, several participants and Professor Shenoy thought that the KU group had the best presentation and investment advice.

By far the most exciting parts of the NYC trip were visits with KU Alumni at their respective companies. The first visit was with Christi Wagenaar, an analyst on the sell side for UBS Investment Bank in New York. She spoke to the group about her quest for a job, the struggles and the long hours required to be successful, and the vast amount of knowledge she has gained. She is preparing to attend the Harvard School of Business to complete her MBA in the near future. The second visit was with APM alum Kelly Robin, an analyst on the buy side at U.S. Equity with JP Morgan Asset Management. The visits proved to be extremely beneficial as the KU group asked questions about the industry and the competitive aspects of getting a job in New York. The consensus about finding a job in New York City was that one must be persistent and use all the contacts from the KU School of Business alumni. Additionally, given the opportunity to interview in New York, make sure to meet with as many people as possible. Don't be shy about calling and working the network.

We ended the visit with a dinner with a big group of KU and APM alums including Kelly and Christi. We also got to meet Robert Tracy—Kynikos Associates, Fred Coulson—T H Lee Putnam, Ryan

Sprott—CFSB, Andrew Frisbie—FMCG, Ryan Bailes—Bank of America Securities, and Brett Young—RBC Dain Rauscher.

Such a positive experience has led to plans for a follow-up trip in the Fall semester of 2005 for KU students. The trip also resulted in one of the group's members, Elizabeth White, beginning work as a high yield debt analyst with Bank of America Securities. Perhaps this experience will lead to an annual trip to New York for KU APM students, and create an even larger alumni network to aid future APM graduates.

Source: APM Newsletter Q2 2005, Stern Summit on Global Business, by Group 5: Carolyn Mohr, Elizabeth White, Marcelo Moreira, Peggy Cameron, and Jamie Melzer, http://www.business.ku.edu/_FileLibrary/PageFile/351/APM-News2005Q2.mht

The runner-up in the competition was a recommendation from Boston University to buy International Paper. Table 13.4 shows how the recommendations stacked up.

We assume that an Inergy investor would put half of her holdings in NRGP when it IPOed three months after this presentation. The APM's class actual CAGR on this investment is 50 percent since April 2003. Since a good portion of that return is from dividends, it's a relatively low-risk investment.

Quick Notes

Garmin We've mentioned Garmin (GRMN) before. We could have talked about Garmin in the last chapter about international investing. Garmin's corporate headquarters is in Olathe, Kansas, a Kansas City suburb. The company is incorporated in the Cayman Islands and has major operations in the United Kingdom, Taiwan, and Oregon. Garmin designs and manufactures all kinds of global positioning systems. It has grown since its IPO in December 2000 from sales of $345 million to almost $2 billion in sales in

TABLE 13.4 Compound Annual Growth Rate, April 12, 2005–June 2007

	WellPoint (WLP)	International Paper (IP)	Inergy Investment	SP 500
CAGR	0.11	0.10	0.22	0.11

TABLE 13.5   Garmin's Valuation Measures, 2002–2007

	Mar-07	Dec-06	Dec-05	Dec-04	Dec-03	Dec-02
EBITDA ($million)	615	597	380	305	244	186
Net income ($million)	566	514	311	206	179	143
Dividend/Share	0.50	0.50	0.25	0.25	0.25	0.00
Share price[a]	54.15	55.66	32.83	29.85	26.50	14.12
Market cap ($million)	11,711	12,028	7,096	6,467	5,733	3,048
TEV ($million)	11,138	11,618	6,729	6,153	5,405	2,738
Dividend Yield (%)	0.92	0.90	0.76	0.84	0.94	0.00
TEV/EBITDA	18.10	19.45	17.73	20.20	22.14	14.74
P/E	20.67	23.40	22.80	31.44	32.09	21.34
Earnings growth (%)	45.28	64.91	50.79	15.24	24.24	25.71
PEG	0.46	0.36	0.45	2.06	1.32	0.83

[a]Split adjusted before August 15, 2006.

the spring of 2007. That's a compound annual growth rate of 32 percent. Earnings have grown almost as fast at 29 percent.

The growth is even more remarkable because Garmin has had virtually no debt.[1] Garmin's growth has all been financed with cash flow. Table 13.5 shows some of the valuation metrics for Garmin. Garmin has never been a "cheap" stock based on P/E or TEV/EBITDA. Since it is a growth stock, it's better to look at the PEG ratio (P/E to growth in earnings). Based on its PEG ratio, Garmin did look much cheaper when we bought the stock in December 2002.

Group 3 in the fall 2002 class recommended a Garmin buy. The group members were Rosalie Ast, Cara Lance, Todd Ludgate, and Matt Taylor. Matt worked at the Johnson County Executive Airport while he was in school. Garmin executives flew in and out of the airport, but he also noticed that lots of the small planes were being retrofitted with new Garmin GPS cockpits. Matt talked to some of the executives and became convinced that this company was one to buy. He sold the idea to group, and the group sold it to the class. Since 2002 we've made a 42.1 percent annual compound return. We've bought calls and pursued a covered call strategy on less than half of our position over the last year. Most have worked out okay, except for the July 2007 $60 calls. We gave up $22 a share on that one! Ouch!

---

[1] It did have $40 million in debt when it went public in 2000. The company paid it all off by 2003.

Kevin Rauckman, Garmin CFO, is a University of Kansas graduate. He has come to class on quite a few occasions to make his investor presentation. In December 2004 Garmin hosted the class at its headquarters for an analyst day. We were impressed with the lean management team and stewardship of the company's funds, especially when the head of investor relations told us she'd be happy when they could fly to Taiwan in business class. The company executives, including the CEO, always fly coach.

Kansas City Southern   Kansas City Southern (KSU) was added to the portfolio in December 2006 based on the recommendation of fall 2006 Group 6 with members Steve Baru, Jeremy Simmons, and Matt Terrill. We don't have a contact with the company yet, but we're working with Steve to develop one. A couple of months after we bought our position in, news reports came in that Warren Buffett had been building a stake in Burlington Northern. All railroad stocks surged on the news.

The group's investment thesis for the purchase was based on five points:

1. Exclusivity of Mexico–Kansas City rail line
2. Operating efficiencies (speed and load)
3. Pricing power
4. Burgeoning Asian trade
5. Strained California ports equals growth of key Mexican port

The group pointed out that U.S. ports are overloaded and that Kansas City Southern has a key rail line coming to the United States from the Pacific side of Mexico. All of those Asian imports have to get to the United States somehow. With lower rates than U.S. ports, the Mexican port with the Kansas City connection is set to take off.

From December 2006 to the end of July 2007, the stock has increased 23 percent.

WRAPPING UP

The examples that we used in this chapter all produced really good returns for the APM portfolio. We also want to show that local investing doesn't always lead to the highest returns. The rest of the local returns are in Table 13.6. Sprint and Payless Cashways were big losers, but we didn't exactly clean up on any of these. The only current holding in the portfolio is NIC, Inc. We decided not to invest in Applebee's in fall 2004. The share price at

TABLE 13.6 APM Returns on Other Local Investments

Company	Cerner Corp	Equity Office Properties	H & R Block	NIC Inc.	Payless Cashways	Protection One	Sprint	Westar Energy	Yellow Corp.
Return: CAGR (%)	10.6	3.7	7.6	22.3	−33.7	3.6	−41.0	16.0	−6.8

that time was close to $25. In July 2007, when the announcement came that IHOP was offering to buy Applebee's, the bid was $25.50.

There's been some criticism that investors shouldn't favor local companies. APM has had some very good returns on local companies, but local companies have returned about the same as the portfolio overall. When we see something good locally, we go after it!

CHAPTER 14

Making Corporate Governance Pay

Corporate governance is all the rage. Companies like to boast about their rankings, how many independent directors they have, and how they have put in place all of the requirements of Sarbanes-Oxley. Corporate governance became the rage after some big corporate meltdowns in 2002; Enron, Tyco, Adelphia, WorldCom, and Global Crossing, easily surpassed previous scandals in terms of lost shareholder wealth, jobs, and executive criminal trials. Corporate governance checks and balances failed big time, but what should concern investors today is the many small failures of corporate governance that still persist.

Congress and regulators had plenty of laws before the scandals, but big scandals provide politicians a big stage and an opportunity to tell voters that they are there to make sure these things don't happen again. But we've had scandals, big shareholder frauds, and meltdowns since public markets began. Sarbanes-Oxley (SOX) won't cure that; in fact, most of SOX succeeded only in adding a lot of additional cost to most corporations. Accounting firms are cleaning up with the added SOX audits that are required. Probably the only provision in the bill that was really beneficial to public shareholders was the statements signed by the chief financial officer (CFO) and the chief executive officer (CEO) that they know what is in the financial statements and they are responsible. No longer can a CEO say, as Ken Lay did, that he or she didn't really understand or know what was going on with all that financial stuff.

There probably aren't any laws that can be passed that will make CEOs take care of the corporation's money as if it were their own, if they are not so inclined. The board of directors is supposed to make sure that things don't get too far out of line. Its job is to make sure that the company is run in the shareholders' long-term interest. CEOs, as managers of companies, may be more interested in their salary, their new corporate jet, their new corporate vacation home, and the like. The board is supposed to balance keeping a ~~great manager versus the cost of keeping him or her. Of course, this great~~ manager is probably a buddy of the several board members, and the board members get paid rather well for showing up at six or seven meetings a year. Now with video or telephone conferencing, directors don't even have to be physically at the meeting.

In this chapter we discuss what we see as the biggest corporate governance issues: independent directors and corporate compensation. We'll also discuss corporate activism and prove some examples of the APM class's engagement in corporate activism. We've been involved in letter-writing campaigns to Oplink (OPLK) and chinadotcom, now called CDC Corp. (CHINA), among others. We've also invested in Tyco and Enron.

BOARD ISSUES

One of the biggest jobs of the board is to set the compensation for the CEO and other senior management. The job is almost always delegated to a compensation committee comprised of independent directors. Before we address the compensation issue, we need to see why the way most of the world thinks about "independent" board members is a problem and not the solution that it's touted to be.

Independent Board Members

It's easier to define independent board members by what they're not than by what they are. An independent board member

- Doesn't work for the company
- Isn't a big customer or supplier
- Isn't the company's lawyer, banker, or consultant
- Isn't an interlocking director
- Doesn't own more than 5 percent of the company's shares

Here is one definition of an independent director from the Council of Institutional Investors:

> *An independent director is someone whose only nontrivial professional, familial or financial connection to the corporation, its chairman, CEO or any other executive officer is his or her directorship.*
>
> *Stated most simply, an independent director is a person whose directorship constitutes his or her only connection to the corporation.*
>
> *Source:* www.cii.org/policies/ind_dir_defn.htm

The idea is that an independent director is someone who'll be fair and honest and isn't unduly attached to a management's point of view. These directors are supposed to provide impartial advice, direction, and monitoring. Unfortunately, while it sounds good in theory, it doesn't work too well in practice.

Most board members have big, high-pressure, full-time jobs outside of being a director. Retired executives who serve as board members might be on several boards, have a consulting practice, or just might want to spend some time on their golf game. Being a board member isn't their highest priority. To help make it a bigger priority, cash compensation has been replaced with a mix of stock and stock option compensation. The idea is that directors can make big money if they successfully participate in getting the company's share price to go up.

If the company has a great CEO who's honest, capable, visionary, and the share price is going up, being an independent director has to be one of the greatest jobs of all time. You go to meetings, listen to the CEO report what she's doing, say "great job," and try to stay out of the way. Perhaps you worry a little about the CEO leaving and put something in place so that doesn't happen. You've done your job, collected your pay, and expended little effort other than getting to the meeting to see the other directors and listen to the CEO report on the wonderful job she's doing. As Nell Minow and Bob Monks report, their late friend and chairman of the National Association of Corporate Directors Tom Horton said, "The most important attribute of a corporate director is the ability to yawn with your mouth closed."[1]

Fast forward a year. The CEO dies suddenly of a massive heart attack. She was only 50; who could have predicted such a thing? Now the board members have to earn their keep. They've got to find a new CEO quickly. They appoint an interim and hire an executive search firm to find the perfect candidate. A few extra conference calls, perhaps a few recommendations to give to the search firm. Now the search firm brings the board a list of candidates, and the board settles on a highly qualified individual. To induce the person to move they only had to double his salary, which was three times the previous CEO's salary, but the directors know they've got to pay to get the best person for the job.

Knowing that you've got a great new CEO, you, as a director, can sit back, relax, and settle in to your former routine as an independent director. Why would you want to work too hard for the shareholders? You've got a

---

[1] Robert A. G. Monks and Nell Minow, *Corporate Governance, 3rd Edition.* (Malden, MA Blackwell Publishing, 2004), 197.

cash salary, some upside in the options and stock holdings, but they aren't a huge holding for you. If there aren't any fires to put out, why should you go looking for them?

As an independent director, it's easiest to believe everything the CEO reports to you. Confrontations aren't pleasant, and other board members won't thank you. What's the payoff for questioning or doubting management? You could have a big fight on your hands. You could be labeled as a troublemaker board member and lose potential seats on other boards. You might get a slight increase in share price somewhere down the road after a lot of grief. In the meantime, a board fight would probably decrease share price for a while. What's the payoff for sitting back and doing just a little? No grief, pretty good pay. You might lose a little on the stock and option holdings, but hey, they're just a little sweetener. It's easier just to get along with everybody.

In this scenario, we're assuming that the independent director is a pretty wealthy former corporate executive who may socialize with the CEO or other board members. Warren Buffett in his 2002 shareholder letter addresses this "collegiality" issue. He also addresses two another "independence issues." What about board members who are receiving a substantial chunk of their income from being members of boards? Are they truly independent? APM ran into that issue with Wilshire Financial, now called Beverly Hills Bancorp (BHBC).

EXCERPT FROM 2002 LETTER TO BERKSHIRE HATHAWAY SHAREHOLDERS

...Why have intelligent and decent directors failed so miserably? The answer lies not in inadequate laws—it's always been clear that directors are obligated to represent the interests of shareholders—but rather in what I'd call "boardroom atmosphere."

It's almost impossible, for example, in a boardroom populated by well-mannered people, to raise the question of whether the CEO should be replaced. It's equally awkward to question a proposed acquisition that has been endorsed by the CEO, particularly when his inside staff and outside advisors are present and unanimously support his decision. (They wouldn't be in the room if they didn't.) Finally, when the compensation committee—armed, as always, with support from a high-paid consultant—reports on a megagrant of options to the CEO, it would be like belching at the dinner table for a director to suggest that the committee reconsider.

These "social" difficulties argue for outside directors regularly meeting without the CEO—a reform that is being instituted and that I enthusiastically endorse. I doubt, however, that most of the other new governance rules and recommendations will provide benefits commensurate with the monetary and other costs they impose.

The current cry is for "independent" directors. It is certainly true that it is desirable to have directors who think and speak independently—but they must also be business-savvy, interested and shareholder-oriented. In my 1993 commentary, those are the three qualities I described as essential.

Rules that have been proposed and that are almost certain to go into effect will require changes in Berkshire's board, obliging us to add directors who meet the codified requirements for "independence." Doing so, we will add a test that we believe is important, but far from determinative, in fostering independence: We will select directors who have huge and true ownership interests (that is, stock that they or their family have purchased, not been given by Berkshire or received via options), expecting those interests to influence their actions to a degree that dwarfs other considerations such as prestige and board fees....

That gets to an often-overlooked point about directors' compensation, which at public companies averages perhaps $50,000 annually. It baffles me how the many directors who look to these dollars for perhaps 20% or more of their annual income can be considered independent when Ron Olson, for example, who is on our board, may be deemed not independent because he receives a tiny percentage of his very large income from Berkshire legal fees.... At Berkshire, wanting our fees to be meaningless to our directors, we pay them only a pittance.

Additionally, not wanting to insulate our directors from any corporate disaster we might have, we don't provide them with officers' and directors' liability insurance (an unorthodoxy that, not so incidentally, has saved our shareholders many millions of dollars over the years). Basically, we want the behavior of our directors to be driven by the effect their decisions will have on their family's net worth, not by their compensation. That's the equation for Charlie and me as managers, and we think it's the right one for Berkshire directors as well. To find new directors, we will look through our shareholders list for people who directly, or in their family, have had large Berkshire holdings—in the millions of dollars—for a long time.

Individuals making that cut should automatically meet two of our tests, namely that they be interested in Berkshire and shareholder-oriented. In our third test, we will look for business savvy, a competence that is far from commonplace.

Source: 2002 Letter to Shareholders by Warren Buffett.
www.berkshirehathaway.com/letters/2002pdf.pdf

We're not saying that all directors on boards are lazy. We are saying that it's easier not to raise a fuss and to get along with people. In a close call it's easier to give someone the benefit of the doubt so a good person may not speak up. On Enron's board, there were many leading lights and very smart people. They were probably good people, too. No one spoke up.

In 1999 the APM class invested in Wilshire Financial as it was emerging from bankruptcy as Wilshire REIT. The former CEO, Andy Wiederhorn, was not too far away from going to jail. The court appointed most of the board. The board did a creditable job hiring a new CEO, Steve Glennon, and getting the company back up and running. There were two main parts of the business: a bank in Beverly Hills and a loan servicing business. The bank was a wholesale bank that primarily funded its commercial lending operations with wholesale certificates of deposit and repurchase (repo) borrowings.

It was pretty clear that the bank was very profitable. It was not clear how profitable the loan servicing business was. The company's headquarters were in Portland, Oregon. The bank was in Southern California. Most of the court-appointed board members were middle-class professionals from the Portland area. For several years beginning in 2001, the board refused any offers for the loan servicing business. After a concerted push by some large shareholders to lobby and remove some board members (not the APM class this time), the loan servicing business was finally sold for $48 million in 2004. The price of the stock rose from $6 per share at the end of 2003 to $10 per share shortly after the announcement.

The other issue that Mr. Buffett addresses is the 5 percent plus rule when defining an independent board member. Who better to represent shareholders than a large shareholder who is not part of the management team? A big shareholder's interests are certainly more aligned with the rest of the shareholders than someone who receives cash and only a few shares in compensation. Such a person wouldn't be afraid to call the CEO on the carpet if things don't quite add up or ask hard questions that more collegial colleagues might let slide.

But there's a but. You do need to be careful whom you call a 5 percent shareholder. The SEC requires anyone who accumulates more than a 5 percent holding to be identified in Part III of the 10-K under "Security Ownership of Certain Beneficial Owners and Management—Identification of owners of 5 percent or more of registrant's stock in addition to listing the amount and percent of each class of stock held by officers and directors." If a shareholder crosses over the 10 percent mark, he or she must file a Form 3 or 4 within 48 hours. Here's what the "but" is. The SEC filing requirements only apply to long positions in equity securities. Frank Partnoy, author of *Fiasco: The Inside Story of a Wall Street Trader* and a KU grad, visited the APM class and pointed out an instance in which a shareholder accumulated a 10 percent position and had filed as a 10 percent owner.[2] However, he had hedged the position with options, so he basically had no economic interest in the firm. He did get a board seat and voted to buy a company he did have an interest in. After the acquisition at an inflated price, he resigned his director position. All of it was perfectly legal. It could play out the other way also. Someone could accumulate a large position by buying a combination of call options and equity, staying just below the equity filing requirements.

One final point about independent directors: Consultants rank corporate governance and compile scores that they publish. Berkshire Hathaway doesn't get high marks because the consultants can't check off the independent directors' box on their rating form. Now, lots of companies are paying lip service to corporate governance. They want to make sure that their boxes all get checked off, never mind the substance. It's not surprising that Warren Buffett is one of the few to speak up when things just don't make sense.

CEO Compensation

Setting CEO compensation is a major task of a board's compensation committee. Today, because it's a "best practice" box that can be checked off, most compensation committees are made up of independent board members. Because the directors want to make sure that they've got all their bases covered, they hire a consultant to help them sort through the task of compensating the CEO and other members of senior management. The compensation consultants provide a survey of CEO pay for comparable companies. They also provide advice on what form the pay should take: salary, bonus, stock, stock options, stock appreciation rights (SARs), phantom stock, insurance policies, severance pay, and more.

---

[2] Frank Partnoy, *Fiasco: The Inside Story of a Wall Street Trader* (New York: Penguin Books, 1999).

The consultants answer all the questions, collect their fees, and walk away. Now it's up to the compensation committee of the board to set the pay. These board members may have been involved in hiring the CEO, too. Can they say "We think our CEO and management team are below average, so we'll set their compensation below the average of the consultants survey"? Of course not. It's just like Garrison Keillor's Lake Wobegon, "where all the women are strong, all the men are good-looking, and all the children are above average." Each year salaries are typically set at a certain percentile of the survey, but no one's going to set their CEO's salary below average. Even average would be an insult and won't reflect well on the board that hired the CEO, so salaries are set at the 60th, 70th, or 80th percentile. The next year the consultant is armed with a new salary survey that's higher than the one from the previous year. Pretty soon you see a price spiral in CEO pay.

It's not in any CEO's interest to stop the race to the top. It's really not in board members' interests either because board salaries and other compensation are set in the same way with many of the same consultants. It's not clear how shareholders can force companies to break out of the cycle. One way is for large institutional investors who control large blocks of shares to force change. In the past, when confronted with a problem CEO, a large institution would simply sell its shares quietly over time. Some institutions have started to vote their proxies and make their voices heard. Institutional Shareholder Services (ISS) is one of several consultants that rate governance and advise large institutions (for a fee) on the most shareholder-friendly way to vote.

CORPORATE ACTIVISTS

In Chapter 12 we mentioned Brad Shoup and T. Boone Pickens. Brad is a KU grad and former employee of Pickens, one of the original corporate raiders. Corporate raiders have been both praised and vilified. In the 1980s lots of companies were fat, happy, and complacent. Employees didn't move around much, benefits were generous, the leveraged buyout (LBO) was beginning to rise on the horizon, and some large shareholders together with a few Wall Street types were starting to agitate for leaner, meaner corporations with higher profits. T. Boone Pickens, Frank Lorenzo, and Carl Icahn teamed up with Wall Street deal makers like Henry Kravis, Michael Milken, and Nicholas Brady to squeeze some of the fat out of public corporations.

In an LBO, the company is refinanced using a large portion of debt, many times high-yield debt or junk bonds. The idea is that the debt will be paid off quickly with the sale of underperforming assets in the company. It is hoped that the new, lean company will be more profitable because the excess has been trimmed away. The sounds easy, but trimming excess also means that workers' benefits are cut and many jobs are lost. The raiders are vilified by those who lose their jobs and praised by investors who make money on the deals. It's the little guy versus Wall Street, or blue collar versus white, and it can cause a lot of hard feelings.

One of the key ideas that Brad Shoup has discussed with the class is using the carrot before you use the stick with a company. Companies fight hostile initiatives with shareholders' money. Getting in a fight with a company is similar to being taxed twice. You pay for your own fight and you pay for them to fight you also.

Oplink Campaign

Oplink is an optical technology company that produces designs in California and manufactures in China. It trades on NASDAQ and is headquartered in California. It IPOed in the October 2000 at a split adjusted price of $239.75 By the end of 2001, the stock traded around $13. In June 2004, the class purchased shares at $13.64. The investment thesis was that Verizon and SBC announced plans to spend billions of dollars to build the last mile of fiber networks. Oplink was positioned as the low cost provider of optical cable. The company had a strong balance sheet with $1.26 per share in cash. We hoped that the re-emergence of tech and a share buyback would make the stock price pop once again. To help bring about the share buyback, we decided to try some corporate activism.

The APM class may not have a lot of clout, but we do have numbers. With 20 to 30 students each semester we can write a lot of letters. In the fall 2005 class we mounted a letter-writing campaign to convince Oplink's board that they should ask for Chairman Chang's resignation, repurchase additional shares with their excess cash, and make sure that there were no conflicts of interest in Chang's hedge fund with the acquisitions that Oplink was planning.

Table 14.1 outlines the first letter-writing assignment. Initially each group wrote to a different board member urging the board to buy back shares instead of continuing to make unprofitable acquisitions.

TABLE 14.1   Fall 2005 Letter-Writing Campaign to Oplink's Board

Board Member or Officer	Group
Joseph Y. Liu: Chief Executive, President, and Director	1, 2
Bruce D. Horn: Chief Financial Officer and Treasurer	3
Herbert Chang: Chairman of Board of Directors	5
Chieh Chang: Director	6
Jesse W. Jack: Director	7
Leonard J. LeBlanc: Director	4

In addition to each group's letter, Joan Huber, a teaching assistant for the class, wrote an excellent letter to the chairman of the board, Herbert Chang. (See Figure 14.1.) After the first set of letters, we wrote a subsequent set based on some specific information addressed in a conference call.

Oplink Letter-Writing Assignment II

- Groups 5, 6, and 7. Letters to Herbert Chang asking for his resignation. Trace his transactions over the last few years. Also document his remuneration for serving as an Oplink board member. Include questions about his stock sales. Has he exercised any of his options?
- Groups 1 and 2. Get the name of the person on the conference call who asked the question about the Dutch auction. Contact him if possible to let him know that we support this action. Write up an explanation of how a Dutch auction works and how it would benefit shareholders. Write a letter to Leonard LeBlanc to show him the benefit of a Dutch auction.
- Groups 3 and 4. Investigate Herbert Chang's hedge fund, Investar. What investments has the fund made? Estimate how successful they have been. Has Investar had any investments in companies that Oplink has done business with or thought about acquiring? Provide a report and possibly a letter to the Oplink, CEO if appropriate. (You may want to split up the companies that they have invested in between your two groups and pool your results.)

While this initiative may not seem like a big deal, ones like it can serve as a wake-up call to the board. Board members, especially in small companies, are not used to getting much feedback or scrutiny of their filings. Just the fact that several people are paying attention and putting some issues on the table may make other board members less hesitant to bring up the issues. We weren't the only ones with questions about Oplink. Questions from other callers on the conference call showed more awareness of some of Chang's questionable transactions.

Around the same time of our second letter-writing campaign, Kent nominated Corey Johnson, an APM student, to Oplink's board. Corey wrote a letter to the board accepting the nomination. At the time, Corey was a JD/MBA student who had worked in Hallmark's fast-track leadership development program. He had graduated from the University of Missouri and had been a member of the varsity football team. While he was in the KU JD/MBA program, he worked in Missouri's public defender program and in the Johnson County District Attorney's Office. He would receive his graduate degrees in the next semester.

October 18, 2005

Mr. Herbert Chang
Chairman of the Board
Oplink Communications Inc.
c/o InveStar Capital, Inc.
Room 1201, 12Fl., 333, Keelung Road, Sec.1
Taipei, Taiwan

Re: Oplink Decisions & Board of Directors Membership

Dear Mr. Chang,

This letter is on behalf of the APM Portfolio held by the Endowment Association at the University of Kansas. Others representing and writing on behalf of this sizeable holding in the APM Portfolio have attempted to communicate with you about issues related to Oplink by recent letters, but no one has had a response from you in any form. This action does not bode well in terms of a Board member's alignment with shareholders' interests. This is especially troubling since Oplink has substantially underperformed the NASDAQ Telecommunications Index since its IPO in 2000, all during your tenure as Board Member and also Board Chairman. One would think that you would be more open to communication about ways to improve performance and shareholder value.

Therefore, I would like to address the following issues:

- Cash/Share Buyback

Oplink holds a large amount of cash/cash equivalents on the balance sheet. This is excessive for what is needed for operations, especially since the company is cash flow positive. It also is more than necessary for prudent acquisitions, and possibly relieves management of strict fiscal responsibility, making it easier for them to execute imprudent acquisitions because "there is more where that came from." We observe that the company has been trading slightly above its cash value. Holding so much cash is not congruent with investors in a growth industry. Shareholders interested in owning a company like Oplink do not intend to hold a firm operating like a bank. If suitable and prudent uses for this cash cannot be found, then the Board should have enough confidence in the company to vote that it reinvest a significant amount of cash in itself, i.e., buy back shares. This would be a low risk option and accretive to shareholder value. The current prices should be compelling.

- Your Managed Funds' Divestiture of Large fraction of their Holdings

Since the IPO, the entities that you represent, InveStar Capital and Forefront Venture partners has decreased its holdings from ~24 million shares to ~13 million shares, with ~800 thousand options unexercised. The most recent reduction of your holdings was as recent as late May in the amount of ~1.5 million shares. The disposal of shares by funds you control has been consistent and relentless. This hardly represents a vote of confidence in the company. If you do not have confidence in the company either to continue to hold shares or vote to repurchase shares, perhaps you should not serve on the Board, and in particular, as its Chairman.

FIGURE 14.1 Joan Huber's Letter to Oplink's Chairman, October 18, 2005 (*Continues*)

- Nominating Yourself to a New Three Year Term with no Alternatives

As Chairman of the Nominating and Governance Committee and given the underperformance of the company on your watch, there should be a legitimate attempt to find fresh experience and ideas from other sources. Also, the Board or this Committee, which you head, seems to have little interest in input from shareholders since the company's Proxy states "The Nominating and Corporate Governance Committee has not determined whether it will consider nominees recommended by stockholders (as opposed to formally nominated) or, if so, what procedures stockholders would follow in submitting recommendations." It would be appropriate for a slate of possible nominees to be put on the ballot so that there is a choice for shareholders.

- Compensation

Given the size of the company and recent performance, the $20,000 annual cash compensation is prudent. However, the size of the 72,000 annual option grants seems excessive. Although the option grants are supposed to align the Board with shareholders' interests, they appear not to have accomplished this goal and should be reduced to 20,000 per member per year. You are in a position as Chairman of the Compensation Committee to recommend this action.

- Conflict of Interest

Your Venture funds are on record as holding over a dozen privately held companies in the same Communication and Networking space as Oplink. It could be in your Venture funds' interests to vote that Oplink use some of its cash to invest in or acquire one of your holdings. Your funds also are on record as having a long history of selling its venture investments to publicly held companies. This does not fit with the OPLK Proxy statement about independent directors: "A material relationship is one which impairs or inhibits, or has the potential to inhibit, a director's exercise of critical and disinterested judgment on behalf of the Company and its stockholders." Surely as Chairman of the Corporate Governance Committee you can appreciate how your activities may not be consistent with good Corporate Governance.

In short, we believe that there is much reason for you to propose and vote for a substantial share buyback. We request that you do this in the amount of an $80 million commitment. We also recommend that you take action in revising the way Board Members are nominated, that you provide a reasonable slate of nominees from which the shareholders choose, and that your committee have a clear path by which shareholders can nominate their own candidates.

If you cannot see the merit in these actions, then we must believe that there are other motivations involved in your decisions rather than your independent position on the Board. In this case, we respectfully request that you resign your position on the Oplink Board of Directors.

Sincerely,

Joan Huber
APM Portfolio
University of Kansas

FIGURE 14.1 (*Continued*)

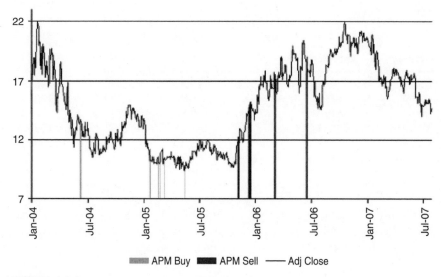

FIGURE 14.2 Oplink Share Price, 2004–2007

Oplink did buy back some shares, never quite as many as we hoped for. The stock never rebounded to its 2000 heights. Oplink's board of directors hasn't changed too much. Herbert Chang didn't resign until February 16, 2006. He was replaced as chairman by Leonard LeBlanc who has served on the board since 2000. In July 2007 the price was still only $14.72. Figure 14.2 shows the share price from the beginning of 2004 to mid-2007. APM managed to earn an annual compound return of 39 percent on holdings that we bought in 2004 and sold in 2005–06.

WRAPPING UP

The class was involved in a similar and more intense campaign that lasted over several semesters with chinadotcom (now CDC Corp.). The company was making some poor acquisitions, and we urged management to use the cash it had available to buy back shares instead. The result was similar to Oplink's, although the class earned quite a bit more on chinadotcom.

We were also invested in Enron at two different times—once as the company was failing, and earlier in 1999. Table 14.2 shows the transactions. The last sell was a great learning experience. We should have sold when the

TABLE 14.2   Enron Transactions

Date	Transaction	Shares	Share Price	Total	Cumulative Shares
1/6/99	BUY	260	29.81	−7,750	260
3/15/00	SELL	−60	70.00	4,200	200
1/4/01	SELL	−200	83.94	16,773	0
9/20/01	BUY	100	31.95	−3,202	100
10/10/01	BUY	100	33.50	−3,357	200
11/27/01	SELL	−200	4.98	982	0

first whiff of trouble was in the air. Of course, hindsight is 20/20. One of Frank Partnoy's comments from class: "If things are too hard for you to understand, it's probably because management wants it that way."

CHAPTER 15

It's All About Who You Know

Information is the lifeblood of investing. With the Internet, investment information is everywhere. It's prepackaged and easy to find. Access like that would have been unthinkable 10 years ago. It is invaluable, but at the same time because everyone has it, it's lost some measure of its value. You have to have it, but now you need to know "what else." The what else is people to put the information in historical and relative context, people to remind us that mass processing of numbers by a standardized program obscures some important points, people to help us "get close to the information."

Since 1994 APM has had a lot of students, speakers, and friends involved with the class. The network gets bigger and bigger. It gets a little easier to pick up the phone and ask an alum what's going on in the oil industry or what's really went down with the Harmon deal. Some of the student groups have stayed close for many years. It's easy to get great speakers to come to class every semester, people know what a great opportunity it is. With every newsletter, we get more alumni with news to update. Careers and families are mostly going well.

In this chapter we want to document and thank those who have made intellectual and financial contributions that have contributed to APM's success. The students, alumni, speakers, and benefactors are all part of the network that makes the APM program. The students shoulder the burden during the semester. The alumni who stay involved provide a balanced perspective. The speakers make the program relevant and provide the type of significant learning experience that makes the students want to continue to stay involved as alumni. Our benefactors provide everything from access to professional financial tools to new networking and employment opportunities for the students.

APM STUDENTS

The APM students are hardworking, talented, and always ready to help. Not only have they made the class a success, but they work hard on the quarterly newsletters, they make our annual golf tournament a fun and profitable, they struggle with their cases, and they make sure the speakers and visitors to class feel welcome and appreciated. They come to class well prepared and eager to engage in a discussion about the portfolio.

They are also apprehensive and a little unsure of themselves initially. That feeling probably serves them well. A little humility in investing does us all good. We can't possibly know it all. We need to be open to learning from the speakers and other members of the class. The students are the bedrock. They are the reason that we're all here. Each semester the new group gets to build on the shoulders of the previous semester. They start off a little wobbly while they negotiate the workload and the overload of new information, but by the end of the semester they are a solid pyramid of APM analysts ready to lead the next group of students through the hoops.

Student Portfolio Returns

The students are always in a hurry to make their mark on the portfolio. Many of them come to class itching to trade, but as we learned from the early years of the class, it's better to go slow with trading at the beginning of the semester. Since 2003 we've had student groups make recommendations at the end of the semester. Each group recommends one trading idea. It can be a short, an option strategy, or most commonly, a long investment in a stock.

The average return on those stocks the class didn't buy was –1.4 percent. The average return on the stocks the class did buy was 22.1 percent. The comparison isn't quite fair for those we didn't buy because when we calculate the return, we assume that we still hold the stock today. We might have sold it earlier as we have with many of the recommendations that we did buy. We didn't pick all of the big winners, but we did manage to avoid the biggest losers. Table 15.1 summarizes the returns by class and group. Table 15.2 shows the stock recommendations. Virtually all of those are long positions.

Our apologies to the class of spring 2004. We have great records for the other semesters, but we only have a couple of the recommendations from that class. I know that we missed buying one stock that did well from that class because we hear from Jeremy Lill and Willie Chang periodically about our mistake!

TABLE 15.1 Return on Recommendations by Group and Semester

Semester	Group								Average			
	1	2	3	4	5	6	7	8	Buys	No. Buys	Overall Average	Difference Buy – No Buy
Fall 2003	**3.2**	*3.1*	**57.4**	*41.7*					**57.4**	16.0	26.4	41.4
Fall 2004	**2.0**	*47.8*	*-40.3*	*21.0*					**23.6**	-40.3	7.6	63.9
Spring 2005	**15.5**	*13.2*	*1.2*	*-5.6*	*23.8*	*-6.7*	*4.5*		**21.7**	1.3	6.6	20.4
Fall 2005	*114.3*	*39.5*	*15.0*	*13.2*	*6.8*	*11.0*	*-56.4*		**12.1**	26.0	20.5	-14.0
Spring 2006	**38.8**	*12.7*	*16.1*	*-46.8*	*-25.3*	*33.1*	*0.0*	**90.7**	**41.7**	3.2	14.9	38.6
Fall 2006	**2.5**	*-31.0*	*-1.9*	*4.9*	*-15.6*	*21.6*	*-32.2*		**10.0**	-11.8	-7.4	21.8
Spring 2007	*5.5*	*6.8*	*-32.0*	*-25.6*	*1.5*	*1.7*			*-12.0*	-4.6	-7.0	-7.4
All semesters	**32.4**	**13.1**	**2.2**	**0.4**	**-1.8**	**12.2**	**-21.0**	**90.7**	**22.1**	-1.4	8.8	23.5

Italic font: Compound annual return on stocks we didn't buy from date recommended to July 31, 2007. Bold font: Compound annual return on stocks we did buy based on group recommendations.

TABLE 15.2 Recommendations by Group and Semesters

Semester	1	2	3	4	5	6	7	8
Fall 2003	**LKQX**	EK	**PCTI**	LOUD				
Fall 2004	**TSCO**	**LKQX**	LEV	MFW				
Spring 2005	**WGO**	DVA	HD	**BBY**	EGOV	**INFY**	HRL	
Fall 2005	**EVST**	KONA	**MRH**	**SGMS**	ENDP	**BUD**	GB:PRTY	
Spring 2006	**LAYN**	**BXXX**	EVVV	**LOW**	GLT	**CRDN**	ELOS	
Fall 2006	**GB:TSCO**	**BECN**	GCFB	**DEO**	PSS	**KSU**	ICO	RIO
Spring 2007	**TWI**	CROX	FCSX	**IBKR**	OKE	**ADY**		

Bold font: Stocks we bought.

You can see that we missed some other good recommendations. Loudeye (LOUD) from Group 4 for the fall 2003 semester had a 42 percent return through October 16, 2006, when it was taken over by Nokia. Other outsize performers that we missed were Everlast (EVST) and Kona Grill Inc. (Kona), Layne Christensen Co. (LAYN), and Ceradyne Inc. (CRDN). The groups that recommended them have the satisfaction of saying "I told you so."

All Class Recommendations

Table 15.3 shows all of the recommendations that we bought since the fall 2003 class (except spring 2004).

Table 15.4 shows all of the recommendations that we didn't buy since the fall 2003 class (except spring 2004). We should note that Group 3 in the fall 2004 class prepared their recommendation and presentation on Levitt Corp. (LEV). A few days or even the evening before their presentations, the students discovered some information that led them to change their buy recommendation. They went ahead with the presentation but told the class not to buy unless certain conditions held. Those conditions did not occur, so we never bought. Something similar happened with Group 3 in the spring 2006 class and ev3, Inc. (EVVV). What is it with those Group 3's!

APM Teaching Assistants

The APM teaching assistants (TAs) are a special group of students who come back after they have taken the class to help with additional portfolio duties, organization, and serve as additional assistance for the current students. At the beginning of the semester, when things can seem overwhelming, they help remind the students that they can survive and thrive. The alumni TAs have become great resources as they have progressed through their careers. They've come in as speakers, e-mailed us to alert us to some special market situations that the students should be aware of, helped with job contacts, facilitated access to companies and corporate leaders, and more. Other alumni have helped with all of these things, but the TAs have more than one semester to bond so they turn out to be some of our most loyal alumni.

They are gluttons for punishment. One semester of hard work isn't enough for them. They come back to do it all again and more. They are the glue that helps keep the students together and the instructors organized. When we forget to mention in class that special key assumption that helps make sense of a complicated case, they step in and let the students know.

TABLE 15.3   APM Student Group Recommendation Buys

Semester	Group	Ticker	Recommended Price	Buy Price	Current Price	Buy Date	Total Return in %	Compound Annual Average Return in %[1]	Still Own?
Fall 03	3	PCTI	9.15	10.56	8.40	11/2003	(23.30)	(20.49)	No
Fall 03	1	LKQX	17.59	17.49	28.59	11/2004	106.66	47.85	Yes
Fall 04	1	TSCO	36.37	33.09	51.93	11/2004	1.96		No
Fall 04	2	LKQX	18.16	17.49	28.59	11/2004	106.66	47.85	Yes
Fall 04	4	MFW	13.16	13.45	65.29	12/2004	22.36	21.03	No
Spring 05	5	EGOV	4.64	4.29	6.80	05/2005	46.76	23.81	Yes
Spring 05	1	WGO	30.41	29.96	29.94	11/2005	17.17	15.52	No
Fall 05	3	MRH	19.28	17.04	17.87	12/2005	14.96	14.97	No
Fall 05	4	SGMS	28.37	27.11	36.78	12/2005	22.69	13.22	Yes
Fall 05	6	BUD	43.50	43.17	50.00	12/2005	18.52	11.05	Yes
Spring 06	7	ELOS	25.76	26.49	24.73	05/2006	(0.00)	(0.01)	No
Spring 06	2	BXXX	11.85	12.69	13.02	05/2006	9.60	12.75	Yes
Spring 06	8	RIO	51.52	46.33	51.21	05/2006	113.24	91.03	Yes
Fall 06	6	KSU	26.77	28.23	40.94	12/2006	21.61		Yes
Fall 06	4	DEO	77.42	78.83	85.02	1/2007	4.90		Yes
Spring 07	4	IBKR	23.27	32.72	23.41	05/2007	(25.64)		Yes
Spring 07	6	ADY	17.83	18.19	18.50	05/2007	1.70		Yes

[1]Compound Annual Return is not calculated for holdings less than one year.

TABLE 15.4 APM Student Group Recommendation We Didn't Buy

Semester	Group	Ticker	Price at Recommendation	Recommendation Date	Current Price	Compound Annual Average Return in %
Fall 03	2	ED	24.01	12/2003	45.01	18.77
Fall 03	4	LOUD*	1.64	11/2003	4.50	41.73
Fall 04	3	LEV	26.00	11/2004	6.43	-40.30
Spring 05	2	DVA	40.30	05/2005	53.22	13.19
Spring 05	3	HD	36.75	05/2005	37.79	1.25
Spring 05	4	BBY	50.34	05/2005	44.19	-5.64
Spring 05	6	INFY	58.01	05/2005	49.69	-6.66
Spring 05	7	HRL	31.78	05/2005	35.05	4.46
Fall 05	1	EVST	8.94	12/2005	31.70	114.53
Fall 05	2	KONA	10.78	12/2005	18.74	39.58
Fall 05	5	ENDP	30.10	12/2005	33.57	6.77
Fall 05	7	GB:PRTY	117.75	12/2005	29.69	-56.43
Spring 06	1	LAYN	30.03	05/2006	45.31	38.85
Spring 06	3	EVVV	13.47	05/2006	16.25	16.16
Spring 06	4	LOW	62.32	05/2006	28.22	-46.87
Spring 06	5	GLT	19.42	05/2006	13.48	-25.33
Spring 06	6	CRDN	52.00	05/2006	74.47	33.20
Fall 06	1	GB:TSCO	397.50	12/2006	407.61	3.87
Fall 06	3	GCFB	5.25	12/2006	5.15	-2.87
Fall 06	5	PSS	30.84	12/2006	26.03	-22.79
Fall 06	7	ICO	5.87	12/2006	3.98	-44.72
Spring 07	1	TWI	23.05	05/2007	29.56	5.46
Spring 07	2	CROX	55.88	05/2007	59.68	6.80
Spring 07	3	FCSX	72.26	05/2007	49.17	-31.95
Spring 07	5	OKE	48.00	05/2007	48.71	1.48

*Loudeye (LOUD)) was taken over by Nokia in 2006 at $4.50/share. Return is based on acquisition date of October 16, 2006.

APM Teaching Assistants

Todd Preheim	1995–Fall	Joan Huber	2003 to 2006–Spring
Dan Drake	1996–Spring	David Brown	2004–Fall
Scott Jones	1996–Spring	Tim Burger	2005–Fall
Doug Davidson	1996–Spring	Jamie Melzer	2005–Fall
Joe Searle	1996–Spring	Jason Mitchell	2005–Fall to 2006–Spring
Ryan Sprott	1996–Spring	Megan Wood	2005–Fall
Jessica Reuss	1996–Fall	Kyle Bateman	2006–Spring
Regev Allon	1996–Fall	Hunter Davis	2006–Spring
Tom Rawlings	1996–Fall	Lindsay Phillips	2006–Spring
Ozel Soykan	1996–Fall	Aaron Arnett	2006–Fall
Matt Moore	1997–Fall	Craig McKim	2006–Fall
Charles Perraudin	1997–Fall	Patrick Nehls	2006–Fall
David Reynoldson	1997/8–Fall	Paul O'Connell	2006–Fall
Joshua Selzer	1997/8–Fall	Adam Hall	2007–Spring
Bart Baldwin	2000–Spring	Ryan Patton	2007–Spring
Jeremy Glauner	2000–Spring	Michael Raupp	2007–Spring
Michael Gentry	2001–Fall	Matt Brunner	2007–Fall
Brendan Woodbury	2001–Fall	Brad Boeshaar	2007–Fall

APM SPEAKERS

The speakers who come to class are the backbone of the students' experience. Without speakers who are generous with time and energy, the APM class would be just another class. The speakers provide a broad perspective. They also provide an incentive for students always to present their best work. No one wants to look bad in front of the guests.

Speakers are a great shortcut in getting close to the information. They participate in the process in several ways. They initiate case ideas, they make sure that the students focus on the right details, and after the students write the cases, they come in and discuss what they've written. This collaborative process makes for a richer discussion. The immediate feedback on the students' ideas helps them deepen their understanding. A chief executive can explain why the company acted a certain way or resolve certain types of uncertainty.

One example of this information came in a class visit from the chief financial officer (CFO) of NIC, Inc. Some groups had written in their cases that they were concerned about the revenue stream because they had read press releases announcing that a certain contract was up for rebid. The CFO, Eric Bur, pointed out that by reading the request for proposals (RFP), you can tell who would get the bid. NIC, Inc. is just about the only company that has a revenue-sharing model for state contracts. If the RFP specifies the NIC business model, then it's virtually a sure thing. He also mentioned that NIC has never lost a rebid on one of its current clients. Information like that casts a whole new light on how to interpret press releases.

Over the years, we estimate that 145 different professionals have been associated with the class. We've visited them, they've spoken in class, or we've arranged a video conference or a conference call. Lots of the speakers have come multiple times. We estimate that we've had 252 separate visits. Table 15.5 breaks down the speakers by position. We've had 20 different CEOs speak in class. Several of them are CEOs of Fortune 500 companies; others are CEOs of smaller firms. All of them have to deal with myriad management problems and have given APM students a taste of what it's like. We've had many other senior corporate officers, including CFOs, executive vice presidents, and more. From the buy side we've had portfolio managers and research analysts. From investment banks we've had managing directors and analysts. The Other category includes securities regulators, entrepreneurs, activist investors, real estate developers, and all sorts of interesting people who can help sort out investment ideas.

We'd like to especially thank those most frequent APM speakers over the years. Table 15.6 lists those speakers who visited class three times or more. They've provided support in many ways, but being in class and available has been a boon to the students.

TABLE 15.5 Speakers in the APM Class by Position and Number of Visits

Position	Visitors	Visits
Analyst	27	29
Chairman	1	1
Chief executive officer	20	51
Chief financial officer	20	33
Chief operating officer	2	3
Managing director	3	3
Portfolio manager	16	45
President	6	7
Professor	7	21
Treasurer	1	1
Vice president	17	34
Other	25	24
Total	**145**	**252**

TABLE 15.6 Frequent APM Speakers

Times in Class	Name	Company	Title
8	Scott Jones	Prairie Wind Capital	Principal
6	John Dicus	Capitol Federal	Chief executive officer
6	Steve Farley	Labrador Partners	Principal
6	Todd Preheim	Campanile Capital	Principal
6	Brad Shoup	BCS Capital	Principal
6	David Walthall	Heritage Media	Chief executive officer
5	Victor Almeida	Internacional de Ceramica	Chief executive officer
5	Steve Glennon	Wilshire Financial	Chief executive officer
4	Todd Banks	Blackthorn Capital	Principal
4	Gene Diederich	A. G. Edwards - St. Louis	Executive vice president
4	Mark Fleischhauer	Jayhawk Capital	Senior vice president
4	Frank Whitsell	Security Benefit Group	Senior research analyst
4	Jim Wineland	Waddell & Reed	Senior vice president—portfolio manager
3	Jeff Davis	KU Endowment Association	Chief financial officer
3	Kent Gasaway	Kornitzer Capital	Senior vice president—portfolio manager
3	Scott Hartman	Novastar	Chief executive officer
3	Marc Hensel	Plains Explorations	Vice president—mergers and acquisitions
3	Michael Lamb	Wealth Monitors	Chief executive officer
3	Derek Palaschuk	SOHU	Chief financial officer
3	Jim Sight		Independent investor
3	Tim Webster	American Italian Pasta	Chief executive officer
3	Brett Young	RBC Dain Rauscher	Vice president

Note: We've listed the title and affiliation at the time of their last visit.

THE LAST WORD

There really are no last words when we're dealing with a constantly changing investment scene and with constantly engaging students. Investing is dynamic, and guiding students along the path of making investment decisions is also a dynamic and rewarding experience. We hope that others can benefit from our experiences in the process of educating our APM students to be better investors.

There are no shortcuts to getting rich, no secret handshakes that will magically transform someone into an investment guru. Building investment experience comes from hard work. Good investment insights are built from learning from a network of individuals with a wide variety of views and from a healthy dose of common sense. These are the ingredients that the University of Kansas APM class tries to cultivate. These are the ingredients that all successful investors share.

Index

Applied Portfolio Management on the Web

Investors interested in following the University of Kansas APM class and its investment portfolio should visit www.business.ku.edu/apm

There, investors can view information about the APM class portfolio using the "Portfolio" quick link. Included via this link are an annual report, portfolio holdings, APM performance graphs relative to portfolio benchmarks, additional portfolio information about buy and sell activity on individual stocks, and a market capitalization summary. Investors also may access specific information about the APM class and student research on specific companies via the "Class" and "Research" website quick links.

■ ■ ■

Investors who wish to support the APM program, after reading the book, may voluntarily do so. They can make a check donation payable to the **KU Endowment Association McCarthy Fund** and mail to: School of Business Endowment, Applied Portfolio Management, c/o Gregory J. Lamb, KU School of Business, 1300 Sunnyside Avenue, Lawrence, Kansas 66045-7585.